T0116249

ROUTLEDGE LIBRARY EDITIONS:
COMPARATIVE EDUCATION

Volume 13

THE UNIFICATION OF GERMAN EDUCATION

THE UNIFICATION OF GERMAN EDUCATION

VAL D. RUST AND DIANE RUST

Routledge
Taylor & Francis Group

LONDON AND NEW YORK

First published in 1995 by Garland Publishing, Inc.

This edition first published in 2018
by Routledge
2 Park Square, Milton Park, Abingdon, Oxon OX14 4RN

and by Routledge
711 Third Avenue, New York, NY 10017

Routledge is an imprint of the Taylor & Francis Group, an informa business

British Library Cataloguing in Publication Data
A catalogue record for this book is available from the British Library

ISBN: 978-1-138-54113-9 (Set)
ISBN: 978-1-351-00358-2 (Set) (ebk)
ISBN: 978-1-138-54412-3 (Volume 13) (hbk)
ISBN: 978-1-138-54494-9 (Volume 13) (pbk)
ISBN: 978-1-351-00466-4 (Volume 13) (ebk)

Publisher's Note
The publisher has gone to great lengths to ensure the quality of this reprint but points out that some imperfections in the original copies may be apparent.

Disclaimer
The publisher has made every effort to trace copyright holders and would welcome correspondence from those they have been unable to trace.

THE UNIFICATION OF GERMAN EDUCATION

Val D. Rust
Diane Rust

GARLAND PUBLISHING, Inc.
New York & London / 1995

Library of Congress Cataloging-in-Publication Data

Rust, Val Dean.
  The unification of German education / by Val D.
Rust and Diane Rust.
      p.   cm. — (Garland reference library of social
science ; vol. 960. Reference books in international
education ; vol. 32)
    Includes bibliographical references (p.) and index.
    ISBN 0-8153-1705-0 (alk. paper)
    1. Education—Germany—History—20th century.
  2. Education and state—Germany—History—20th
century. 3. Education—Social aspects—Germany—
History—20th century. 4. Germany—History—Uni-
fication, 1990. I. Rust, Diane. II. Title. III. Series:
Garland reference library of social science ; v. 960.
IV. Series: Garland reference library of social science.
Reference books in international education ; vol. 32.
LA721.83.R87 1995
370'.943'09049—dc20   94–26651
                                                                      CIP

Printed on acid-free, 250-year-life paper
Manufactured in the United States of America

DEDICATED TO

Helen Abbott Harding
A builder of relationships

SERIES EDITOR'S FOREWORD

This series of scholarly works in comparative and international education has grown well beyond the initial conception of a collection of reference books. Although retaining its original purpose of providing a resource to scholars, students, and a variety of other professionals who need to understand the role played by education in various societies or regions of the world, it also strives to provide up-to-date information on a wide variety of selected educational issues, problems and experiments within an international context.

Contributors to this series are well-known scholars who have devoted their professional lives to the study of their specialization. Without exception these men and women possess an intimate understanding of the subject of their research and writing. Without exception they have not only studied their subject in dusty archives, but they have also lived and travelled widely in their quest for knowledge. In short, they are "experts" in the best sense of that often overused word.

In our increasingly interdependent world, it is now widely understood that it is a matter of survival that we not only understand better what makes other societies tick, but that we also make a serious effort to understand how others, be they Japanese, German or Chilean, attempt to solve the same kinds of educational problems that we face in North America. As the late George Z.F. Bereday wrote: "[E]ducation is a mirror held against the face of a people. Nations may put on blustering shows of strength to conceal public weakness, erect grand facades to conceal shabby back-yards, and profess peace while secretly arming for conquest, but how they take care of their children tells unerringly who they are" (*Comparative Method in Education,* New York: Holt, Rinehart & Winston, 1964, p. 5).

Perhaps equally important, however, is the valuable perspective that studying another education system (or its problems) provides us in understanding our own system (or its problems). To step outside of our own limited experience and our commonly held assumptions about schools and learning in order to look back at our system in contrast to another places it in a very different light. To learn, for example, how the Soviet Union or Belgium handles the education of a multilingual society; how the French provide for the funding of a public education; or how the Japanese control admissions into their universities enables us to understand that there are alternatives to our own familiar way of doing things. Not that we can often "borrow" directly from other societies; indeed, educational arrangements are inevitably a reflection of deeply rooted political, economic and cultural factors that are unique to a society. But a conscious recognition that there are other ways of doing things can serve to open our minds and provoke our imaginations in ways that can result in new approaches that we would not have otherwise considered.

Since this series is intended to be a useful research tool, the editor and contributors welcome suggestions for future volumes as well as ways in which this series can be improved.

Edward R. Beauchamp
University of Hawaii

CONTENTS

ACKNOWLEDGMENTS

Val D. Rust was the recipient of a Fulbright research grant the 1991/92 academic year, and he served as a guest professor at Humboldt University in the former East Berlin where he was associated with the *Abteilung Erziehungswissenschaft*. After returning to the University of California, Los Angeles, Val D. Rust also received support from the Academic Senate of UCLA to continue his research on the unification process of the two Germanys. We should like to give a special thanks to the people at Humboldt University for their gracious hospitality during the year and to those people in the schools and other educational institutions who provided great time and energy to help us become informed of the situation. The writing of this book has been a privilege.

PREFACE

This study is an outgrowth of a research project undertaken shortly after the collapse of the German Democratic Republic (GDR). Shortly after the Berlin Wall opened, one of the authors was able to visit the GDR and gain a brief but important glimpse of developments taking place. In the summer of 1991 both authors moved to East Germany where they lived for a year. Humboldt University in East Berlin had granted Val D. Rust a visiting professorship with funds from the Fulbright Commission. Both were able to spend the year engaged in researching the changes taking place. Diane Rust accepted an invitation to teach English in two *Gesamtschulen* when the new curriculum and new organizational structure and learning materials were tried for the first time in East Berlin schools, and so gained a perspective as an insider of the struggles and stresses as well as satisfactions that educators, pupils, and parents experienced. During the year she undertook the difficult task of interviewing the parents of her pupils to gain some sense of the educational changes taking place from the vantage point of the parents. Through the cooperation of school officials in East Berlin, a large number of schools were visited, some over the entire year, so that an intimate acquaintance with the school could be gained. During the year, Val D. Rust was invited to give lectures at many of the institutions of higher learning in the old German Democratic Republic. He always accepted these invitations on condition that the people in the cities where the institutions are located would make arrangements for him and the other author to visit two or three schools in the area. Given this format, he was able to make acquaintance with cities such as Rostock, Zwickau, Freiberg, Dresden, Magdeburg, Leipzig, and Potsdam and enter into long and fruitful discussions with school people as well. Other professional contacts provided the opportunity to visit many other cities and their schools. Even chance visits to schools where the family happened to be on holiday or traveling usually proved to be successful and productive. As a consequence, more than one hundred different institutions were visited during the time. Many schools arranged meetings with faculty members, students, and even parents. At least one formal interview with a teacher or headmaster was arranged at each school to discuss the evolution of that particular educational institution over the past decade. These interviews often required more than one appointment and they lasted from two to six hours. Our interest was to gain a perspective of changes that have been taking place in East Germany, by looking carefully at individual schools, vocational training centers, teacher training colleges, or universities. Because we were able to visit more than one hundred educational institutions, we feel we were able to gain a broad picture of the situation from the roots up. Although this book offers a general overview of conditions and events of the recent past, the reader must keep in mind that our perspective is ultimately on the individual educational institution and the teachers and students of those institutions. We admit to a certain bias in our study. During our year of visiting the new states of East Germany we came to gain a high regard for the professional and humane orientation demonstrated by these educators. The reader will recognize reflections of that appreciation in the report.

Even though our basic starting point was at the local level, we asked questions that are typically considered as macro-analytic. That is, three basic questions came into consideration. The first asks about the conditions in which educational policy is successfully formulated. The second asks about the conditions in which that educational policy is implemented. The third asks about the consequences of successfully implemented educational reform. Consequently, given our basic data source it was impossible to rely heavily on conventional macro and micro analytic distinctions.

The book is organized around five considerations. In the first section, we provide the context for the study. Following an introductory chapter where we discuss certain theoretical and methodological issues related to education and social change in Germany, we then give an historical analysis of the divisions and bonds that have characterized Germany and German education over the years (Chapter II). Following that, two lengthy chapters lay out the basic legal and organizational framework for education in both the old Federal Republic of Germany (Chapter III) and the German Democratic Republic (Chapter IV). We conclude this section with a discussion of certain characteristics of the teachers in the two Germanys (Chapter V).

In the second section, we look at the growing crisis in East Germany during the 1980s, which led to the collapse of the state regime at the end of 1989 (Chapter VI). We show here what happened in schools and what educators experienced during the crisis. In Chapter VII we explore the vital period immediately following the collapse and the ways in which educators responded in a time when hierarchical authority had broken down throughout the entire state. At this time it was yet unclear what would happen to East Germany. Our interest was to determine the direction that teachers and other educators wanted to take education when that crucial decision seemed to rest with them alone.

In the third section we consider how East Germany was so quickly incorporated into the Federal Republic of Germany. In Chapter VIII we discuss the first phase lasting from the spring of 1990, when it became apparent that the two republics would be united until final preparations for formal unification in October of that same year. In Chapter IX we give our attention to the formation of the provisional school laws in the five new states. In so doing we attempt to provide some comparative perspective of these laws and some areas which deviate from the West German tradition. In Chapter X we discuss the successes and failures of the new school provisions and the prospects faced by pupils and teachers.

In the fourth section, we deal with four special cases of gender issues related to work and education (Chapter XI), family education (Chapter XII), with what Germans call free-time education (Chapter XIII), and with the rising concern about extremism and the foreigner in Germany (Chapter XIV), and what is presently happening in relation to these issues in a unified Germany.

In the final section we attempt to place the unification of East and West German education in context of the tendency toward a unified Europe (Chapter XV).

At the end of the book we have included the entire copy of the new school law for the state of Saxony-Anhalt. This law provides a detailed account of educational provisions and it typifies the laws established in each of the five new states of Germany.

Section I

The Context

Chapter I

Education and Social Change in Germany

Some years ago Ivan Illich pointed out that in the modern world school had replaced the church as the harbinger of some of life's fundamental purposes. School had become the institution that approved particular rites of passage. It both determined what station in life a person would attain and conveyed the basic values of society (Illich, 1970). When the Berlin Wall was breached on 9 November 1989, and the East Germans were quickly joined with the West Germans, it came as no surprise that one of the issues which stirred the passions of the Germans was the kind of schooling that would characterize the newly unified Germany. That struggle has been, in many respects, a microcosmic play of the larger social, political, and economic drama taking place in unified Germany.

The unification process of the German Democratic Republic and the Federal Republic of Germany provides an opportunity to explore serious issues related to the change process in education. It casts the historical focus of educational reform in Europe in a new light. In the past the major debates related to social and educational change in Europe have revolved around two conflicting interpretations concerning the relationship schools have with society. On the one hand, most proponents of change assume that schools can act as a stimulus to social improvement. On the other hand, certain scholars believe that school reform is limited to boundaries set by broader social, political, and economic forces.

The notion that schools can act as an agent of social change is attractive to those trying to understand the change process. It has been especially attractive to those interested in cultural and humanitarian improvement. Such scholars wish to change schools so that they are more capable of reducing social class divisions and enhancing relations between social groups, of improving life chances, and of ensuring greater social justice. Those scholars dealing with Europe typically focus on the conventional model of schooling in Europe, pointing out that the Europeans created different types of schools with the intention that each school type would serve and reinforce a different social class. Historically, the agenda of those wanting structural reform in education in various societies of Europe has been to create some sort of unified school, that would serve the entire pupil population and contribute to cultural integration. It was thought that a common school would bring about greater equality of educational opportunity and facilitate social mobility among all peoples.[1]

Germany has been the focus of much attention in this regard because school reformers have attempted to create an educational institution that would be an instrument of bettering social conditions. In other words, schooling would influence change in the very social and political fabric of the nation.

After World War I, when the German government collapsed and the Weimar Republic came into being, educators caught up in the progressive education movement (*Reformbewegung*) banded together to undermine the old educational establishment and begin building a new tradition. A National Assembly was convened in June 1920 with the intention of restructuring schools. As a result, for the first time in Germany's history, a common primary school was mandated which would serve as an integrative force for all social classes in the country.

Following World War II, the four occupational powers were intent on using the schools as an instrument to "democratize" the Germans. In May 1945, they came together at Potsdam and decided what was to occur. German "militarism" and "Naziism" were to be rooted out of the German people and replaced by a "democratic and peaceful foundation" (quoted in Deuerlein 1957, p. 248). America and the Soviet Union strongly asserted their ideas about schools. Thus, one

---

[1]Such a claim has recently been challenged by Leschinsky and Meyer (1990), who provide evidence that the diversified system of West Germany is providing as much equality of educational opportunity as those systems that have gone comprehensive.

outcome of the Potsdam Agreement was that traditional class oriented schools be replaced by a unified, comprehensive school.[2]

There have always been people, among them scholars, who have challenged the assumption that schools could be used as an instrument of social change. Some of the research activities of the authors of this volume have supported such a point of view. For example, Rust (1968) compared common school reform endeavors in nineteenth century United States with early twentieth century German common school reforms and found that American reformers were successful in bringing about reforms, while the German reformers, just as energetic and committed, were marginally so. He found the main reasons for this difference in success was that American reformers showed that their reform endeavors were consistent with the dominant ideological and value commitments of the American people, whereas the German reformers had attempted to change some of the fundamental social relations and values that existed in Germany. Thus, their reform activities were not very successful.

Marxist tradition has held the point of view that schools are little more than instruments of the larger society. In Germany, following World War I, a group of educators calling themselves the Association of Radical School Reformers,[3] called for the overthrow of the capitalistic state because "the dominant capitalistic system compels the edu-

---

[2]Although we concentrate here on Germany, the examples we could draw on could be large. For example, the assumption that schools could be used as an instrument of change was so great that it was incorporated into the modernization agenda of social scientists in the 1950s and 60s. The so-called "mobilization model" of Karl Deutsch (1953) typifies the sentiments of social science researchers who wanted to accelerate the modernization process of the developing world. The basic notion behind Deutsch's model was that social, political, and economic processes were bracketed together as a society develops, including urban/rural, religious/secular, fatalistic/rationality shifts and increasing consumption of communication, material goods, and schooling. Because most of these processes were seen to change simultaneously in the modernization process, it was reasoned that changing one process could act as a catalyst for change of the other processes. Schooling was seen as just such a potential catalyst.

[3]*Bund Entschiedener Schulreformer.*

cational institutions into a form which makes them an effective tool of world reaction" (Lask, 1926).

The "success" of the Soviet Union in transforming East German education following World War II could be attributed to the thorough and coercive reorientation of its social, political, and economic institutions. With the emergence of the Socialist Unity Party in 1946 and the founding of the German Democratic Republic in 1949, capitalism was, indeed, eliminated from the East German economy and the country was incorporated completely into the pervasive Soviet ideology. In contrast, the American occupying force was just as committed to school reform as were the Soviets, but a strong argument could be made that they were so respectful of traditional German political and economic norms that only minor parts of their comprehensive schooling agenda were adopted by the Germans.

These theoretical beliefs about the relationship of school to society has taken on new vigor in recent years. One of the important claims of so-called conflict theorists of the 1970s and early 1980s was to solidify the assumption that schools could not be used as instruments of social change. For example, Martin Carnoy and Henry Levin (1976) developed what they called the "correspondence principle" and argued as follows:

> ...schools exist as an agent of the larger social, economic, and political context which fosters them. Accordingly, they correspond to the institutions of the larger society and serve the functions assigned to them for reproducing the social, economic, and political relationships reflected by the prevailing institutions and ideologies.

The implications of such a point of view are important. It suggests that schools serve only to reinforce the existing social order and that stable and enduring educational systems are those which closely mirror the social, economic, and political conditions of the society of which they are a part. If change occurs in these broader spheres, we can expect change to occur in education; the latter with the intent to bring schools in line with social conditions and economic demands. It would be unlikely that school reforms would extend beyond the limits of the social order. This does not mean that attempts at school reforms do not take place, but they are only accepted if they "correspond to modifications in the larger social order" (Carnoy & Levin, 1977, p. 43).

If the basic claims of Carnoy and Levin were used as a paradigm for that which happened to schools during the unification process of East and West Germany, they would require some refinement. For example, these authors focused only on emerging needs for change and assumed a common starting point. That is, traditional school systems would correspond with the broader social context and changes in schools would occur only as society evolved. However, in a historical study of Norwegian school reform, Rust (1989) found that early nineteenth century Norwegian schools, such as they were at the time Norway gained independence from Denmark in 1814, did not reflect the broader social value system at all. The schools in the country had been imposed by the Danes during their 400 year colonial reign, and they reflected the continental model that reinforced distinct social divisions unknown in Norway. Successful fundamental reforms of Norwegian schools happened because they pointed toward bringing the schools into harmony with general social conditions. In other words, school reformers were not trying to change society in any fundamental way.

Toward a New Paradigm of Change

At the time Eastern Europe collapsed, each of the two schools of thought outlined above were strong voices in school policy and academic literature. However, the 1989 revolution in Eastern Europe, including East Germany, has created difficulty for social scientists advocating these theories, because conventional social theory appears insufficiently developed to cope with the apparent panoply of dimensions and processes involved in the collapse of the East German regime and the rapid unification of the two Germanys. The collapse itself was so unusual that social scientists were as surprised as political analysts and the media. In other words, their tools of analysis had not given them the slightest insight into the processes of change that were at work.

The conventional debate, whether schools exist as an agent of social reform or whether school reform is largely conditioned by its social, political, and economic context, has been subsumed into a much larger argument related to educational reform. We shall mention but three major factors in the current debate. First, social theory on which school reform is based has taken for granted that the larger social context would be quite stable and non-revolutionary. Certainly, the evolutionary theorists, such as modernization theorists, systems analysts, structural functionalists, and others have operated on the assumption that social systems would evolve gradually and slowly, but most conflict theorists also have assumed that conflict in regions such as North America and Europe were contained and regulated rather than chaotic and revolutionary. Social science paradigms based on assumptions of stability have not been very helpful in attempts to understand what has happened in Eastern Europe, where everything has been in a state of disruption. The revolution of Eastern Europe certainly was stimulated by individuals such as Gorbachev and Yeltsin, and yet even they have been swept into events that went far beyond their control, and we all have been forced to consider reform in the context of conditions of high disequilibrium. Second, it has become increasingly clear that the separation of social, political, and economic institutions from local groups, institutions, and individuals in the form of "macro-studies" as opposed to "micro-studies" is not only arbitrary but distorting of our ability to understand the nature of social reality. Third, in Eastern Europe the orderly but spontaneous transformation of systems, including the educational enterprise, has forced us to take seriously the possibility that organization is not necessarily something imposed by some larger authority or by a defined power but includes a self-organizing process of myriad individual acts that constitute almost an unconscious organizing capacity. Let us consider these and other factors in greater detail.

Disequilibrium and Change

Events such as those taking place in Eastern Europe are helping us begin to construct a new paradigm for change. All of Eastern Europe finds itself in a period of turbulence. In the struggle to understand what is taking place, we are finding a new type of literature that suggests that constructive and positive change is most likely to occur during periods of disequilibrium and turbulence. In the past we have usually thought of chaotic social conditions as frightening and disorienting, but we are finally beginning to understand that all social systems operate in a condition that is not static nor in a state of equilibrium. In fact, from the perspective of the new literature, equilibrium is actually seen as a state of entropy, a state of death. All living, developing systems exhibit so-called autopoietic characteristics. That is, they are continually renewing themselves, but the renewal process is regulated such that upgrading and downgrading processes operate simultaneously so that the integrity of their structure and functions is maintained. Social systems, as all systems, will do everything possible to preserve themselves (Krohn, Küppers and Nowotny, 1980), but there is great possibility that the perturbation may reach a breaking point where the system simply collapses. Events in Eastern Europe have been painful and difficult. The outcome may not be something better than existed in the recent past. However, there also appears to exist a self-organizing capacity of most systems that includes their ability to adjust to extensive external shifts, so that self-preservation ultimately means the emergence of quite new orientations and configurations of the system itself. Eastern Europe may emerge with social systems more humane, vital, and life-enhancing than in the previous social system. Our point here is that disequilibrium is a condition of life, it is the condition under which development and growth actually take place. Turbulence is precarious, but it has great positive potential (Schieve & Allen, 1987; Prigogine and Stengers, 1989; Maruyama, 1981; and Haken, 1988).

Earlier in this chapter, we stated that the periods immediately following the two world wars were times when significant change occurred in German education. Those were periods of great disequilibrium and disorientation, but also times when the possibility of constructive change existed. Some important insights must be mentioned. First, even in times of relative stability a certain level of turbulence is present. Even in relatively stable North America and Western Europe, nonlinear, complex, and turbulent conditions with their amplifying causal loops exist. These are usually the most conducive for growth and development. For example, the stock market is characterized more by gradual inclines and declines than violent shifts, but underneath that stability, one can observe on any given day the chaotic, confusing actions on the stock exchange floor. Schools have the appearance of great stability if one measures the number of courses taught, the grading curve, and the school leaving process, but every teacher knows he/she is constantly working on the edge of bedlam. Second, to speak of disequilibrium and turbulence should not be interpreted to mean there is no order and control. Anarchy is not characteristic of growth and development. Doyne Farmer claims the ideal dynamics of change are "at the edge of chaos" (quoted in Waldrop, 1992, p. 294). Evolution thrives in social systems that are active at the bottom levels of the organizational structure. However, this creativity and renewal process requires external resources. A living cell is self-organizational but it exists in a dense web of stimulation, energy, and regulation from the larger system. A school may operate with great creativity and growth, but only if it receives the resources and support from the central office that is necessary for it to thrive.

This newer thinking is not a pessimistic view of total indeterminacy in periods of great turbulence but the realization that by better understanding how change takes place, we know where intervention is possible and where prediction and intervention is problematic. Because these newer theoretical orientations are coming forth from so many disciplines, the terms used are often not consistent. One hears about chaos, transformation, self-organization, catastrophe, dissipative organizations, autopoiesis, and synergetics. But these terms reject similar ideas, and they form the foundation for newer thinking that deals with change and its connection to very unstable conditions.

Relationship of Schools to Society

Certain contemporary scholars are providing new paradigms that help us redefine the relationship schools have with society. Here we shall rely on the work of Michel Foucault, who has chosen to focus his work on the relationships between individuals, groups, and institutions such as factories, hospitals, schools, families. At the same time, Foucault attended to the aims of the larger state apparatus. In the process Foucault has helped us discard the conventional separation of macro from micro analysis and put behind assumptions that power is associated only with formal hierarchical relationships. Foucault has conceptualized notions of power that constitute a radical break with all previous ideas of power. He claims power is not something an individual, group or institution possesses. Rather, power is a label we use to describe the process of social relationships. For Foucault power is not a general system of domination exerted by one group over another, nor is it a unified state apparatus, but must be understood as the multiplicity of power relationships at work in a particular geographic region. There is a constant struggle in these relationships which strengthens, weakens, and transforms them.

In his analysis of power relationships, Foucault (1978, pp. 92-3) asserts that power

> must be understood in the first instance as the multiplicity of force relations immanent in the sphere in which they operate and which constitute their own organization; the process which, through ceaseless struggles and confrontations, transforms, strengthens, or reverses them; or on the contrary, the disjunctions and contradictions which isolate them from one another; and lastly, as the strategies in which they effect.

Here Foucault argues that it might be advantageous to begin on the fringes of what is typically understood as power centers. Using the metaphor of the human body, Foucault argues that power must include an understanding of the "capillaries"; it must be analyzed at its extremities. He maintains that power is not located mainly at the top of an administrative hierarchy but it permeates the entire system. At the same time power is contingent, imprecise, and relational. It does not exist as a substantive entity but as a mode of action. The exercise of power is "always a way of acting upon an acting subject or acting subjects by virtue of their acting or being capable of action." To govern, for example, is "to structure the possible field of action of others," so it is always relational; however, power does not just come down from formal influence points in the environment but from the bottom up through any system. According to Foucault:

> power must be analyzed as something which circulates, or rather as something which only functions in the form of a chain. It is never localized here or there, never in any body's hands, never appropriated as a commodity or piece of wealth. Power is employed and exercised through a net-like organization (Foucault, 1972, p. 98).

Any establishment is maintained by a network of habitual behaviors, socialized bodies, and other forms of control that permeate the entire system. Central power is only one dimension of this network of relationships. Power is not simply a relationship of dominance and submission. It is closely bound to the concept of freedom, for freedom is power's permanent support. If conditions do away with all choices so that behavior and options are determined and coerced, then a power relationship disappears, it becomes a relationship of compulsion and coercion. Foucault gives his attention to prisons, brothels, and mental institutions, and he finds that even in these institutions, all participants maintain power relationships, not coercion relationships, in that everyone exercises options and makes choices. The system is maintained on the basis of these choices. We could look at power relationships in education in the same manner. These must include local material educational institutions, which might be considered the "capillaries" of any national educational system. Those capillaries are the individual schools, and the teachers and pupils, who give those schools their life and vitality. Their stability and viability depend on the support local participants provide to system maintenance. Our age has been characterized by its densely regulated, "disciplined" nature.

However, such power relationships also give rise to Foucault's concept of resistance. As long as a power relationship exists there must be some possibility of insubordination, resistance or escape. In every situation of power, a point exists at which the supportive relationship ceases and struggle and opposition take over. If insubordination is quelled completely, then the power relationship becomes one of total subservience. In totalitarian states power relationships may indeed turn into total compulsion, but on the slightest sign of weakness or openness from the oppressor, the power relationship may again emerge and resistance or escape may begin anew. Foucault's concepts prove helpful in understanding the sudden and total collapse of the last empire in the modern world: the Soviet block.

We noted above that power is always unstable, in that its distribution is in a constant state of flux. This may mean that arbitrary and complete power may, indeed, be so arranged that we can talk of a "top-down" imposition of change. However, we might also talk of "institution-based" change. Even when top-down power relationships exist, it must be understood that influence emanates not just from the formal hierarchy but from various centralized points in the environment. In the case of education, countless cases exist of centrally decided and developed innovations that are imposed on local educational institutions. In such cases, the educational change strategy is particularly one-sided and comes from political and administrative bodies that might be considered "environmental" influences from the perspective of the individual school. This was certainly the case in East Germany following World War II, when the Soviet Union and its designated German officials dictated the nature of schooling. Schools were fundamentally changed and the school community was expected to adopt those changes without alteration. In such an extreme context, one would expect to find extensive submission on the part of local participants, who would feel compelled to adopt administrative mandates with little adaptation to local needs; however, one would also expect to find seeds of resistance and insubordination that would flower at the slightest sign of openness and weakness.

On the other hand, many examples exist of power relationships in which the local educational institutions take responsibility for defining their own innovations or adapting ideas and practices found in the environment, including central administrative initiatives. In these cases the local institution would adapt "environmental" initiatives to meet their own development needs and improve their own practice.

Even though the two above extremes suggest contradictory processes, Foucault would undoubtedly hold that "superstructure" and "base" are both involved in all innovative processes. Dalin has called this process a "mutual adaptation and development" process, whereby power relationships include the local institution's ability of responding to external initiatives while simultaneously creating and developing ways to improve itself. A continual dialogue goes on between every institution and its environment, and the discourse between the two affects the types of change that occur.

Contingent Development

If the dialogue between each institution and its environment is imbalanced, the outcome of that dialogue will depend on the location of power. If the superstructure dominates the dialogue, the outcome will be quite different than if the base dominates. If environmental influences are dominant, regardless of the content of this influence, the local institutions would likely respond in a mechanistic fashion, and the innovation would appear to be rigidly controlled to function in a defined manner. The classic examples of this type of response are in what is referred to as totalitarian social systems. In East Germany following World War II, the Soviet regime instituted rigidly controlled and defined subsystems, including schools. These schools were relatively closed and maintained limited interaction with the environment other than what was allowed by the Soviet leaders. The schools operated with few decision-making levels and had clearly defined goals that were prescribed to them. They had little or no room for self-direction. Consequently, they behaved mechanistically and exhibited little system dynamics. Consequently, once they were in place, they had great difficulty to change and innovate. The type of power relationships that are established have a great deal to do with the consequences. Immediately following World War II, the Soviet Union dictated the nature of schooling at the local level. The Soviet Union was successful in establishing its educational aims in the schools, and the consequences were predictable. Schools conformed, teachers behaved according to strict regulations and guidelines, and pupils were obedient and industrious.

Such outcomes, as noted in totalitarian systems, would also be predicted in systems that might be defined as democratic if environmental influences so dominate that those in local educational institutions have little recourse but to respond in a mechanistic and deterministic fashion or to resist and subvert such initiatives. We anticipate that this type of behavior is prevalent in the current context of the new states of Germany where schools, teachers and pupils are not expected to operate on the basis of autonomy, critical thought, and independence but according to directives imposed on them.

Even if local units exercise extensive decision-making properties, there is no assurance that those institutions are innovative and creative. They might adopt what can be described as "maximum maintenance" of the *status quo*, in that they have no capacity for self-renewal. They could also exhibit the capacity for internal creativity but not be open to external influences. They could, though, be highly self-directive, in a constant state of change, and engaged in a continual dialogue with their environments to satisfy mutual needs and interests. These could be designated as examples of "mutual adaptation and development" processes. Under these conditions there is a capacity at the local level for orderly transformation. These local entities are usually dependent on important inputs from central and regional leaders. Rust and Dalin have long held that creative schools are those which are able to respond to environmental stimulus, but have internal capacity to initiate and innovate (Dalin & Rust, 1983).

In the change literature of the West, it has become increasingly clear that the school must be central in any effective change process (Dalin & Rust, 1983). At the same time, schools must always be viewed as subsystems of much larger systems. They are never completely autonomous and must work in conjunction with the rest of the system which plays a large role in their ability to survive and thrive. It is usually the larger system that ensures that the school has the funds and other resources to carry out its work. The larger system also provides the framework within which a school is allowed to operate and the standards it is expected to maintain. Within the change process, there are two ways a school may be seen as part of the larger system. Most of the change literature deals with schools as institutions that are expected to adopt change suggested from external sources. To institutionalize change is, in other words, to change according to some grand design, to take on the characteristics of a policy or some project. However, there is a second type of institutionalization, and that is to create a framework, to bring about a working model, and to help the school develop the capacity to engage in its own development process (Rolff, 1991). In this sense, the larger system is a support system rather than a directing system.

The literature on change has concluded that centralized change processes that impose themselves on the schools will be met with excessive and usually effective reactions against these processes. For this reason schools have been characterized as extremely stable and almost static, in nature (Dalin, 1973; 1978).

In this model, central authorities have the responsibility to provide the conditions that facilitate development at the local level, to help release self-organizing capacity, and to intervene in such a way that micro-structures operate in productive and constructive ways. We maintain, then, that in periods of great instability, there is a clear, important need for central and regional leadership to work jointly with local entities, schools in this case.

The three theoretical themes outlined above will appear throughout this volume. The contemporary German educational reform process provides a good opportunity to contribute to a more balanced discussion of change theory.

Chapter II

The Politics of Division and Unification

World War II and Its Aftermath

The sudden fall of the Berlin Wall in November 1989, destined education, among other aspects of East German life, to change. That West Germany would serve as the primary model for this restructuring soon became clear. It is, therefore, imperative to describe the systems which existed in the East and the West and how, through the machinations of politics and the influence of society, they came to be what they were.

In 1945, Germany was divided by the four victorious powers. The Soviet Union took over approximately one third of the county and gave it to Poland. Then the remainder was divided into four zones of occupation. Among the occupiers, the Soviet Union gained access to the largest land mass because the Americans and English agreed to turn over territory which they occupied in return for the right to share control of Berlin, which lay in the Soviet zone. Because of the ability of the French, British, and Americans to come to harmonious agreement, their occupation zones were eventually transformed into an independent Federal Republic of Germany (FRG) in 1949.

The Soviet zone of occupation took quite a different direction of development and soon after the FRG was created, the Soviet Union established the German Democratic Republic (GDR), which was patterned after the Soviet Union. This action set a precedence in resolving occupational conflicts between the communist sphere of influence and the Western European and American spheres of influence.[1] Consequently, a similar division took place when North and South Korea were established in 1953, and North and South Vietnam were established in 1954. Although dividing a county seems a curious way to resolve conflict, it was possible here because Germany had never been able to establish a culture so unified that the Germans would refuse to allow themselves to be divided by the occupational forces.

There was not enough commonality politically and culturally among the various German regions to ensure a unified state. Twice a tenuous German political unity had been created--once in 1871 under Otto von Bismarck and again, this time more strongly, during the National Socialist period. That political fusion had proved so catastrophic to Germany as well as the rest of the world, that Germans inclined to a unified state had little reason to argue that the precedent set in National Socialist times justified the continued unity of Germany at the end of World War II.

Because German culture has always been fragmented and diverse, to speak of pluralistic German cultures rather than a single, unitary Germany is more accurate. Popular press books such as Rudolf W. Leonhardt's *X-mal Deutschland* (1960) illustrate Germany's infatuation with its own diversity. Of course, this diversity manifested itself in the kinds of educational traditions that emerged. For example, in the nineteenth century, even though the *Gymnasium* had a rather uniform external structure in the various German regions, important differences existed in the inner context and ambiance. In Prussia, each *Gymnasium* enjoyed a relatively large amount of freedom in the way it was run. This extended to the point that each institution took great responsibility for the content of its prescribed courses and the conducting of its school leaving examination. In Bavaria, there was such tight control over content and

---

[1]Of course, divisions of territory has characterized much of the world's political history. For example, the Iranians and Russians divided Azerbaijan in 1827 in the so-called Turkmanchai Peace Treaty, and the Azeri people remain divided to this day.

the examination structure that each institution was constrained to follow central mandates precisely. These traditions carried into the contemporary world. East Germany, which included the Saxons, Prussians, Thuringians, Pomeranians, and Mecklenburgers, was as diverse as West Germany, but diversity was glossed over and subverted by the German Democratic Republic, a government as centralized as the Nazi regime.

All occupying powers attempted to impose themselves to some degree on their respective zones of occupation. One of the targets of all occupying powers was the schools, which had long been used in various German states to foster the objectives of the regime in power. This is certainly not a unique situation in modern Germany. In fact, public education, as we know it today, came into being in most modern states in order to foster a sense of national pride and commitment on the part of state subjects. The schools had certainly been used by the Prussians in their attempt to revitalize a patriotic state following the defeat of the Prussians to Napoleon at Jena in 1806. Just prior to turn of this century, Kaiser Wilhelm II had circulated a formal decree that history instruction was to be employed in the German schools to thwart the expansion of socialistic and communistic ideas (In Berthold and Schepp, 1973). And the National Socialists had dedicated the schools to the service of Hitler and his political machine in an attempt to create a Germany built on folk and racial foundation. The National Socialists infiltrated all professions, but Franklin Littell observed that "the school teachers were perhaps the worst of the lot" (1960, p. 117).

The Soviet Union was the most thorough of the occupational powers in that it attempted to alter the very nature of German society. To ensure that socialism would become a reality, the Soviets and their German collaborators instituted and integrated a highly centralized state. The central organ of this state was the Socialist Unity Party (SED), which had been formed in 1946 as an amalgam of the German Communist Party (KPD) and the German Socialist Party (SPD). It maintained a firm grip on all affairs of the East German state, and used the schools as an instrument of this transformation.

Even before the GDR had been organized, the Soviets had thoroughly cleaned house regarding education. The Germans had long given their teachers the role of "civil servants." One of the criteria for being a civil servant was that they be willing to support the regime, which meant that teachers had, by definition, been supporters of the National Socialist regime. Because the Soviet Union had terminated all civil servants, there was a severe need for teachers in the Soviet zone of occupation. The solution to this problem was to appoint "new teachers" (*Neulehrer*), young people, many without a higher education qualification, who were pressed into service and into a special, short-term teacher training program. This training program included an intense indoctrination program to attract teachers to socialism and create a mechanism for the socialist transformation of East Germany.

East German education was used to instill the "educational ideas and experiences of the German and international socialist working class movements from Karl Marx to the present and with the ideas of Marxism-Leninism." It was dedicated to rooting out fascism, that was connected with capitalist imperialism, and instilling in its place an anti-fascist democratic order based on the fundamentals of socialism (Abusch, 1966, p. 10). The state dedicated East Germany's educational program to the elimination of all bias against the working class and set out to ensure educational advantage for the children of this class.

The West Germans did not escape change; however, they did have their way in education. Those in control acceded to German insistence that the educational system existing prior to the Nazi period be re-instituted but with certain modifications. Most West Germans had been psychologically devastated by the atrocities that had taken place in the previous twelve years, and they attempted to grasp onto the few cultural traditions in which the Germans could take pride. For more than a century Germans had been the undisputed world leaders of the world in educational programs, and they demanded that they be given the right to restore this source of pride in the Western zones.

One of the most important means of "democratizing" West Germany on the part of the Western occupation forces was to decentralize the political structure by instituting a federated nation. The notion of federation resonated among Germans because it recalled the many small kingdoms and principalities that had comprised Germany before Bismarck's unification in 1871 (Merkl, 1963, pp. 28-35). The political parties, too, that emerged after the war favored some sort of federation, although some Christian Democrats (CDU), particularly those sympathetic to France West of the Rhine, tended to favor being part of a united Europe. Others in Bavaria, long known as a renegade state, argued for restoration of Bavaria's autonomy as a separate nation. At the first convention of the Social Democrats (SPD) in 1946, Kurt Schumacher, the party chairman, proposed a German political structure that would be "as federalist as possible and as centralist as necessary" (SPD, 1947, p. 128). The Western occupation forces had wisely adjusted most of the original zonal borders to conform in general with historical groupings, such as the Bavarians, the Hessens, and the Lower Saxons, although some arbitrary clusterings, such as the northern part of Rhineland, Westphalia and Lippe were thrown together. In addition, an enclave in the Bremen-Bremerhaven area was created to give the American zone a seaport. The outcome of all this was a Federal Republic of Germany with eleven *Länder*,[2] held together by a rather weak central state and having what was thought to be a transitional constitution, the Basic Law,[3] as its legal base.

The next chapter shall show that it is possible to speak of a West German system of education, yet compared to the highly centralized East German tradition, it seems to differ significantly from state (*Land*) to state. These differences are important in our analysis of education. When the East German regime collapsed in 1989, East Germany was broken into five new federal states (East Berlin was united with West Berlin). Because of the federal system of education

---

[2]Baden-Württemberg, Bavaria, Berlin, Bremen, Hamburg, Hesse, Lower Saxony, North-Rhine-Westphalia, Rhineland-Palatinate, Saarland, Schleswig-Holstein.
[3]*Grundgesetz*.

they had adopted, it fell to these new Eastern states to develop their own systems; therefore, each initiated a partnership agreement with one of the original states of West Germany with the intention of exchanging information and patterning its educational laws and system to a great extent on the partner state's.

West German Political Diversity

Certain generalizations can be made about regional differences in West Germany by looking at political party affiliations within these areas. This is so, because "political parties in Germany are far more cohesive organizations both electorally and legislatively than they are in the United States" (Cerny, 1978, preface). In West Germany four major political parties have come to dominate: the Christian Democratic Union (CDU) and its sister the Christian Social Union (CSU) in Bavaria; the Social Democratic Party (SPD); the Free Democratic Party (FDP); and the Green Party.

Figure
The Political Spectrum of the Political Parties of the old Federal Republic of Germany

Conservative				Liberal
CSU	CDU	FDP	SPD	GREENS

In political position, the CDU/CSU parties have been the most conservative, while the FDP is the center party and usually brokers its way by establishing itself as a coalition party with one of the major parties. The SPD identifies as a liberal party. The Green Party is the newest, smallest, and most liberal in that originally its strongest position was environmental protection.

Those states where the strongest party is Social Democratic (SPD) are Bremen (46.5%), Saarland (43.5%), and North-Rhine-Westphalia (43.2%), while those where the strongest party is Christian Democratic (CDU/CSU) are Bavaria (55.1%), Baden-Württemberg (46.7%), and Rhineland-Palatinate (45.1%).[4] The three Christian Democrat states just named constitute the southern-most region of the Federal Republic, and they have the reputation of being the most conservative among the states. They are heavily Catholic, and their leaders take pride in their allegiance to the conservative impulses of the Church. Bavaria, especially, has a strong history of a constitutional monarchy, a marker of a conservative tradition. The three city states of Bremen, Hamburg, and Berlin are among the most liberal, yet North-Rhine-Westphalia is also very liberal. Even though that state is Catholic, it is the major industrial area of West Germany, the most densely populated, containing more than 21% of the total population (16,954 in 1989) of the old FRG, and it is dominated by labor interests.

Each state in the Federal Republic based its schools on the educational system that had existed during the Weimar period, some two decades earlier. The authority structure in the federated educational system extended from the beginning of compulsory schooling through the universities and other institutions of higher learning.

In the next decades, East and West Germany evolved political processes and educational systems that became increasingly different, largely because the FRG was tightly bound to the United States and Western Europe and their free enterprise economies, while the GDR was bound to the Soviet Union and Eastern Europe and their socialist economies.

---

[4]In countries with multi-party systems 40-50% of the electorate is usually a strong indicator.

Chapter III

Education in the Federal Republic of Germany

Young people in the Federal Republic of Germany enjoy one of the prestigious educational systems internationally. They remain in school as long as any group in the world, score well on international achievement tests, and enjoy great benefits from success in school. The corporate system of Germany has built schooling into its formula for success.

Legal Provisions for a Federated West German Education

The state and law have played an important role in the context of the Federal Republic. In fact, Article 7 (1) of the Basic Law of the Federal Republic states explicitly that "the entire educational system is under the supervision of the state." Debates have gone on for years about the meaning of this statement, but Mitter (1994, p.1) explains that jurisprudential literature has typically interpreted it to mean that the educational system is under an "all-embracing state control through decision-making administrative authorities according to the valid laws, decrees, and orders." As we shall see, state control does not mean the state has a complete monopoly over education although such a condition exists with regard to preschooling. There have always been a small number of private schools, but these have also been under tight regulation of the state.

Mitter (1994) also points out that the federated nature of German education does not present a paradox to the state monopoly of education. It only means that each state operates its individual, centralized monopoly over education. We shall also see that the tendency has been toward extreme amounts of centralization in the Federal Republic over the years, so that considerable uniformity exists among the various states, which have voluntarily entered into treaties and agreements to conform with each other in almost every essential aspect of education.

Article 30 of the Basic Law, the constitution of the Federal Republic of Germany, stipulates that "the discharge of state functions is the concern of the states *(Länder)*, insofar as the Basic Law does not otherwise prescribe or permit." Some functions were defined as the responsibility of the central government, such as foreign relations, the military, currency, postal service and railways, but "cultural functions," such as the radio, television, libraries, theater, and education became largely a undertaking of each of the states. Almost all education programs--preschools, primary schools, secondary schools, and institutions of higher learning--fell under the definition of cultural functions and have become the states' responsibility. In fact, the Ministry responsible for education in each state is known as the *Kultusministerium* because it oversees museums, theater, and so forth. In this volume, however, it will be called the Ministry of Education.

At the time the Basic Law was written, religious instruction, vocational education, and research support were reserved for central government responsibility. Religious instruction is ensured by the Basic Law as a part of public school programs (Art. 7: 3); however, parents have the right to decide whether the child shall receive it (Art. 7: 2). Vocational education in Germany has long been a matter involving labor unions and economic enterprises, and the Basic Law specifies all law related to these aspects of German society are a matter of the central government (Art. 74: 11, 12). Over time the central government has also assumed greater and greater responsibility for higher education, and the Basic Law was amended between 1969 and 1971 to allow central control to go far beyond research support into matters such as administrative organization, student admissions policies, and student support (Baumert and Others, 1990, pp. 54-7). The Structural Law for Higher Education *(Hochschulrahmengesetz)*, passed in 1976, brought about great central control in organization of institutions, administrative structure, admissions requirements, faculty regulations, and programs of studies.

Other Basic Law provisions have also affected education, even though education is, by and large, the responsibility of the state. For example, parents are given responsibility for the "care and upbringing of children," which has been interpreted to mean that parents are ultimately responsible for the type of formal education their child will receive, though the state "watches over their performance" (Art. 6: 2). Parental responsibility is particularly evident in child rearing prior to compulsory attendance at school, religious instruction and private schooling.

The status and competence of teachers is also a federal issue. German secondary teachers had long enjoyed the role of civil servants,[1] and this continued under the Basic Law with the stipulation that those entrusted to public service would be pledged to "service and loyalty by public law" (Art. 33: 4), and that this service be regulated according to "traditional principles concerning the status of professional civil servants" (Art. 33: 5). These provisions ensure that all teachers, no matter which state they live in, would enjoy a secure and respected place in society. Comparative data show that relative to other occupations, West German teachers have one of the highest salaries in the world. For example, the highest secondary teacher salaries in West Germany are more than double the industrial worker average (Bell, 1978, p. 78). German teachers recognize this standing. A teacher, Walter Kempowski (1979), remarked in *Der Spiegel*: "When it comes to time and money, the West German teacher is better off than any others in the entire world." In addition, West German teachers are protected by the Basic Law in their right "freely to express and to disseminate their opinion" (Art. 5: 1) and to exercise the traditional "freedom of teaching" (Art. 5: 3).[2] In all states, teach-

---

[1]There remains a strong status, qualification, and salary difference between primary and secondary teachers.

[2]Recall the basic rights of the German academic of *Lehrfreiheit* and *Lernfreiheit*, although strain was experienced in this commitment during the tumultuous student movement of the late 1960s and 70s, which tightened the reigns of freedom,

ers are seen as independent, autonomous professionals, who are responsible for their instruction and means of going about it.

Although teachers were given constitutional independence and autonomy does not mean that they have always exercised such independence and autonomy. Following World War II, German political elites were hypersensitive about the fragility of the German democracy, and they went to great extremes to develop institutional rules that substantially and effectively reduced the potential for the rise of extreme anti-democratic political activities. Serious concerns continue to plague the Germans, who repeatedly demonstrate that many are vulnerable to extremist tendencies. Yet teachers have followed restraint and have gradually developed norms of behavior in the schools that are consistent with conventional wisdom related to democratic behavior and the conduct of schooling. Within our theoretical framework, we would postulate that the resistance West Germans showed toward Western allied attempts to "democratize" the Germans by changing their educational system in some fundamental way, may have contributed significantly to the German's ability to act in a manner consistent with democratic traditions.

Education is mainly a function of the states, and from the beginning of the FRG, state Ministers of Education knew that they needed to coordinate aspects of education among themselves. Consequently, a Standing Conference of State Ministers of Education was founded in 1949.[3] This Standing Conference was not intended to compel any one state to comply with central mandates but to allow the states to regulate parts of the education system that would benefit from coordination. For example, all states found it helpful to stagger summer vacation periods so that holiday areas would not be overcrowded. It was also necessary to choose somebody who could represent Germany in international contacts and decisions.

---

in that freedom of teaching was widely interpreted in such a way that it did not absolve teachers from declaring allegiance to the Basic Law (Art 5: 3).

[3]*Ständige Konferenz der Kultusminister der Länder in der Bundesrepublik Deutschland.*

The Standing Conference came to decisions by consensus. Significant agreements included the Düsseldorf and Hamburg Treaties.

Düsseldorf Treaty of 1955

The first major unifying document, known as the Düsseldorf Treaty,[4] was drawn up in 1955. Its purpose was to integrate the basic educational and examination structure so that courses taken or examinations passed at any given school would have the same content and value. After World War II, certain differences among schools had evolved that were disturbing to many Germans. For example, the city state of Berlin had moved deliberately toward a common secondary school, whereas other states remained more or less committed to the three different school types beyond the primary school: the *Hauptschule* (main school), the *Realschule* (secondary general school), and the *Gymnasium*. At the Düsseldorf conference the three school types were made mandatory, so that if a family moved from one state to another, sufficient commonality would exist between schools that the children would not be disadvantaged.

In addition, each of the three types of secondary schools was assigned a specific role. For example, the *Gymnasium* was to qualify its graduates for admission to the university. Thus, any school whose main function was to do this would carry the name *Gymnasium*.

Hamburg Treaty of 1964

In the unification of East and West Germany, the most important agreement made by the Standing Conference of Ministers was the Hamburg Treaty of 1964. It became the school law imposed on the new East German states as they sorted out their educational options and wrote their individual school laws. The Unification Treaty between East and West Germany (Art. 37, sec. 4) stipulated that the

---

[4]*Abkommen zwischen den Ländern der Bundesrepublik zur Vereinheitlichung auf dem Gebiete des Schulwesens vom 17. Februar 1955.*

school system in each of the five new states would conform to the agreement the Education Ministers of the old states (FRG) made in 1964.

Over the years a number of difficult issues faced states of the FRG related to equality of educational opportunity and recognition of each other's educational programs. One important issue discussed above was the mobility of West German families. This and other problems had been approached in the Düsseldorf Treaty of 1955 but remained unsettled.

Therefore, the Ministers of Education from all eleven states engaged in a long and tedious process of decision making that resulted in the Hamburg Treaty of 1964. It mandated that the school laws of all eleven states be brought into conformity with the Treaty, which provides the basic organizational structure for all schooling, including the following provisions:

- **The beginning and ending of the school year** (Art. 1): The school year begins in all states of the Federal Republic after 1 August of any year and concludes on 31 July of the following year.
- **The beginning and length of compulsory attendance** (Art. 2): Compulsory attendance at school will be required on 1 August for all pupils, who have reached their sixth birthday by 30 June of any year. Full-time compulsory attendance ends at the conclusion of nine years of schooling. Attendance for a tenth full-time school year is permitted for all pupils.
- **Length of vacations** (Art. 3): The total number of vacation days in all states of the Federal Republic shall be 75 work days each school year. In general, the following vacation periods shall exist: fall, Christmas, Easter, Whitsuntide, and summer. The dates and length of vacations must be decided in consultation with the Standing Conference of Ministers. In general, summer vacation lasts six weeks and takes place on a rolling basis from 15 June until 15 September. The date is pushed back in each state every year.

- **The types of the different educational institutions and the organizational forms** (Art. 4, 5, 6, 7, 8, 9, 10, 11): There are a number of different types of schools. The *Grundschule* (primary school) is a general school serving all pupils at the primary level. At the conclusion of primary school, pupils pass on to a support or an orientation level of secondary school or directly to one of several secondary school types: the *Hauptschule* (main school), the *Realschule* (secondary general school), the *Gymnasium*, or the *Gesamtschule* (comprehensive school). The *Abendschule* (evening school) is a part of the second educational track, which has the label *Abendhauptschule, Abendrealschule,* or *Abendgymnasium.* If a state wishes to make provision for vocationally oriented secondary students to receive a school-leaving certificate qualifying for higher education, the state may provide a *Kolleg* (college). Provisions for the *Sonderschule* (special education school) and *Fachhochschule* (advanced technical school) are possible. Provision for transfer between schools should be assured. The Hamburg Treaty does not describe the comprehensive schools, which are considered to be experimental schools in the FRG, and which require special agreements with the state Ministers of Education.
- **Foreign language in the different school types** (Art. 9, 10, 13, 14): The *Hauptschule* and *Realschule* will offer one foreign language, generally English, that begins in grade five. At the *Realschule* a second foreign language can be offered as an elective subject. The *Gymnasium* offers the first foreign language in grade five and the second foreign language (English, French, or Latin) in grade seven. Any foreign language beyond the first foreign language must begin by grade nine.
- **Acceptance of school-leaving certificates of specific school forms** (Art. 17): Most school-leaving certificates qualifying for higher education of one state are accepted by other states. A number of school-leaving certificates are named: the

Hauptschulabschluß, Realschulabschluß, the *Abitur (Gymnasiumabschluß),* and the *Fachhochschulreife,* which provides the *Abitur* along with a vocational qualification. It is not necessary to attend a specific school type to obtain a specific school-leaving certificate. There exist many avenues toward these aims.

- **Reciprocal recognition of school examinations** (Art. 18): A condition for reciprocal recognition of state examinations is that the first state examination (in higher education) be conducted according to the guidelines of the Standing Conference of Ministers. The second state examination, a professional qualification, must also be conducted according to agreements reached. Reciprocity exists for leaving certificates from the comprehensive school, special schools, private schools, other technical and higher education certificates.

- **Designation of marks for report cards and school-leaving examinations** (Art. 19): The entire FRG is bound to the following marks for Report Cards and School Examinations: very good (1), good (2), satisfactory (3), sufficient (4), deficient (5), failure (6).

While many of the agreements reached in Hamburg pose little difficulty for the new states of Germany, some present great hardship. These include a provision for a 13 year *Gymnasium* prior to the *Abitur,* whereas East Germany had provision for a 12 year *Gymnasium.* Also the Hamburg Treaty had no provision for a polytechnical school similar to that which was universal in East Germany.

The Education System in 1989

Even though the West German school system had a great number of differences at the time of the collapse, these differences were mainly quantitative rather than qualitative. Therefore, that which is described here is the general framework of the school structure.

Pre-School Education

Nursery schools have existed in Germany since the beginning of the nineteenth century, but they have not been a part of the formal education structure. At the time the FRG was established, people took for granted that the young child should be in the home under family care, particularly the mother's. Some formal programs for children ages three to six existed to "supplement" the work of the family, to act as a bridge from family to school, and to help children who did not have a proper family environment in which to grow. Because pre-schooling was regarded as an adjunct to the family, it fell within the realm of the Ministry of Social Welfare and not the Ministry of Education. Attendance at nursery school has not been mandatory, and most programs run only three hours or half a day. Almost all of the teaching personnel have been *Erzieherinnen* (female educators), who have attended a vocational school rather than a teacher training college or university. Most nursery schools are sponsored by Catholic and Protestant welfare associations; however, local communities are increasingly involved in establishing them. At the end of 1989, the time of East Germany's collapse, approximately 30% of all nursery schools were run by local communities.

At the FRG's beginning in 1949, it was the exceptional child who attended a nursery school. By 1960 approximately 32% of all children in the three to six age group were enrolled and in the late sixties the percentages climbed dramatically, so that by the end of the 1970s almost 80% of the children were attending (Baumert and Others, 1990, p. 162). A number of reasons exist for this dramatic shift. First, the number of children born dropped almost in half during this period, while the number of places available remained stable. In 1965, for example, more than 1,000,000 children were born, while in 1990, approximately 600,000 births were recorded (Baumert and Others, 1990, p. 164). Second, the number of women entering the work force increased. In 1957 32.5% of all women held jobs outside the home, rising to 43.3% by 1987 (Baumert and Others, 1990, p. 145). With more mothers working, children needed watching for part or all of the day, and nursery schools became an important choice for these women. Third, pre-school education began to be seen as a part of formal education and an important step in the schooling process that provided:

- support and complementary child rearing experiences;
- preparatory experiences for formal schooling;
- day-care for mothers who were now in the workforce;
- extra stimulation for children who came from environments that were not rich in basic learning opportunities;
- a model for child rearing (Liegle, 1990).

Nursery school education has been the one sphere of schooling lying beyond firm state regulation. Statements of aims, content, and methods have been considered advisory rather than regulatory. Yet its nature is defined--not by rules but by the tradition of free play and social development through activities that children choose for themselves. In the past twenty years, however, a growing emphasis on "school preparation" has brought reading and numbers into nursery schools. Even so, situational learning rather than normal learning has characterized nursery school programs.

Primary Schooling

The *Volksschule* historically provided formal schooling for most children. At the end of World War II, however, the lower level of the *Volksschule* came to serve as the common school for all children. The foundation for this common school had been laid at the beginning of the Weimar Period although a parallel school for the elites did exist. After the war, these elite schools were prohibited by the Basic Law (Art. 7: 6), making the lower level of the *Volksschule* a true common school, now known as the *Grundschule* (foundation school). From the beginning of the FRG, variation in the number of years of common schooling has existed from state to state. Whereas most of the states chose a four year foundation school, the city states of Berlin, Bremen and Hamburg opted for a six year program.

Parents are required to register their six-year-olds at the neighborhood *Grundschule*. Because of the shrinking birthrate in West Germany, the size of the classes has changed dramatically over the years. Whereas over four million children attended the common school in 1973, only 1.8 million went in 1987. Accordingly, the number of pupils in a typical classroom dropped from 31 to 20 (Baumert and Others 1990, p. 166).

After World War II, the *common school* was expected to impart general education to pupils heading toward the *Gymnasium* (university preparation), the *Realschule* (secondary general school), and the *Hauptschule* (foundation for vocational training). Moreover, the common school was to be free of social class distinction. These expectations have not fully been met. In particular, country schools and those which remained attached to the upper level of the old *Volksschule* have not adequately served pupils with academic potential. These are still general schools which focus on pupils learning to be good, obedient citizens and competent workers.

By and large, though, the *Grundschule* has been able to successfully impart the basics of reading, writing, arithmetic, social relations, awareness of the world and its interconnectedness, and proper manners and behavior.

Another fundamental task of the *Grundschule* has been to help decide for which type of secondary school each pupil would be suited. This was a new responsibility for the school since its task had always been to serve those who were not destined for academics. With this new obligation, most common schools have emphasized academics more--development in the mother tongue, foreign languages, and introduction to natural and social sciences. In addition, it has adopted more sophisticated teaching strategies such as inquiry learning, cooperative learning, problem solving, individualized instruction, etc. Because of the focus on equality of educational opportunity, the school has given increasing attention to compensatory education--special assistance to children with learning difficulties and other problems.

The final decision about further education for each pupil is not made definitely during the brief time in the common school. Policies have emerged, which have cushioned this transition process. Transfer from primary to secondary school, for example, was originally accomplished by an entrance examination, essentially an intelligence or aptitude test. This type of selection procedure was recognized as too narrow, so in most states, these examinations have been discontinued. A procedure has evolved which allows the teachers to develop profiles of pupil performance and potential. These are communicated to parents with a recommended placement at the secondary level. However, parents are allowed to challenge this recommendation and apply for a different kind of placement. In most instances, these applications have been honored although children must be observed for a time to evaluate their performance. Most secondary schools, though, have adopted one or two "observation years," which allow them to make adjustments in pupil placements and transfer pupils appropriately.

Secondary Education

General secondary education has been realized in several different school types. In the past, they were meant to satisfy the schooling requirements of different social classes and occupational groups: the *Hauptschule* (main school), which originally satisfied eight years of schooling, though that time has been extended to nine or ten years of schooling; the *Realschule* (secondary general school), which satisfied ten years of schooling; the *Gymnasium*, which satisfied thirteen years of schooling. More recently, a school has emerged, known as the *Gesamtschule* (comprehensive school), which has usually put the lower secondary part of all three school programs under a single roof.

At the beginning of the FRG, the proportion of pupils attending each of these schools was quite different than it is today. Figure 1 shows that almost three-fourths of all fourteen-year-old pupils were enrolled in the *Hauptschule*. By 1987 the percentage had fallen dramatically to just over a third. At the same time, the number of pupils in the *Realschule* and *Gymnasium* has gone up in proportion, so that by 1987 approximately 27% attended each of these school types.

The increases in *Realschule* and *Gymnasium* enrollments have been one way West Germans have responded to the reform impulses taking place throughout Western Europe. To increase educational opportunities, do away with early selection procedures, and raise educational standards for all children, countries such as Great Britain and Sweden have moved deliberately toward the type of comprehensive secondary school, which offers the curricula of the major types of secondary schools under one roof. Pupils then are "tracked" into the academic, technical, and pre-vocational levels, but with more flexibility than had been the case in separated schools.

West Germany, however, has chosen to retain its three-part school structure. This has not been without major debate. Particularly during the 1960s and 70s, discussion took place concerning adoption of a general secondary school. The group taking the lead in this movement was the so-called *Deutscher Bildungsrat* (German Educational Council), which was a group of prominent public figures called together in 1965 in a joint agreement between the states and the federal government to suggest educational reform. The Educational Council met in two five year terms, then was disbanded in 1975 because it had stirred up such controversy. Its initial reform proposal was published at the end of its first five-year term (Deutscher Bildungsrat, 1970), recommending that West Germany adopt a comprehensive secondary school similar to that emerging in other countries of Western Europe. This would serve as a common school for all pupils from grades 5 through 10 and would take on the status of the lower secondary school. Its explicit goal was to satisfy the "demand for equality of opportunity" and to raise the general education of everyone (Deutscher Bildungsrat, 1969, p. 21). At the beginning the plan met with general support, but within a short time people began to have serious reservations. By the time the formal plan was formulated in

1973, the sentiment was so strong against it that it never went beyond the experimental stage of development.

On the surface it would appear that West Germany abandoned its quest for greater social justice in education. It chose, however, to go about social justice in a different way than nations adopting the comprehensive school. Certain findings backed the decision. Achim Leschinsky and Karl Ulrich Mayer (1990) published a study of social effects of the comprehensive school in France, Great Britain, and Sweden. They conclude that incorporation of these schools has not achieved the social equity desired; the elites continue to dominate the academic tracks.

Figure 1

The percentage of students entering the *Hauptschule, Realschule,* and *Gymnasium* in 1952, 1960, 1970, 1980, and 1987.

	1952	1960	1970	1980	1987
Hauptschule	73	45	49	40	36
Realschule	6	10	18	26	27
Gymnasium	11	14	19	25	27

Even though West Germany continues to maintain a school structure that reflects a social class bias, the expanding enrollments in the elite schools have been dramatic; what is more, the majority of students in the *Gymnasium* have been coming from the middle and lower social strata. Another aim of the reform was to raise the standard of education for all pupils. Leschinsky and Mayer found that the numbers of pupils passing through schools is such that the *Realschule* leaving certificate has essentially become the minimum standard for almost all pupils. In other words, the general education of most West German young people has increased in the past two decades. They conclude that the aims of social equity and equal opportunity may not be tied as closely to the particular features of the school structure as has been thought.

The three school types, the main school, the *Realschule*, and the *Gymnasium* have also evolved to the point where they all offer a general common curriculum, which consists of German, foreign language, social sciences, mathematics, natural sciences, art and music, physical education, religion/ethics, and a few elective courses. The number of hours varies greatly between school types and between states, but the courses of study have a striking uniformity in subject and content. It is important to take a closer look, however, at the specific school types involved in secondary education.

The Hauptschule

The *Hauptschule* (main school) represents one of the dilemmas of the German school system. At one time, it serviced most of the young people and was regarded as a secondary common school; however, over the years fewer and fewer young people enroll, so that now just over a third of fourteen-year-olds attend. It has become the school of last resort for most young people and has been populated by pupils who are the most difficult to handle--those who are discontented and not very competent academically. In addition, it is still thought of as the old upper level of the *Volksschule* and has had a difficult time shedding its reputation as a school for the lower classes and establishing its identity as a true secondary school. As long as it remains physically connected with the primary school, it is difficult to change the way it is viewed. Gradually, though, some change has been taking place. Berlin, Bremen and North-Rhine-Westphalia have extended the compulsory school time to ten years, so the *Hauptschule* in these states, now one to two years longer than before, has developed new curricula. In Hamburg and Hesse the *Hauptschule* now serves unemployed youth who have completed their compulsory schooling. Consequently, it involves itself in vocational training and the transition from school to work. In the countryside, though, the old *Volksschule* model still remains. Relatively few children now live in the country, though, thus the separation of the primary and secondary sections has been considerably reduced (Baumert and Others, 1990, p. 236).

In urban areas, a more recent development has created severe problems. Approximately 8% of the population in the old states of Germany are foreigners. In the past, these were "guestworkers," men who worked for a time and then returned to their own countries. But increasingly these foreigners are political asylum seekers or people with families who wish to live more secure lives economically. Since the collapse of the Berlin Wall, more than one million asylum seekers have entered Germany, and their numbers have put stress on all public systems including the school system (Nelan, 1993, p. 39). The children of guestworkers and asylum seekers have largely been channeled into the *Hauptschule*, so that in some cities, many of these schools are dominated by the children of the foreign born.

The *Hauptschule* curriculum has been altered to make it more interesting and challenging than in prior years. Previously it focused on what pupils could learn through their own experiences--a concrete relationship to the pupil's everyday life. It now emphasizes more theoretical, scientific, and abstract concepts, which are broken down into subject fields taught by teachers who are specialists. This change has been particularly evident in natural science subjects (physics, chemistry, and biology) and mathematics. English as a foreign language has also become available in most schools. The school has developed a differentiated curriculum, so that certain accelerated classes are available. Also a new vocational subject, *Arbeitslehre* (career education), introduces pupils to the way economics and the work world function in modern society although this course has been difficult to realize in the manner originally planned. Finally, limited elective courses are available that meet specific interests and intellectual capacities. Of course, the old subjects of religion, German, history, social studies, geography, music, drawing, and physical education continue, though less time is given to them.

Upon completion of school, young people can qualify for two types of leaving certificates: the *Hauptschule* and the *Realschule* leaving certificates. In the mid-1970s three quarters of all leaving certificates were for the *Hauptschule*. By 1987 the majority were for the *Realschule*. This suggests that the quality and focus of the *Hauptschule* has changed to overlap the *Realschule* program in significant ways.

The Realschule

The *Realschule* (secondary general school) can be loosely described as a school which has been attended by those who are destined for middle-level occupations. Pupils completing the *Realschule* will have been in formal schooling for at least ten years. The number of pupils attending the school has traditionally been very limited. In the early years of the FRG, the number of fourteen year olds attending the *Realschule* was only about 6%. Over the years, however, the percentage of pupils has increased rapidly to the point that by 1987, 27% of all fourteen year olds were attending this school. This increase is consistent with the general trend toward upward mobility and the desire of working class families to have their children in white collar professions, such as sales, nursing, technical occupations, and middle-level management positions.

The *Realschule* begins in the fifth grade in those states where the primary school is only four years, and in the seventh grade in those states where the primary school extends to six years. It then runs until the ninth or tenth grade, depending on the regulations of the state in question. The fifth and sixth grades have been defined as observation years, which allows a child, who may have been placed in the wrong type of school, to be transferred without time penalty to the *Hauptschule* or the *Gymnasium*.

The curriculum of the *Realschule* has been more varied and extensive than that of the *Hauptschule*. In North-Rhine Westphalia, pupils have been able to concentrate on special subjects, such as technology, economics, nutrition and home economics. In other states, pupils may take special subjects in bookkeeping, accounting, shorthand, typing, woodworking, drafting, and metalworking. While the general subjects have been, by and large, the same as in the

Hauptschule, pupils take many more hours of German, English, mathematics, physics, and other subjects.

The secondary general school leaving certificate (*Realschulabschluß*) is earned by examination.

The Gymnasium

The *Gymnasium* has been the academic secondary school in the FRG. Historically, its main task has been to prepare pupils for study at institutions of higher learning. It has required one of the longest and most rigorous secondary schooling programs in the world. Pupils must successfully complete thirteen years of schooling before receiving the secondary school leaving certificate. Even to be promoted from one year to the next has not been an easy matter for pupils. If they fail any aspect of their program, they have been expected to repeat the full year. Almost a quarter of a century ago, Rolf Dahrendorf (1966) scandalized German educators by publicizing that retentions had been so pervasive that the average *Gymnasium* leaver was 20.4 years old.

In the past the *Gymnasium* served as the school for the small elite group. In the early 1950s barely 5% of an age group could claim to have completed the *Abitur*, which is the *Gymnasium's* school leaving certificate. At the time of the collapse of East Germany, approximately 25% of an age group could make that claim. This general expansion was not by conscious design but was a consequence of events that opened up the most conservative institution in German education.

In the nineteenth century, the *Gymnasium* offered a single, classical program of studies. Only at the turn of this century did modern languages and mathematics/natural science become Gymnasial programs. In the early days of the FRG, these three types were the only legitimate forms of academic schooling,[5] though more recently other

---

[5]*Altsprachliches Gymnasium, Neusprachliches Gymnasium*, and *Mathematischnaturwissenschaftliches Gymnasium*.

types have emerged, including those for economics, social sciences, fine arts and art history, education studies, agriculture, domestic sciences, and physical education. At one time, pupils enrolled in a single *Gymnasium* that would take them through the entire program. Recent reforms have attempted to make the lower level of the *Gymnasium* more general so that a pupil would only begin to specialize in the later part of the lower level, then transfer to the special program at the upper secondary level. This arrangement has permitted more flexibility and has allowed students to transfer from one type of program to another with relative ease, at least in the early stages of secondary study.

The curriculum has always been academic. Practical studies have had little place in the program, and the program bias has always been toward languages and literature. In fact, the distinguishing characteristic of the *Gymnasium* is its foreign language offerings. The first foreign language is begun in the fifth grade and is continued for up to eight years. The second foreign language is usually begun in the seventh grade and lasts for six years, and the optional third foreign language is begun in the ninth grade and may last for four. Any foreign language study must begin by the ninth grade. In a modern language program, the first foreign language has usually been English, though French has often been available in states such as Saarland near the French border.

The first foreign language of the classical program has always been Latin. Even in the classical program, the second foreign language has been a modern language, then Greek has been started in the ninth grade. If a pupil anticipates transferring to the *Gymnasium* from the *Hauptschule* or *Realschule*, he must take foreign languages in a proper sequence. This means that almost all transfers take place by the seventh grade. In fact, the typical transfers have been downward, out of the *Gymnasium*. It has been common knowledge that only about half of those who begin a *Gymnasium* ever move on to the upper secondary level at the *Gymnasium* and obtain the *Abitur*.

The Upper Level of the Gymnasium

Grades 11-13 have constituted the upper level of the *Gymnasium*. It has recently undergone important changes. An important characteristic of German schooling has long been the age-group class where all members of a class group have taken the courses together. Of course, exceptions exist, usually involving foreign language instruction. A pupil might, for example, take French rather than English. The age-group class, however, has been such a part of schooling, that if a pupil failed any course in a given year, he would be assigned to a lower age-group class and repeat a full year. In 1977 the Standing Conference of Ministers (1978) issued recommendations for a fundamental reform of the upper secondary level. The reform has replaced age-group classes at the upper secondary level with a program of individualized studies, in which a pupil may pursue a broad range of courses with differing degrees of difficulty and concentration.

The guidelines of the Standing Conference stipulated that individualized learning begin in grade eleven; however, during the first semester the age-group class would be held together while the pupils were exposed to the choices available. In the second semester, the age-group class influence would be reduced, and in grade twelve would be done away with entirely. This did not mean that pupils had complete choice of courses--choice was for larger thematic units that involved set courses.

The *Gymnasium* terminates with the leaving examination. To be eligible for this examination, pupils have been required to complete a prescribed number of compulsory courses and attain a certain total number of points from marks received in these courses. At the time of the collapse, the typical *Abitur* examination required that the pupil be examined in four subjects, most of which were through written examinations. One of these subjects was German, mathematics, or the first foreign language. The pupil could select either a scientific or art subject for the oral examination. Generally, the teachers have had some control over the content of the examinations, but the Standing

Conference of Ministers has attempted to ensure some uniformity among the schools and the states by providing a list detailing the purposes of the examination, the content the different subjects shall cover, and the form the examination shall take.

In spite of the variety of special subjects available to pupils, West Germans have remained committed to the notion that the *Gymnasium* provide a sound general education (*Allgemeinbildung*) for its pupils. In fact, another term for the *Abitur* is "maturity examination," that reflects this resolution. There are some, who have claimed that the knowledge explosion has made it impossible to ensure a basic general knowledge for all, or even to define what that would be. The basic sentiment has remained, however, that the *Gymnasium* provides a general education.

The Gesamtschule

Since the mid-1960s debate about the *Gesamtschule* has continued in West Germany. The *Gesamtschule* was intended to integrate the three lower secondary institutions into a single school, at least from grades 5 to 10 although most added an upper secondary school for inclined pupils to obtain the *Abitur*. Two types of *Gesamtschulen* have been typical: the integrated *Gesamtschule*, housing all three school types under one roof, and the cooperative *Gesamtschule*, consisting of the three separate types of schools under a single central administration that allowed cooperation in programs of courses and pupil offerings.

In those early years, the *Gesamtschule* was considered to be an experimental institution, though its advocates considered it to be an experiment in the Swedish and Norwegian comprehensive school sense. In Scandinavia policy makers relied on research and technology as a means of demonstrating how new forms of schooling would be demonstrably better than old forms. Pedagogy was not simply thought of as an expression of some ideological bias or based on some particular political faction. Education would be based on scientific evidence and reform proposals would be based on experimental proof.

The comprehensive school experiments in Sweden and Norway were conducted with the belief that the government would try out new school forms and educational methods before these would be mandated by law. Experimentation as an appropriate mode of inquiry had become generally popular following World War II (e.g., Hitpass, 1980).

Germans, particularly in the city states of Berlin, Bremen, and Hamburg, assumed their comprehensive school experiments were to demonstrate the advantages of what they believed to be the school of the future. By 1975, at least 216 comprehensive schools had been established (Köhler & Schreier, 1990, p. 120). Unfortunately, the ambitions of the educational researchers were somewhat beyond the capacity of experimentation. It would be impossible to "prove" the value of one institution over another. Ultimately, the decision as to what school form would be adopted would be a political decision. In the mid-1970s the comprehensive school became a central political issue in the political campaign. Election outcomes indicated that the *Gesamtschule* would not replace the old system. However, the *Gesamtschule* remained an experimental institution, and in 1982 the Standing Conference of Ministers agreed to recognize the leaving certificates of the *Gesamtschule* as a regular part of the West German system. Thus, the *Gesamtschule* eventually went beyond the experimental stage and became an alternative to the three part school structure, albeit a modest alternative at least in numbers of *Gesamtschulen*. As of 1987, there were 365 *Gesamtschulen* to 2,455 *Gymnasien*, 2,593 *Realschulen*, and 2,304 *Hauptschulen* (Köhler & Schreier, 1990, p. 120).

The distinguishing characteristic of the *Gesamtschule* has been its commitment to grouping, which meets the individual needs of its pupils. In contrast, the purpose of the three other school types has long been to provide a rather uniform school curriculum to a specific type of student. The *Gesamtschule*, though, has brought different types of students together in the same school. In the first two grades of the secondary level, the *Gesamtschule* has retained its observation plan, so the students have been heterogeneously grouped during the fifth and sixth grades; however, the last three years of the program has seen a differentiated structure based on student ability and interest, that offers programs similar to those in the *Gymnasium*, *Realschule*, and *Hauptschule*. The *Gesamtschule* has attempted to retain the age-group class by placing each child in a heterogeneous group that attends classes like history, geography, social studies, and music/art together. Then the group breaks up into ability sections for specific subjects, including the first foreign language, mathematics, German, and the natural sciences.

Special Education

Throughout the years of the FRG, recognizing the different talents, needs, and interests of pupils and providing schooling to suit these requirements have been central to reform. Such improvements have come slower for children with learning and behavior problems, brain dysfunction, physical and mental handicaps, and non-German children with limited proficiency in the language.

A report put out by the Committee on Special Education, part of the Education Council, presented objectives that meant to integrate more special education children into regular schools and to develop curricula to help them in ways they need, not just carry them along. It suggested that:

- Diagnostic procedures used to classify pupils with learning disabilities and to evaluate their later progress be made more effective;
- Return to primary school or the *Hauptschule* be made easier for children who attended a special school and who show improvement;
- Teaching methods be developed which allow a portion of the children suffering under more serious learning disabilities to

remain in primary school or the *Hauptschule* and find help there;

- Contact be promoted between the pupils at special schools and the children in regular schools in order to break down prejudice and resentment (Max Planck Institute for Human Development and Education, 1979).

Since the end of World War II until 1973, Turks, Greeks, Yugoslavs, Spaniards, and Italians were invited by the German government to increase the work force needed for the rebuilding of the country and for the great industrial expansion. These "guest workers" (*Gastarbeiter*) were expected to stay a few years and then return to their own countries. Many did but many stayed on and established families. The Max Planck Institute reports that in 1979, every tenth child under 15 and every seventh child under 7 was non-German. Even though many of these children were born in the Federal Republic, the law does not give them German citizenship. So these children who live between cultures, so to speak, are growing up without equal access to the most desirable in German life. They are overrepresented in primary and *Hauptschulen* and underrepresented in *Gymnasien* and *Realschulen*. A lower proportion than German children fail to obtain a leaving certificate or to attend vocational school. Studies reported by the Max Planck Institute term this a social-minority problem having to do mainly with Turks, Yugoslavs, Greeks, Italians, and Spaniards. Americans, Japanese, and other West European children do much better.

Reform attempts were begun late, the problem of citizenship still remains, and many families have been indecisive whether they would stay or go back to their mother countries. Nevertheless, progress has been made. Special funds exist for intensive tutoring of non-German children in German and in other subjects. Special preparatory courses are offered teachers to prepare them to help these children better. Finally, supplemental funds have been allocated for teaching materials especially developed for these children.

Vocational Education

In West Germany young people could become skilled in a craft in two major ways: attending full-time vocational schools and entering an apprenticeship system. The number of pupils in full-time vocational schools has been relatively small. In 1987 approximately 302,000 students were attending special vocational schools *(Berufsfachschulen)*, while another 110,000 were attending school services in health *(Schulen des Gesundheitswesens)*. In contrast, 1,740,000 persons were in apprenticeship positions.

In 1987, nearly 70% of all school leavers, approximately the numbers above, who completed the nine year *Hauptschule*, the ten year *Realschule*, and the thirteen year *Gymnasium* moved on through vocational education and training. In the two decades prior to that time, the average starting age for apprenticeship rose significantly, from about fifteen to eighteen years of age, because a growing number of young people have remained in full-time general education or even full-time vocational school before moving into the vocational training programs. Those in training have included a increasing number of young people who have completed the 13 year *Gymnasium*, which has until recently remained exclusively in the academic sphere. In fact, some apprentices have even attended the university. As recently as 1970, over 70% of all apprentices were *Hauptschule* graduates, and almost no one had attended the *Gymnasium*. In 1987, the percentages changed to only about one third *Hauptschule* leavers and almost one fifth *Gymnasium* graduates. That approximately 40% of all university students have taken apprenticeship training before entering the university is indicative of the melding of the practical and academic world. Seen in another way, those going into the vocational sphere are more highly skilled, at least in terms of formal education, than apprentices of the past (Schmidt, 1992).

Apprenticeship has been labeled "the dual system" in West Germany, because practical training is had at the work places (80% of the training time) and theoretical training is given in vocational training schools. "The characteristic feature of this system is that the provision of knowledge and skills is linked to the acquisition of the required job experience" (Deutscher Industrie- und Handelstag, 1988, p. 5). The dual system has relied on a joint venture between private enterprise and public vocational training. While on-the-job training has been offered by the private sector, formal education has been conducted by the federal government. The entire process has been monitored by the Chamber of Crafts and Industry.

Apprentice training has usually run for a three year period. The young person has worked on-the-job for three to four days a week and has spent the remaining one or two days in formal instruction. The practical training has been carried out by certified instructors in accordance with a curriculum that has been defined by the Federal Institute for Vocational Training, in cooperation with the employer's organizations and trade unions. Locally, the responsibility for guaranteeing the quality of apprenticeship training has rested in the hands of business organizations. In 1992 there were 380 different occupations available in which training could be received. Approximately half of the apprentices have been in industry and commerce, while another 36% have been in handcrafts occupations, and less than 3% have been in agriculture (Statistisches Bundesamt, 1987). In recent years the number of occupations for which training has been available has shrunk. In 1971 there were more than 600 recognized occupations for which youth could qualify.

The number of occupations has declined because of a radical restructuring of occupations. Most trade union members, employers, and vocational school people agree that the old system of training has not worked as well as it could. Because society is interactive and everything effects everything else, they claim this must be reflected in work organization. Consequently, the new vocational education must be inter-connective and no longer made up of isolated training programs. The whole is different from the sum of its parts. This requires that training must be broadly based, marked by a high level of professional competence and the development of personal characteristics such as the ability to cooperate and self-reliance (Rolff, 1988, p. 51). In addition, workers must understand the organization in which they work--a helicopter's view of the situation rather than a worm's eye view (Schmidt, 1992).

This orientation implies changes in training practice from principally narrow work specialization of the past toward greater unity and integration. The practical solution to this reform has been to reduce the number of occupational categories and insist that all training have a broad, more general foundation to help future workers see how their jobs fit in to all aspects of the company and beyond. Because of recent changes in training, apprentices in similar occupations have begun to share the same training, general education, and occupational education for the first year and a half. In the next half year they have become more specialized, but continue clustered training with certain related occupations. Only in the final year and a half has training become highly specialized (Munch, 1990, pp. 321-22). The new changes in Germany's apprenticeship program is also viewed more and more as the beginning of life-long learning, rather than terminal training.

Teacher Education

Pedagogy, as a special field of study, is long on tradition in Germany. Prospective teachers learn theory as well as engage in practice, the relative importance of each varying according to the level of training involved. The two basic models of teacher preparation are best represented by the training taken by future *Gymnasium* teachers and that offered to *primary* teachers.

Those wishing to become teachers at the *Gymnasium* have typically followed the regular higher education program of studies for two fields. This means students have been expected to attend the university for eight to twelve semesters and conclude with a state examination. Students and professors take for granted that their study is not oriented to the practice of teaching itself but focused on scientific inquiry. Every university offers pedagogical studies, but students who take these courses also confront a strong scientific orientation rather than one designed to prepare them for teaching. Once a student has completed the university program, he or she has been deemed qualified to teach, but only on a provisional basis. During the first two years of practice, the student has entered the second stage of teacher preparation, which is specifically directed to school practice. In fact, this stage has not been connected with the university at all. Individual school districts have long conducted this program which has required that the provisional teacher engage in a two-year intensive experience completed by an examination.

The pre-professional experience of the primary teacher has been quite different. Historically, those wishing to be a part of this school, did not even complete the *Gymnasium*, but entered teaching as an apprentice. This meant that those connected with the two types of institutions never crossed paths. The *Gymnasium* teachers had attended the *Gymnasium* and the university, while the primary teachers had attended the *Volksschule* or *Hauptschule* and the teacher training program. The backgrounds of primary teachers was finally altered after World War I, when the *Reichsschulkonferenz* of 1920 mandated that all prospective *Volksschule* teachers must obtain the *Abitur* prior to being admitted to the teacher training program.

Initially, prospective *Volksschule* teachers attended a teacher preparation seminary, which was eventually upgraded to a teacher training institute and then the teacher training college (*Pädagogische Hochschule*). This meant that they had been given higher education status. In 1960 there were 77 teacher training colleges in the Federal Republic of Germany. Even though these institutions had gained higher education status, they remained directed toward practice and attempted to help young prospective teachers gain the skills necessary to act in the classroom. The recent trend has been to break down the isolation of the teacher training college and integrate it with the general university. In 1970 the number of separate colleges had been reduced to 32, to 13 in 1980, and to 9 in 1987 (Peisert, 1990, p. 408). This has often been a painful and difficult process because the university has expected the college to become scientifically oriented, while those at the college wished to keep their commitment to prepare teachers for actual practice.

An ongoing difficulty with teacher training has been defining appropriate training for teachers in the *Realschule* and *Gesamtschule*. The conventional solution has been a middle-ground approach. For example, a *Realschule* teacher must complete three years of education at a university, then transfer to a teacher training college for an additional three semesters, where he or she focuses on pedagogy and practice.

Higher Education

In West Germany, science-oriented institutions and technical institutes (*Fachhochschulen*) have made up the higher educational system. In 1987 there were approximately 120 of the first type, including 20 established universities, 15 newer universities, 12 technical universities, 6 comprehensive institutions of higher education, and 15 specialized institutions of higher education. At the same time, approximately 120 *Fachhochschulen* were in existence, including 26 institutes with multiple study areas, 14 with two, and 10 with just one. The major study areas most often represented include 20 for technology, 18 for social sciences, 4 for economics, 7 for art and design. All but 13 institutes have enrolled fewer than 7,000 students, so they have been relatively small compared with the major established universities where enrollments average 26,000 or more--Munich University has 62,000 students, and the Free University of Berlin has 58,000 students. Approximately one million students were enrolled in research institutions, while less than 300,000 were in *Fachhochschulen* (Peisert, 1990, pp. 408-11).

The above numbers represent a dramatic shift in the nature of higher education in West Germany. The university of the nineteenth century was specifically for the elites of German society. As late as 1960 the route to institutions of higher education was through the *Gymnasium* and the *Abitur*. Until recently, anyone possessing the *Abitur* was qualified to enter any field of study available at the university, regardless of the secondary school track the student had taken. As the university shifted from an elite institution to a mass institution, it has become necessary to restrict the number of students in specific programs. This is known as the *numerus clausus*, which has allowed a university to determine the number of places available and allow only that number of qualified students to enter the program. Most fields of study controlled by *numerus clausus* specify that a maximum of 5% of all allocated places be open to non-German students.

Traditionally, the *Abitur* was the only way to higher education, but in the 1950s a second possibility arose. Those who completed the lesser school-leaving certificates and entered vocational training, were allowed to proceed onto technical schools and *Fach-hochschulen*, where they could eventually qualify to transfer to the university. This has become known as the second educational track (*Zweiter Bildungsweg*). Because approximately 40% of all students in higher education have gone through a vocational education program, the importance of the second educational track has taken on more and more significance.

There is a marked difference in the socio-economic background of students at the *Fachhochschule* and those at research institutions. This is best illustrated by the numbers of students from working class families in the two types of institutions. Whereas one student in five at the *Fachhochschule* has come from working-class backgrounds, only one student in ten at the university has come from this social class. Actually, the representation of working-class families was much higher at both institutions in the 1970s but in the 80s it fell back again. The participation of females at research institutions (41%) is much higher than at *Fachhochschulen* (29%), but this can best be explained by the fact that most of the fields of study at the technical institutes focus on more traditional male occupations.

In West Germany, students have been admitted directly into their particular field of study. The assumption has been that general education studies are mainly completed in secondary school, so traditionally, general education courses are sparse in higher education. The programs at the *Fachhochschulen* are more concentrated than at the university. Students typically spend three or four years at these institutions. When they complete the program, they are then eligible to transfer to the university. Because much of their previous studies count for university also, they can complete the five or six year university program rather quickly. Occupation expectations remain more limited for graduates of technical institutes. Those finishing the university expect positions equivalent to the highest levels of civil servant status. There are more than 320 different fields of study in higher education in West Germany. In the classical sense, higher education in West Germany is committed to the notion of *Lehrfreiheit* (freedom to teach) and *Lernfreiheit,* (freedom to learn), but in recent years certain regulations have interfered with these commitments, particularly as it relates to examinations. Students must pursue a specific number of courses and engage in specific readings if they expect to pass the examination structure.

Foreign Students

West Germany has been exemplary in terms of its commitment to hosting foreign students. Its institutions of higher learning reserve 6% of all student places for foreigners and even more places are made available in those fields where *numerus clausus* restrictions are not in effect. Only the United States and France can claim to have a greater proportion of foreign students in its institutions of higher learning (Peisert, 1990, p. 456). The figures cited in this section refer only to full-time students who are in residence usually for one or more years. In addition, one must keep in mind that large numbers of exchange arrangements for short-term programs, seminars, and conferences take place each year.

Conditions for admission to an institution of higher learning is an academic background comparable to that of German students. Tradition has established certain guidelines for comparability. For example, students from the United States usually have to have completed two years of university study in order to be admitted in full standing. If there is no such tradition, then potential students must pass an examination that demonstrates equivalency. Students must also demonstrate a sufficient language facility to function in the classroom and access to sufficient funds.

The arrangements of the European Community (EC) are especially important. Whereas about half of all foreign students came from the developing world in 1960, that figure has sunk to about 35%, while students coming from EC countries has risen from 24% to 29% (Baumert and Others, 1990, p. 100). Their participation often comes through EC sponsored programs, such as ERASMUS and COMECON. The objective of the EC is that one tenth of all students in each of the countries of the EC will engage in studies in another EC country. One of the difficulties of such an aim is that study time be recognized in Germany as equivalent to study at a German institution of higher learning. In the past students have not been very successful although some arrangements are now being accepted in terms of institutional partnerships.

Chapter IV

Education in the German Democratic Republic

Introduction

In the last decades, the German Democratic Republic became characterized, both at home and abroad, as an educational society. Almost every citizen in every corner of the country were participating in some sort of educational institution or program from birth until death. Even though the main justification for all this could be attributed political leadership's desire to engage people in life-long ideological indoctrination, there was much more to it than that. This accent on education permeated every dimension of society and was supported well by state resources. Education was to be accessible equally to males and females, as well as all classes of people; nevertheless, certain people had greater advantage and others were deprived of full education.

Marxist/Leninist Ideology in East German Education

The foundation for education in the German Democratic Republic rested on the ideology of Marx and Engels. While it is questionable whether Marx and Engels laid out a full educational scheme, they certainly provided a general basis on which such a program ought to be built. In the twentieth century, a number of educational positions emerged, which were inspired by the ideas of Marx and Engels. The workers' movement (*Arbeiterbewegung*) influenced those that developed in Germany, such as the Eisenach Program (1869), the Gothaer Program (1875), the Erfurt Program (1891), and the Proletarian School Program (1929) (Fischer 1990, pp. 17-9). Perhaps the strongest indigenous German educational movement at the time the GDR was being formed was *Reformpädagogik* (Reform Pedagogy), the German version of progressive education, influential in the United States earlier in the century. In Germany, this movement challenged the elitist classical humanism stressed a child centered program within a democratic comprehensive school. During the Weimar period, reform-oriented educators such as Paul Oestreich, Franz Hilker, Fritz Karsen, Siegfried Kawerau, and Elizabeth Rotten had established the Association of Radical School Reformers.[1] Although the Association did not affiliate with any political party, it leaned toward socialism and used Marxist language in its publications. In the Weimar period it concerned itself mainly with educational developments in the Soviet Union (Rust, 1967, p. 56).

During the first years after World War II, those who identified with the *Reformpädagogik* movement were active in the Soviet occupation zone. But their beliefs were not entirely consistent with the educational ideology of the Soviet Union. Whereas the progressive educators focused on the "child-centered" dimensions of the movement, Soviet socialist education focused on institutional and social imperatives (Alt, 1946).

The progressive educators rapidly lost influence in the Soviet occupation zone, so that when the German Democratic Republic (GDR) was established in 1949, it adopted, in large measure, the educational ideology and practices of the Soviet Union.

The aim of socialist education system was a high educational level of all people, meaning universally educated and highly qualified citizens who are mentally and physically healthy, efficient, cultured and able and ready to fulfill the historic tasks of the time (Education Law, 1965, paragraph 2). Not to be forgotten is the goal of developing in each an all-round and harmoniously developed socialist personality--a person who consciously shapes life in society, changes nature, and leads a full and happy life worthy of a human being.

Educators in the Soviet Occupation Zone were continually exploring practical ways of helping young people develop into ideal

---

[1] *Bund Entschiedener Schulreformer.*

citizens--the socialistic personalities who would one day bring Communism into full flower in Germany. At the Pedagogical Congress of August, 1949, that took place just before the establishment of the German Democratic Republic in October of that year, delegates discussed improving the school performance of children and youth. They searched for means of actualizing the Socialist goal of a high educational level in the citizenry. One suggested tactic was establishing a pupils' free time organization and fostering a close connection between that and school (Ministerium für Volksbildung, 1949, p. 9). The congress report stated that "extracurricular education must support, broaden, deepen, and fortify what is being taught at school" and was to be developed through the establishment of circles, courses, work teams, and Children's Houses in such a way that the interests and inclinations of children are satisfied and that they can unfold their capabilities and their character. (Ministerium für Volksbildung, 1949, p. 174). This was a practical way of building the socialistic personality while following the connection between work/school and leisure time that Marx advocated.

Contained within the ideal of the well-rounded socialistic personality, was the expectation that such people would fulfill the historic tasks of the age, which meant dedicating their time and energies to the building up and support of the socialist state. Therefore, Communistic education of youth during school/work hours as well as during leisure time became a task of the first importance, not just for educators but for society as a whole. (Voß, 1981, p. 265). This could be properly accomplished only when formal schooling and free time or extracurricular education were coordinated. The Program Model of the SED (Programmenentwurf der SED, 1947, p. 148) directed that "schools be developed with all facilities for before and after school care...and with the cooperation of the Friends of the New School...be a cultural focus in the community."

The Friends of the New School was a pedagogical movement in the Soviet zone of Germany during the post-war period whose goal was to give "assistance in the carrying through of extracurricular free time activities." (Richtlinien, 1948). Community organizations and state institutions were represented within this group who wanted to give opportunity for self initiative, activity, and leisure-time opportunities to children (Richtlinien, 1947). Noteworthy is that from the beginning, trusted community organizations were given co-responsibility as education sponsors, and, in addition, these activities were not exclusively for ideological goal setting--something that developed later. The Friends of the New School set precedence for cooperative efforts between schools/youth organizations and other groups, including sponsorships of firms of the various pupil work teams set up by the Pioneer organization (Gräßler & Raabe, 1991, pp. 5-6).

Education in the GDR went through phases, but for all intents and purposes, the system that existed in 1989 was already in place by 1961/62. The two most significant educational laws that determined education in 1989 were the Education Law of 1965 and the Higher Education Law of 1967.

Education went far beyond the formal schooling at primary, secondary and higher levels. The German Democratic Republic established a plan of life-long informal, nonformal, and formal education that was as extensive as any in the world. Fischer (1992, pp. 57-8) claims that three elements characterized the system. First, whereas conventional education had been based on social class, the new foundation was the common school. Every effort would be given to bring all young people into the same institution, giving them a common educational experience, and helping them to learn how to work as a single social unit.

The system was centered around the ten year general polytechnical secondary school, that would be attended by all young people.[2] This school actually served as both the primary and lower secondary school, satisfying the ten years of compulsory school attendance. According to informants in East Germany, schools in the mid-1980s were stable and effective institutions. Because education was a high priority in the old East German regime, great resources were avail-

---

[2]*Polytechnische Oberschule* (POS).

able to schools. In return, they were expected to conform to a tightly defined role, which over time led to schooling being uniform and conformist. The curriculum was explicitly defined by central authorities, and very little innovation and experimentation was acceptable. All young people in the ten-year school were expected to take nearly the same program of studies. Instruction was ordered and formal, and it was also expected to be ideologically supportive of the regime. Second, all education was under the jurisdiction of the state. One of the first decrees the Soviet Union made after the revolution in 1918 was to remove the control of schools from the church and place them under the control of regional and local councils (Bereday, Brickman & Read, 1969, p. 60), because they were seen as vestiges of capitalistic free enterprise and the ruling class. For this reason, the German Democratic Republic eliminated almost all private schools. Third, education was made "worldly" in that all connections with religion were severed. Not only were private religious schools taken over by the state, but religious instruction, which had been a central aspect of all school curricula, was cut out. Fourth, education was free. That tradition existed for compulsory school in Germany prior to World War II, but East Germany extended it to pre-schooling, to vocational training, and to higher education.

Tight Supervision by Socialist Unity Party (SED)

While the formal management structure of education in the German Democratic Republic is difficult to frame, the informal power structure was clear and simple. The most prominent feature of management was the extent of tight central control throughout the country. Education was intended to serve the needs of socialist society as defined by the Socialist Unity Party (*Sozialistische Einheitspartei Deutschland*--SED). Its more bureaucratic branches were charged with putting the policies into practice. The formal power structure of education was lodged in a three part, hierarchical organization as outlined in Figure 1.

The real power behind Education lay with the Socialist Unity Party (Figure 1, left), moved through the Council of Ministers to the ministries. The Council of Ministers coordinated, planned, and managed the economic and social aspects of education. The ministries took over certain responsibilities delegated by the Council of Ministers. The most important of these ministries was the Ministry of Education; however, the State Planning Commission planned and guided general vocational education, along with a number of subordinate Councils, including a National Economic Council that was responsible for vocational training in industry, an Agricultural Council, and a State Secretariat for Higher and Technical Education which controlled colleges and technical schools of Education (Education Law, 1965, VIII-I-71 to 76).

Figure 1
The Power Structure of Education in the German Democratic Republic.

Socialist Unity Party	Council of Ministers	Ministries of Various Facets of Education
Regional Organs of the Socialist Unity Party	Regional and District Offices of the Council of Ministers	Regional and District Education Offices
Local Organs of the socialist Unity Party	Local Organs of the Council of Ministers	Local Education Offices

Connected to these groups were several offices which oversaw matters related to practice and educational structure. The most important was the Academy of Pedagogical Sciences (*Akademie der Pädagogischen Wissenschaften*), located in East Berlin next door to the Ministry of Education and subject to that ministry. It had heavy research responsibilities, but its main function was to realize the German Democratic Republic's political and ideological policies in school practice. It developed curricula for the country, wrote textbooks, created programs for further education of teachers, etc. It had published more than 300 books and more than 1,000 doctoral research and *Habilitation* works. It was also responsible for the major educational libraries of the country. At its peak it maintained a staff of approximately 800 researchers and professionals and published a number of journals (Kossakowski, 1992, p. 88).

The above structure was duplicated at the regional level, and again at the town or district level. A general party structure, which answered to the party structure at the regional level, a town or district executive committee that answered to the regional executive committee, and a local school administrative office, which answered to the regional school administrative office. Because our interest in this study is focused on the local school, the main observation necessary is that the local school not only had its formal administrative structure, but it had its school council consisting of members of the SED, with its own school party secretary.

School Leadership

Each school was headed by a School Director, who was formally responsible for the administration of the school. However, it was with the school director that the party hierarchy and the state administrative structure came together. That is, the school director represented both the administrative arm and the party arm in the school. Consequently, the school director was almost always a strong member of the SED or at least a loyal citizen of the GDR. School directors were responsible for the political, educational and organizational climate and structure of the school. The school director was formally recommended by the local school inspector to the local council of ministers, which ensured that the individual was politically acceptable. Even though the school director was often a capable educator, the primary criterion for selection was always that the person was firm believer in socialism as interpreted by the SED. The climate of the school usually was determined by the director, who had great influence on all happenings in the school.

Mainly, most directors acted with positive intent in regard to the children and teachers in their school; however, there were clear cases of discrimination and even vindictive behavior on the part of certain directors. We have interviewed too many people who encountered such problems to dismiss them as distorted narratives of disgruntled individuals. In one case, a young child had the dilemma of choosing between attending young pioneer meetings or religious meetings sponsored by the child's church.[3] This child, who chose to attend the religious meetings, was consequently denied the opportunity to proceed from the POS to the extended upper secondary school (EOS), because the child had not demonstrated adequate civic responsibility.

The most severe cases usually were related to young people who were active in religious organizations, but other cases were plentiful. As an example, Hans B. lived in East Berlin and had been trained in model engineering as a young man. The state was not always able to satisfy its own production needs, and occasionally allowed individuals to establish private firms to products they needed. Because the state had not been very successful in its own attempts to produce model products, Herr B. proposed to the state that he set up a small model building firm. He was given permission to do so, and he became very successful in his small shop. The fact that he owned a business, however, raised him out of the working class; he, along with his wife and three children, became a capitalist in the socialist state. A daughter was identified early as gifted in music and was placed in a special school after regular school hours to receive inten-

---

[3]For a published account of someone who had been denied access to education because of lack of participation in youth groups, see the account of Rainer Eppelmann (Philipsen 1993, pp. 58-9).

sive music training. When the director of the child's regular school became aware of this, suddenly the little girl began receiving poor grades in the regular school. This meant she would be disqualified from attending the special school. The teacher explained to the parents that the director had given her a directive to fail the child, and she felt powerless to do otherwise.

The school director's role in the school was formally clearly defined. However, the director was also obliged to work in harmony with the person in charge of the Free German Youth and the secretary of the School Party Organization of the SED and other groups connected with the school. This inevitably led to stress points because the meetings were not always consensual and harmonious.

We shall mention briefly the three major leadership groups associated with the individual school: the School Party Organization of the SED (*Schulparteiorganisation der SED*), the Union (*Gewerkschaft Unterricht und Erziehung*), and the Parent Assembly (*Elternversammlung*). In almost all schools, a number of the teachers, secretaries, janitorial staff, etc. were typically members of the SED. These members joined together for the School Party Organization of the SED, and they elected one of their members to serve as the local Secretary. That person was one of the most important figures in the school in that he/she acted as the local link to the socialist party, who was responsible for overseeing the progress of the socialist movement in the school.

The so-called comrades (*Genossen*) made certain that instruction and other educational activities of the school maintained a high level of political and value content consistent with socialism. At least once a month a meeting was organized to instruct the school personnel in some aspect of socialist thought. The organization was also responsible for the FDJ and the Pioneer groups. The polytechnical nature of education was continually stressed. It might be instructive to provide a glimpse at one POS in Marzahn, part of East Berlin. That school employed 40 teachers, 14 educators for the younger children, and 6 technical workers. The school was especially active in recruiting SED members and had 21 members just prior to the collapse. This was somewhat higher than the norm, because about one quarter of a school's instructional staff were typically members of the SED. Schools existed which did not even have an SED organization, although it was highly unusual to find such a situation. Schools were required to have at least three active members of the SED before they could constitute a party organization in the school (Laabs, 1987, p. 337).

Closely aligned with the party organization was the Union, known formally as the Union for Instruction and Education. It was formally optional for people to join but in fact almost every member of the school community was a member. Its main purpose was to see to the welfare of the instructional staff. It worked to find living quarters for new teachers, make arrangements for vacations for teachers, care for personnel if they fall ill, make complaints if the School Director did not act responsibly. The Union was also very active. Of the school mentioned above only four of the 60 professional staff were not members of the Union.

One of the important claims socialists can make is that they have long supported the notion of parental representation in schooling matters. Throughout the Soviet Union, parent councils came into existence shortly after the revolution and have remained an important part of the educational enterprise (Günther and Others, 1973, p. 591). With the establishment of the GDR, parental participation was included as a fundamental right and responsibility in the constitution (Article 37).

In all educational establishments parental involvement was strongly encouraged. The purpose of these groups was to develop a strong relationship between home and school and to draw parents into the general educational process, particularly to support the educational processes taking place in the school. Each school maintained a regular schedule of parent meetings, parent conferences with teachers, information bulletins from the school to the home. Contrary to Western European traditions, almost all parents were actively involved in these meetings and conferences.

The School Structure

We shall outline only the major institutions in the formal educational system, but we later shall discuss various other aspects of education where appropriate.

Preschool Education

Preschool education can be divided into two main phases: *Crèches* and Kindergartens.

Crèches or *Kinderkrippen*

From the very beginning of the GDR, the state made full-day infant care available to working mothers and female students. Originally, babies as young as ten weeks of age were taken in, though there had been considerable discussion as to the wisdom of separating such young babies from their mothers. In fact, in 1977, maternity leave was extended from 10 weeks to 20 weeks, so that babies could remain at home with their mothers for a longer period of time. Maternity leave was again extended to 52 weeks in 1988 (Fischer, 1992, p. 55).

Even though *crèches* fell under the responsibility of the Ministry of Health, these institutions for children up to age three, were considered to be part of the formal educational process. Actually, the main educational function crèches fulfilled was to replace what has traditionally been seen as family education; that is, a social education of the child. Its purpose was to nurture a healthy, happy, active, inquisitive child, who feels comfortable in society and has full opportunity to become competent in speaking the mother tongue. Children were to become accustomed to order and regularity in their daily routines and to attain the first stages of independence (School Law, 1965, III-I-2).

Educators (*Erzieherinnen*) worked with small groups of approximately six young children of the same age. The main method of teaching was through play. Basic hygienic habits were also stressed, and children received regular physical examinations by medical doctors. Enrollment was free of charge though parents participated in the costs of meals.

At the beginning of the GDR, relatively few babies were brought to the *crèches*; however, the numbers gradually increased (1965 at 18.7%; 1975 at 50.8%; 1985 at 72.7%) to the point that in 1989 at least 80.2% of all three year-olds were in the crèches (Fischer, 1992, p. 55).

The Kindergarten

Parents could choose to enroll their three year-old children in Kindergarten where they could remain until they began compulsory school. Generally, a child left Kindergarten between 6.3 to 7.3 years of age to enroll in the polytechnical secondary school (POS). Kindergartens were considered to be the first stage of formal schooling. Even though they were state supervised and determined, different groups were actual sponsors. The most usual sponsor was the community (85.7% of the children). Firms sponsored Kindergartens for 12.1% of the children and churches for just 2.1%. All kindergartens were given precise and detailed outlines that they were expected to follow (Fischer, 1991, p. 56).

The primary aims of kindergarten were the children's healthy physical and mental development, including "attentiveness, imagination, memory and intellectual power," their ability to speak the mother tongue "clearly and coherently," their awareness of "socialist life and of nature," and their acquaintance with "simple time, quantitative and special concepts." Children were to paint, model and build, sing, and dance to awaken "their sense of the beautiful in nature and in our social life." They were to be educated to love their socialist homeland and to love peace. Order and regularity was reinforced through a well-planned routine (School Law, 1965, III-II-2). Play was the method of learning, and the focus of play was group activity.

Even though enrollment remained optional, tuition was free and the rate of participation in kindergarten was among the highest in the world. Even in 1950 20.5% of eligible children were enrolled. By 1960 this figure had reached 46.1%, by 1970 it was 64.5%, by 1980 it was 92.2% and by 1989 it was 95.1% (Fischer, 1992, p. 56).

The Polytechnical Secondary School (POS)

The Polytechnical Secondary School was the center-piece of the East German educational system. It was a ten-year common school that advocated, to the extent possible, grouping pupils together from all social and economic levels. The only exceptions to this were young people who were placed in special education schools and classes: one type for those not capable of performing in the regular classroom and a second type for those showing exceptional talent in technical subjects, mathematics, natural science, language, art and sports. Approximately 6% of the pupils were judged to be eligible for special education programs of the first type, and a very restricted number of exceptionally talented for the second type.

The teacher/pupil ratio at the POS became more favorable over the years. Because the number of children coming through the school kept decreasing, the Ministry of Education was able to improve this ratio. Whereas it stood at 28.0 pupils per teacher in 1960, that ratio dropped to 26.2 in 1975, and to 19.9 in 1985 (Köhler & Schreier, 1990, p. 121). The POS was articulated from grade to grade and connected to the community and to firms. However, it was broken down into three subdivisions, each with a different emphasis.

Lower Level (grades 1-3)

This level paralleled much of what primary school typically rep-resents--learning to read, to write, and to do arithmetic. Thus, the curriculum centered on the German language and arithmetic compu-tations and the natural numbers, but also on basic artistic under-standing related to singing, music, drawing, painting, and modeling;

on all-round physical education; and on simple economic understanding, including manual training and school gardening, .

Already at this level, pupils were subjected to a gentle indoctrination process, that attempted to instill a love for their "socialist fatherland," to habituate them to behave in a disciplined manner, to internalize diligent and scrupulous learning and working habits, and to instill a sense of the value of socially useful activity (Education Law, 1965, IV-I-14).

Intermediate Level (grades 4-6)

At the intermediate level, the focus was still on the German language, mathematics, manual training and school gardening, art subjects, and physical education, but at a higher level than before. In addition, pupils were introduced to the basic elements of social sciences, foreign languages, vocational education, and natural science, including the notion that laws of nature exist. Theoretically based experiments, observations and investigations were carried out. In social sciences, history and politics were emphasized. Stress was placed on independent thinking, but within the framework of social laws as defined by Marx, Engels, and other foundation thinkers of socialism. It was also at this level that students began their first foreign language, Russian. Emphasis was placed on reading and writing the language. In basic vocational education pupils became acquainted with the most important vocations of their region and how their national economy operated (Education Law, 1965, IV-I-15).

Upper Level (grades 7-10)

At the upper level of the POS, pupils remained in homogeneous groups, but they were encouraged to begin considering their own vocational choices. General and vocational education were combined so that pupils could see the connections between science and mathematics, for example, and practical activities. Scientific development was stressed in all facets of the program, and the content of instruction included the following:

- Mathematics: geometry and other mathematics was taught, with special attention to application of mathematical knowledge to other subjects, vocations, and so forth.
- Natural Sciences: physics, astronomy, chemistry, biology, and physical geography were offered, with emphasis given to theory and the discovery of laws through experiments.
- Polytechnical instruction: pupils were systematically exposed to the scientific-technical, technological, and political-economic foundations of socialist production. In the last two grades, pupils spent time in socialist enterprises discovering the types of occupations that exist and learning to appreciate labor.
- Social Sciences: The main focus was that pupils acquired basic historical and political knowledge related to the advancement of socialism, the rise of the German Democratic Republic, and its historic role in socio-political-economic evolution.
- German: While oral and written expression were further perfected, a major focus was on the humanist literature related to socialist realism.
- Foreign languages: Russian language study was continued, and pupils began their second foreign language, which was obligatory.
- Art: Aesthetics was introduced, including the power to make judgments of artistic works. Pupils were encouraged to become active participants in cultural life.
- Sport instruction: Attention was given to all-sided physical education, though special attention was given to gifted pupils (School Law, 1965, IV-I-16).
- Military Instruction: In grades nine and ten compulsory military instruction was given to all students, with the intention of introducing them to socialist military defense and

knowledge. The program was accompanied by an optional experience in military camp.

Comparison between East and West Germany

A major issue is the relative emphasis given to the different subjects during the first ten years of education in the two Germanys.

Figure 2

Comparison of hours of instruction in Hamburg, Hesse, Bavaria and the GDR.

Subject	Hamburg	Hesse	Bavaria	GDR
German	1,576	1,698	1,621	2,853
Maths	1,458	1,660	1,467	1,926
Natural Sciences	1,379	1,312	1,197	1,249
Social Studies	709	849	772	962
1st For. Language	867	888	849	820
2nd For. Language	355	618	---	392
Polytech./ Career ed.	276	154	618	785
Art/Music	788	1,197	1,235	1,070
Religion	394	772	888	---
Sports	1,024	1,081	1,390	820
Other	866		1,505	214

Source: Mitter, 1990, p. 191.

A wide difference exists in the number of hours devoted to specific subjects in the different states in West Germany, so the comparison has to be made between East German and specific states of the FRG. In Figure 2 above, the number of hours recorded for various subjects in the GDR and three states of the FRG, so that some comparison is possible.

This data indicates that the East German school dedicated much more time to German language than any West German state. In addition, it provided more time to mathematics instruction. In natural sciences, it fell into the general range of West German states, and it devoted a little more time to social studies. In fact, this was the only program in both countries that gave special time (178 hours) to civics education (*Staatsbürgerkunde*). The special feature of East German education was what has been described as polytechnical education. Not surprisingly, the POS devoted more time to such activities than any of the West German states. Surprising also may be the fact that West German schools devoted more time to physical education and sports than did the East German POS.

Extended Secondary School (EOS)

Upon completion of the POS, a limited number of pupils were allowed to proceed on to the Extended Secondary School (*Erweiterte Oberschule*), where they spent two years in a university preparatory program. In the 1960s no more than 10% of an age-group was admitted to the EOS, but this figure even sank slightly over the years, until only 8.3% of an age-group was being admitted in 1980.

Three criteria determined admission to the EOS. First, the pupils were high achievers. Second, the pupils were dependable in their political-ideological orientation. This was one of the most problematic aspects of advancing through the educational system. Young people whose parents were identified as members of the former entrepreneurial class and who were active in religious groups were systematically denied the opportunity of further education. Third, pupils' competencies were in an area important to the economic well-being of the GDR (Baske, 1990, p. 215). This criterion eventually became critical in second foreign language choice. In 1981, it was determined that only those young people who had selected a second foreign language in grade seven would be eligible for admission to the EOS (Fischer, 1991, p. 65).

The program of studies was divided into compulsory subjects and optional subjects. Yet almost all of the subjects were compulsory (31 of 36 hours per week). In two years at the EOS, every pupil would participate in the following number of compulsory weekly hours: German (6), Russian (6), English (5), Latin (9), Greek (6), Mathematics (10), physics (6), chemistry (5), biology (5), geography (2), history (3), civics (3), sports (4), and art (2) (Baske, 1990, p. 213).

At the conclusion of these two years, pupils would take the secondary school leaving examination called the *Abitur*. It consisted of written tests in German, mathematics, Russian, and one natural science subject, and an oral examination in at least two different subjects. The marks given were 1=very good, 2=good, 3=satisfactory, 4=passing, 5=fail.

Special Schools and Classes

The main aim of special education in the GDR was to prepare handicapped pupils for employment and to handle as much independence as possible in day-to-day living. Part of this was to help disabled people develop their personalities in order to take part as fully as possible in socialistic life. Behind the extensive special education system lay the notion that as the socialistic way of life is perfected, fewer and fewer impairments will manifest in people. In the meantime, the pedagogical goal of special education was "the social by-passing of the impairment" (Wygotsky).

The special education system, designed for those whose impairments were too severe to allow attendance at regular schools, was part of the unified socialist education system. Included were schools for the mentally retarded (*Hilfsschulen*), for the hard of hearing, the deaf, visually impaired, blind, physically handicapped, and the learning handicapped (*Ausgleichsschulen*), and special education outpatient counseling centers. In 1989, just over 3% of all pupils attended these institutions (Fischer, 1992). By far the greatest number of special education pupils were placed in one of the two divisions of the *Hilfsschule*. Division I, grades 2 through 8, took pupils with light mental retardation, while Division II, grades 1 through 8, handled those with medium to severe retardation. Often Division II pupils had attended pre-schools or kindergartens connected with the *Hilfsschule* or other special education pre-schools and kindergartens. Both divisions offered two years of vocational training, appropriate to the pupils involved, and many had before and after school care as well as boarding facilities. For leavers of the *Hilfsschule*, further vocational training was also available.

Except for the *Hilfsschulen* and schools for the deaf which developed their own courses, East German special education schools followed the POS curriculum and offered the possibility for pupils to take the *Abitur*. Toward the end of 1989, the Ministry of Education made known their aim to have all lesser impaired children be able to attend their local kindergartens and polytechnical ten-year schools (Fischer, 1989).

In a different vein, one of the most impressive elements of GDR education were special schools and classes for those who demonstrated great potential in science, sport, and culture. The international success the GDR had in sports is probably the most widely known example, but programs also existed for technical subjects, mathematics, natural sciences, linguistics, and art, where young people could receive training in that special talent. Even at a very early age, sometimes preschool age, young people were placed in programs intended to enhance their talents. Entrance was rigorous and many of the young people failed to maintain the appropriate level of development at the rigorous programs. Although great status was given to these young people, they were, at the same time, expected to keep up with courses found in the regular schools. This was not always possible, and a major conflict among pedagogues was how to address special needs while ensuring a broad educational development. This was especially the case, when pedagogical specialists pointed out that the young people were failing to maintain the appropriate standard in the regular program.

Vocational Education

One of the great strengths of East German education was the polyvalent nature of its general education program. The POS was preoccupied with polytechnical education and insisted that every young person become familiar with the work world. Beyond that, however, was a fully developed vocational education enterprise. At the central level stood a State Secretatiat for Vocational Education[4] headed by a State Secretary, who was responsible for vocational training, though the formal authority was vested in a Ministry Council with representatives from various ministries involved in education, commerce, and industry. The State Secretary also had the support of a center, known as the Central Institute for Vocational Education,[5] that had a function similar to the function the Academy of Pedagogical Sciences played for the Ministry of Education. That is, it provided an academic and planning resource for vocational education, developed curricula, training programs, standards, etc.

According to the constitution of the GDR, every young person was guaranteed the right and responsibility to learn a vocation (Art. 25, 4). The main form of vocational training, part-time vocational schools and workstations organized by public firms, handled more than two-thirds of all apprentices. In addition there were municipal vocational schools, which usually placed their pupils in small local firms. East Germany, just as the FRG, sponsored a limited number of full-time vocational schools. In the East two types of these full-time schools existed. One took pupils directly out of the POS and required three or four years of training for full qualification. In 1983 there were 63 schools providing some type of middle-level medical training, 47 pedagogical institutes preparing kindergarten and lower-

---

[4]*Staatssekretariat für Berufsbildung.*
[5]*Zentralinstitut für Berufsbildung.*

level POS teachers, and six centers offering training in theater, ballet, and dance. The other type of full-time vocational school required a previous vocational qualification for admission, but led to higher professional qualifications (Schäfer, 1990, p. 340).

Most vocational training took place through apprenticeships. These training opportunities were published widely; in addition, counseling centers existed to advise pupils about vocational options. Young people were able to apply for any open position; however, the firms themselves were allowed to make the final decision as to which candidates they would select based upon certain criteria, including the candidate's personality, expressed motives for taking part, school record, record of social participation, and state of health.

Vocational education, consisting of practical and theoretical instruction, usually lasted two years and was seen as a vital aspect of socialist life. As forerunner to vocational training, the POS was charged with the responsibility of providing basic understanding of the socialist economy and the various vocations available to the young. The School Law of 1965 spelled out some of the general qualities vocational training was to provide:

> In the training of young people such qualities as diligence, conscientiousness, exactness, a sense of responsibility, independence, punctuality, discipline, order, striving for greater competency, militant support of the new, intolerance of shortcomings in their own work and the work of others, and a conscious opposition to outdated work habits and methods are to be developed (V-I-32-8).

Just as the West Germans, one of the major problems the East Germans faced was a tendency to train young people in narrower, more specific vocation that was not amenable to a rapidly changing technological society. In 1957 there were 972 different vocations for which training was available. By 1967, the number of training options had been reduced to 455, and by 1986 it had been reduced again to 348 (Schäfer, 1990, p. 326).

In the last two decades of the GDR, great efforts had been under way to update and revise the content of training in vocations. For each of the training areas, a vocational training commission had been set with representatives of masters, vocational educators, and social organizations. These had been working together to define the content of each area in both a vertical and horizontal way; that is, each was divided vertically into four levels of training and horizontally, into parts that were general and specific to that vocation. By 1986/87 the content of 78 vocations had been determined; by 1987/88, another 99; and it was anticipated that another 71 would be set by 1988/89, when the collapse occurred (Schäfer, 1990, p. 328).

Vocational Training with Abitur

One of the significant educational innovations East Germans introduced was a vocational training program that provided not only an occupational qualification, but the *Abitur*, that qualified the pupil for study in an institution of higher learning. This program required three years, rather than the regular two year EOS or apprenticeship options, but it opened up a larger number of choices to young people. The percentage of an age-group that was able to take advantage of this shifted between 6.6% and 5.3% over the years, but, in spite of the small numbers, represented a major innovation in the history of German education (Fischer, 1990, pp. 65-6).

Further Education of Workers

The German Democratic Republic maintained an extensive array of further education institutions, including approximately 1,500 so-called industrial academies (*Betriebsakademien*) and approximately 220 folk high schools (*Volkshochschulen*) (Oer, 1990). The industrial academies were available to qualified workers who wished to engage in some type of specialized training, to qualify as a master in a given field, to qualify for study at a technical school or even a university. The folk high schools had a more general purpose in that they provided a general education outlet to people wishing some form of further learning experience. They also allowed people to obtain, retroactive qualifications in school and work, that people had failed to obtain in the regular course of their development. Of course, as in all institutions there was attention given to political and ideological indoctrination.

Teacher Education

At the time the German Democratic Republic was formed, East Germany experienced a dilemma in teacher availability. Under the German Reich prior to the end of World War II, teachers had been defined as civil servants. Then in the Soviet zone of occupation, all civil servants were terminated from their positions as supporters of National Socialism, creating a severe lack of teachers. The short range solution to this dilemma was "new teacher training" (*Neulehrerausbildung*), where young people, most of whom did not have a higher education degree, were pressed into service. At the same time, they were placed in a special, short-term training program. Concurrently, long-range plans were under way to revolutionize the old way of teacher training, that in the eyes of socialists had paralleled the class nature of society.

Previously, *Volksschule* teachers had come from the working classes and had rarely been exposed to any other education that not meant for their social class. Teacher candidates were then channeled right back into the Volksschule after special teacher training. In contrast, the Gymnasial or academic track teachers had come almost exclusively from the elite class and had attended institutions of higher education. East Germans endeavored to break this tradition, but the attempt was not nearly as successful as ideologues would have hoped. Because of the new training, teachers of all sorts, including POS, EOS, kindergarten, and day-care, came to have a great deal in common, but they also had separate qualifications and professional distinctions that disallowed a complete breakdown of status and salary differences.

A number of different types of professional institutions engaged in teacher education. Lower-level POS teachers received a qualification that was not considered equivalent to a full higher education degree. This training was given at 25 Institutes for Teacher Training (*Institute für Lehrerbildung*), which had the status of a technical school. Young people were admitted to the Institutes after completing their POS and remained at the Institute for four years, leaving with a full-teaching qualification for the lower-level of the POS (but not a higher education degree).

Teacher training took place in a number of institutions of higher education. The six universities, two technical universities, the music academy (*Musikhochschule*) in Weimar, and the academy for physical culture all provided various types of teacher education. Eight teacher training colleges existed that were designated as higher education institutions focusing on teacher education. These training colleges also provided teacher training for lower-level teachers, but that training was separate from the training programs for upper-level teachers.

These institutions came under quite different administrative jurisdictions. The institutes for teacher education and the teacher training colleges were under the Ministry of Education, while the general universities and technical universities came under the jurisdiction of the Ministry of Higher and Technical Education. The Franz List Music Academy came under the Ministry of Culture, and the German Academy for Physical Culture came under the Secretary of Physical Culture and Sport. However, the content of their pedagogical programs was similar.

Special training programs and certificates were available for day-care educators and for pioneer leaders at specific Institutes and teacher training colleges. Special education teachers also attended designated programs at the Universities of Berlin, Halle, and Rostock, and the Technical University of Magdeburg. In addition, teachers of vocational schools were trained at various institutions, but special training for technical careers was given at the Technical

University of Dresden and special training for economic careers and medical careers at Humboldt University in Berlin.

Technical and Higher Education

A wide array of institutions of higher education existed in the GDR. The most prominent institutions were six universities that constitute some of the most prestigious institutions of higher learning in German educational history, including Humboldt University in Berlin with more than 20,000 students, Leipzig University with more than 15,000 students, Halle-Wittenberg University, with more than 10,000 students, and Rostock, Jena, and Greifswald Universities, each enrolling less than 10,000. In addition, there were nine technical universities and higher schools, three of which were the established institutions at Dresden with more than 12,000 students and the smaller institutions at Freiberg and Weimar. There were also three medical academies, two agriculture and forestry colleges, three economic and law academies, nine engineering and technical schools, ten pedagogical colleges, and twelve art academies (Rytlewski 1990, p. 422). This represents a striking increase in institutions of higher learning since the early days of the GDR. In 1951 there were only 21 such institutions; in the next twenty years another 23 were begun. By 1970 already, as many existed as nearly 20 years later at the fall of the Berlin Wall (Rytlewski, 1990, p. 422). However, the number of students enrolled in them was generally very small. Only four institutions enrolled more than 10,000 students, three additional institutions enrolled at least 5,000 students, fifteen enrolled from 2,000 to 5,000 students, and 28 institutions, including the engineering, teacher training, and art academies, enrolled less than 2,000 students.

Because of the difficulties East Germans had in maintaining contacts with the West, many assume that higher education was not current according to Western standards. In the 1970s, though, certain spheres of East German education had began to open itself to the West. Those in the Ministry of Higher Education were particularly concerned that socialist higher education confront its own deficiencies and remain competitive with Western institutions. Scholars such as Hans-Dieter Schäfer were given the right to travel and learn of new developments in countries such as the United States.

The traditional route to institutions of higher education for students has been through the *Abitur*, but East Germany began to develop alternative routes. Mention has already been made of the programs that coupled vocational training with the conventional *Abitur*. In addition, a one year preparatory course was developed for those with the *Abitur*, who wished to enter technical and medical programs. Young people, who had completed their vocational training programs were eligible to enter the engineering and technical schools. A three year preparatory program was available in the farming and the crafts departments of colleges, and in an international studies program at Freiberg and Halle Universities. Finally, an alternate examination was available that was comparable to the *Abitur*. In spite of all these options, 75% of all students qualified for higher education studies through the conventional EOS and *Abitur* routes.

Those who completed the lesser school-leaving certificates and entered vocational training were allowed to proceed onto technical schools and technical institutes of higher education, where they could eventually qualify to transfer to the university. This became known as the second educational path (*Zweiter Bildungsweg*). Because approximately 40% of all students in higher education have gone through a vocational education program, the importance of the second educational way has taken on more and more significance.

Chapter V

Teachers and Teaching in the Two Germanys

Introduction

Teachers carry a large responsibility for the growth and development of youth in society. The same holds true for both East and West Germany but in different ways. Before that is explored, it is necessary to ask who the teacher is.

Social Background of Teachers

The policy to ensure children of workers and farmers equal access to post-secondary studies has characterized higher education in the GDR as no other issue. This aim was part of public discourse during the 1950s and early 1960s. As time went on, though, it became more and more complicated to distinguish whether a person was of working class background or not. For example, marriages where one partner was of the working class were typically counted as a working class family, even though the elite parent may have exercised greater influence on the development of the children. Further, political functionaries were automatically counted among the working class, even though they were among elites of society. Finally, workers' children who emerged from higher education institutions wished their children to be counted among the working class in order to retain the advantages being given to that level of society.

Government policy and social class complications aside, university students coming from families having a history of higher education studies were on the increase. In 1979 only 28% of the university students had at least one parent who had obtained a university degree; by 1989, this had risen to 52%. In the same year, though, 65% of medical students could make this claim while those preparing to be teachers had only 21% of mothers and 41% of fathers who had gone through the university (Bathke, 1990, p. 122). In other words, most teacher candidates came from backgrounds that did not include higher education studies. In the extensive interviews conducted in East Germany, we asked teachers about their parents. The responses were uniformly similar. One teacher explained, "My father was an auto mechanic and my mother worked but had not learned a special craft." Fathers were usually described as being a "simple laborer" or a "factory worker," while the mother may have been a "salesperson in a local store" or "a secretary in government office." Of course, there were exceptions. One lower-level POS teacher described his father as the "owner of a private ball bearing firm having 60 employees" and his mother as a specialist in a credit office.

In contrast, students in West German institutions of higher learning rarely came from worker families. In 1969 only 7% of those beginning studies at scientific institutions of higher learning came from families considered to be working class. By 1985, this had risen only to 12%. Historically, most students had always come from the civil servant class, which included educators at all schooling levels (Geißler, 1990, p. 106). Teachers, except those at the *Hauptschule*, generally came from a social background that reflected higher education studies.

Age of Teachers

In the earlier days of the GDR, teachers were relatively young; almost all experienced teachers, considered civil servants under the Nazi regime, had been let go by the new socialist government soon after World Ward II and had been replaced by young inexperienced people. In 1946 more than 90% of all teachers were less than 30 years old. By 1977, however, only 30% of all teachers were less than 30 years old although another third of the teachers was less than 40 years old. Over time, the average age of teachers has slowly risen to the point that it is no longer skewed in the direction of youth. In 1989, 48.8% of all teachers were less than forty years of age. The most prevalent age category was age 40-45, the age of 18.2% of all teachers.

In West Germany, the percentage of teachers in general education institutions under forty years of age was slightly lower than in East Germany (44.4% in 1987). Striking is the small number of West German teachers who are under 30 years of age. In 1987, only 2.9% of all teachers were in this category, and it was dropping rapidly. However, the most prevalent age category was the 35-40 age group, having 26.3% of all teachers (Schulz, 1990, p. 524).

Pupil/Teacher Ratio

In both Germanys the pupil/teacher ratio dropped considerably over time. In 1960 the average number of pupils in the ten year school stood at 28.0, and this number fell to 21 by 1987. In the Upper Secondary School it fell from 25.3 to 16.7. In the *Grund-* and *Hauptschule* the number fell from 33.1 to 17.4, in the *Realschule* it fell from 23.5 to 16.3 and in the *Gymnasium* from 19.9 to 13.5 (Köhler and Schreier, 1990, pp. 120-21). One would conclude that the pupil/teacher ratio in West Germany was generally a bit lower than in East Germany.

Hours of Instruction

In West Germany the number of required hours a teacher instructs each week is determined by the individual state. However, most of the states could be broken down to the following hours:

Grundschule	28
Hauptschule	28
Realschule	27
Gymnasium	24
Gesamtschule	24

It must be understood that instructional hours are only a part of the actual time teachers work. It is estimated that most teachers devote up to 48 hours a week to some type of activity related to their professions, including preparation time, consultation time, correcting papers, meetings, supervision of playgrounds, and so forth (Schulz, 1990, p. 518).

Pay of Teachers

It would be very difficult to make across the board comparisons regarding the pay of East and West German teachers. In East Germany, the salaries of most people were similar. Because the country was strongly socialist, it provided almost all social services, including housing, food, medical care, clothing, travel, summer vacations, education, and recreation facilities for little or no cost. Consequently, the salary one received was of relatively little importance.

In West Germany the pay of teachers has been regulated through federal law, so it has been uniform in all states. Teachers at different school types receive different base pay. *Gymnasium* and vocational school teachers receive generally higher salaries than do primary school and *Realschule* teachers.

It is always difficult to compare salary levels of different nations. One of the typical ways of going about it has been to contrast the salaries of teachers with the average salaries of industrial workers. In international comparisons with industrial workers, West German teachers have been among the highest paid in the world. Both primary and secondary teachers begin teaching with good pay and that increases gradually so that they retire with an excellent pension by international standards (ILO, 1980).

Retirement

In East Germany women teachers were required, by law, to retire at the age of 60, and men at 65. In West Germany all teachers could work until the age of 65 before retiring, although they have been allowed to take early retirement at age 62. If they had worked for 35 years they could receive a pension of 75% of their highest salary, and their marriage partner could receive as much as 60% (Schulz, 1990, p. 518).

Teacher Surplus and Shortage

It is almost impossible to provide quantitative figures for teacher shortages and surpluses in East Germany. By law, any person completing a technical or higher education degree could make claim to an appropriate position. This means that there was no unemployment in East Germany although it was very difficult to match the people available with the positions to be filled. Consequently, teachers were often assigned to positions for which they had little training. Since teaching was not a highly popular occupation among young people, a surplus of teachers didn't exist.

In West Germany there was a dramatic teacher shortage until the approach of the 1980s, when the number of teachers seeking a position began to outnumber the positions available. In 1979, 83.8% of all qualified teachers seeking a position were able to find employment. A year later this had fallen to 75.8%, and a year after that to 63.4%. The percentages continued to fall even more rapidly, so that by 1986 only 11.8% of all teachers seeking a position were able to find employment (Schulz, 1990, p. 522). The situation has not improved much since that time.

Civil Servant Recognition

From the beginning of the GDR, East German teachers had been denied civil servant status. During National Socialism teachers had been considered civil servants, and this status became identified with being a supporter of that regime. In addition, civil service was seen as a part of bourgeois social structure; thus, it was denied to the East German teacher. In contrast, West German teachers had long enjoyed such a high status. In 1987 more than 92% of all teachers in North-

Rhine-Westphalia held civil servant status, which meant that they were entrusted with the right and responsibility to exercise state authority and to be entrusted as public servants "who are pledged to service and loyalty by public law" (Basic Law, article 33 (4)). Because civil servants are restricted in certain forms of free expression, West Germans have struggled with the right teachers have traditionally had to express themselves freely. In the early 1970s at the time of the student movement, the issue of allegiance to the constitution and free speech of teachers was often raised. In several cases teachers were denied civil servant status because they had overstepped the boundaries of propriety in their office as teachers (Baumert and Others, 1990, p. 75). In spite of this, teachers have been given special recognition among civil servants in that they, indeed, possess a certain "pedagogical freedom" that ensures a professional autonomy connected with instruction and education although this autonomy has boundaries in terms of behavior and public expressions.

Value Orientation of Teachers

The major question regarding teachers in the two Germanys is the degree of autonomy they were able to exercise as professional educators. To what degree were they functionaries carrying out the mandates of the state and to what degree were they considered to be professionals, who could make major decisions regarding the choice and organization of curriculum and the carrying out of instruction?

One of the nagging indictments continually made of West German teachers has been that they have been reluctant to discuss aspects of Germany that pose an embarrassment to them. This has been particularly so with regard to the German involvement with National Socialism. The claim is that they have historically made few efforts in their classrooms to preach the anti-fascist message. No grand system of infant care, child care, kindergartens, and youth organizations was established to counteract possible Nazi influence from parents and, equally important, to educate children to a new ideology. Over time, of course, such an indictment takes on less and less meaning. One indirect means of assessing the messages children receive in school would be to review the textbooks that they read. The authors of this volume reviewed 14 of the most recent versions of secondary school history textbooks that deal with the twentieth century, including *Entdecken und Verstehen: Von 1917 bis zur Gegenwart; Erlebnis Geschichte; Fragen an die Geschichte: Die Welt im 20. Jahrhundert; Geschichte: Das 20. Jahrhundert; Geschichte für Morgen; Geschichte heute; Geschichte: Kennen und Verstehen; Geschichtliche Weltkunde: Von der Zeit des Imperialismus bis zur Gegenwart; Lebendige Vergangenheit,* and found extensive and objective treatment of the period of National Socialism in all of them. One can only assume that the texts were read and discussed in class.

No comparative data exists in which both East and West German teachers were asked identical questions under identical conditions. Alan Menlo and Pam Poppleton engaged in a number of international studies of teacher attitudes during the 1980s, and they included West Germany in these reports (e.g., Menlo & Poppleton, 1990). Among the issues they surveyed were attitudes about teaching as work, teaching as a career, and teaching as pedagogy. The West German teachers were like teachers of most other industrialized countries with regard to their attitudes toward teaching as work. Work is an economic imperative, but West German teachers appear to have a relatively high regard for the choice they made to be teachers. If they had the choice to make again, they would likely choose teaching again, whereas teachers in countries such as Great Britain and the United States would be reluctant to make such a choice a second time. West German teachers also experienced somewhat lower levels of stress and higher levels of job satisfaction. One of the main reasons for such a profile appears to be the high salary level of the West German teachers. In fact, they are in the occupation largely because it pays so well, rather than intrinsic means of self-expression or because they feel a duty to give society something. In terms of teaching as a career, the researchers found that West Germans attach great importance to the subject they teach rather than the pastoral or administrative opportunities it offers. Regarding teaching as pedagogy, West German teachers show surprisingly little concern for the pedagogical aspects of teaching, rather they feel obliged to satisfy contractual agreements and do not worry about dealing with unique problems, satisfying individual needs, helping all children to succeed, etc. (Poppleton, 1992).

West German teachers appear to have rather utilitarian values and are not driven by political ideology or cosmic ideals. As was noted above, however, they enjoy civil servant status, which carries with it an inherent right and responsibility to be pledged to service and loyalty to the state and to serve as models of citizenship to their students. West German teachers have resisted the extreme expression of this requirement, while East German teachers had a reputation for being more committed to the ideals of socialism than the broader East German population, mainly because their role was defined by law as being responsible for preparing young people for life in socialism. Section VII, #25, (3) of the 1965 Law on Socialist Education reads:

> The teachers educate their pupils in the spirit of socialism, peace, love of the German Democratic Republic, work and working people. They educate them to be ready to define the achievements of their socialist homeland.

The next article mandates that teachers are to prepare their lessons conscientiously and creatively and carry them through with high quality. In certain respects the demand on teachers to be both creative and to indoctrinate may be a contradiction; however, the most important provision was that they be dedicated to socialism and exert their energies to its growth and development. Few facts are available about the extent to which the East German teachers had internalized socialist ideology. Evidence that could come from East German researchers may not be acceptable because it would be interested primarily in substantiating government claims of high commitment to socialism. Also misleading are certain indicators of allegiance, such as membership in the SED. Many teachers held membership out of political expediency while others believed firmly in the party but were prevented from joining by one circumstance or another. One teacher explained to us that she had planned to join the party in the early 1980s because she had been appointed to be the assistant director, but for health reasons she took a year's leave and didn't get around to joining the party after she returned.

Prior to the collapse it had not been possible for outsiders to gain permission to do survey research with teachers. Some creative work was done by Dietmar Waterkamp, then at the University of Bochum in West Germany, who had questioned hundreds of East German educators among the approximately 200,000 East Germans emigrating to West Germany between 1984 and 1989. He had also gone to summer camp grounds in Hungary prior to the collapse and had talked with vacationing and emigrating East German teachers about their situation. He found, not surprisingly, that those who had left East Germany had rejected the goals of the East German political system. Of those teachers still residing in East Germany, 26.7% maintained a strong loyalty and had their students participate in organized demonstrations. More than half of the teachers demanded that students revere symbols of the state and SED (Waterkamp, 1990).

In our own conversations with East German teachers following the collapse, Waterkamp's findings were generally confirmed. Teachers had usually expressed firm allegiance to the ideals of socialism and a strong identity with the German Democratic Republic. One educator in Dresden explained his development as follows:

> As I came into adulthood, I was attracted to the glowing ideals professed by our state leaders. I had grown up a devoted Catholic, but whereas the Catholic Church spoke of a paradise hereafter, state leaders proclaimed that I could help the state build a paradise here on earth, a paradise where all

could live in a state of equality, community, peace, and brotherly love. I found that very attractive.

A teacher in East Berlin explained:

When I grew up, I came to believe that socialism was very supportive; it was there to serve mankind. We always used the phrase, "For the good of the people" when speaking about the ideals of East German socialism.

Another East Berlin teacher explained:

My parents didn't believe in socialism, and at first I fought it, but I always demanded logic in my life, and as I studied the great literature of socialism, I came to see that it made sense, it was logical, and I came to embrace its ideals as my own.

However, these teachers were also often critical of the regime and the SED as being out of step with reality. They claimed to be often impatient with directives coming from the Ministry of Education and even challenged, behind the classroom door, some of these directives. For example, many of them discussed West German television with their pupils and they left some distasteful aspects of the curriculum out of their lesson plans. In spite of extensive criticism, there appears to have been a sense of accomplishment and effectiveness in the schools. George Lengkeek, from the Netherlands, interviewed a number of history teachers shortly after the collapse, and he found them to express a sense of pride in what they did as teachers in the GDR. That pride was related to the full responsibilities they had as teachers. One teacher, for example, exclaimed how worthwhile *Jugendweihe*, excursions, youth activities, and attempts to come to terms with fascism had been.[1] Teachers were happy with the atmosphere in the classroom and the harmonious relationships they experienced with their colleagues. With regard to history curriculum, a sense of movement and relative openness appeared in the 1986/87 program that encouraged explorations with topics such as religion in history (Lengkeek, 1992).

To satisfy their function as purveyors of socialist ideology, teachers were charged with the responsibility not only of being conscientious classroom instructors but of being active in parents' advisory councils and other groups, of working with other socialist organizations, and of being active with the Free German Youth and the Ernst Thälmann Young Pioneer Organization. In addition, teachers were continually engaged in further education and personal development programs that were intended to ensure that they were dealing competently with the ideological and political aims of schooling.

In actual practice, East German teachers were subjected to a host of regulations that dictated almost everything they did as teachers. The curriculum was detailed explicitly for them, and they were expected to follow it minutely. This was particularly so with regard to socially determined courses such as civics and history, but it extended to other subjects as well. They learned how to behave in order to survive as a teacher.

---

[1]*Jugendweihe* was a GDR substitute for the religious "confirmation" rite of passage for young people at about the age of 14.

Section II

The Collapse and Its Aftermath

Chapter VI

Crisis and Collapse in the 1980s

Introduction

An understanding of the changes taking place in The GDR during the 1980s is only possible within the context of broader international conditions. Considered in retrospect, the collapse of the East German regime was largely a consequence of a much larger drama taking place throughout Central and Eastern Europe. This is not to suggest that important internal activities discussed in this chapter did not come into play, but these activities were engaged in with a keen awareness that the Soviet Union remained the major regional power, and it was always possible that the Soviet Union could assert itself at any time, so events were always tempered by the *Realpolitik* that pervaded Central and Eastern Europe. It is for this reason that Gorbachev's policies of *glasnost* and *perestroika* are now seen to have been so significant in terms of the events of the 1980s in Central and Eastern Europe.

In the Soviet Union the Soviet authorities recognized that both economic and political stability were on the edge of collapse and they began making some gestures toward change without fundamental change. These changes included educational reform, as progressive citizens throughout the region, both within and outside the Soviet Union, grasped the opportunity and began demanding that their region move from a centralized authoritarian government to various versions of representative democracy, stressing self-realizing participation in social life. During the early period of *glasnost* and *perestroika*, the Soviet Union, however, chose to retain its commitment to the ideology it had supported for the past 70 years, and its leaders spoke of a renewal of socialism, rather than of a fundamental shift in orientation. The Central Committee proclaimed that the nation must cleanse itself of Stalin's totalitarian approach and go back to Lenin's more idealistic and humane socialism. However, this occurred in an atmosphere of openness and self-criticism unparalleled in Soviet history. Of course, at this time the underlying economic weaknesses of the Soviet Union were not widely recognized, and Gorbachev's initial aim to continue domination of Eastern Europe was accepted without question. Soon, however, the criticism led to attacks on the ideology of socialism itself. This contributed to instability and chaos within the Soviet Union, causing alarm among political leaders of East Germany, because that instability and chaos represented a threat to their own political control. As political stability and the economy plummeted, the Soviet Union also tempered its orientation. In a speech before the United Nations in December 1988 Gorbachev finally identified himself with "freedom of choice" in terms of decisions being made in Central and Eastern Europe.

In education, a hesitant shift was also under way in the Soviet Union. In March, 1989, at a joint session of the State Committee for Education and the All-Unions-Soviet decisions were made for the Soviet Union to democratize its schools so that a so-called dialectical relationship between unity and differentiation would be realized. What this meant was that a commitment to its unified, comprehensive, polytechnical school was reaffirmed as the basic educational institution of the country, but that the school was expected to concentrate on helping young people become more competitive, competent contributors to the Soviet economy. It was unclear how these two contradictory statements would be achieved.

The reform agenda for the region was being spelled out by a special Committee for Educational Innovation in Moscow, known generally by the acronym of VNIK, which developed a basic reform policy focusing on "democratizing and humanizing" the educational establishment and the educational process (Rust, 1990b).[1] These reform labels had been given a specific meaning by those at VNIK. To democratize education meant to provide choice and the training in making decisions and to support provisions for professional educa-

---

[1] The language of reform that was formulated at this time even penetrated the East German reform discussion shortly after the *Wende* (For example, see Kaltenborn, 1990).

tors to work collaboratively among each other. To humanize education meant, first, to connect the Soviet Union once again with classical European humanism including classical languages and literature and a Western-oriented scientific and historical tradition, and, second, to make the educational process more humane, to become more child-centered (Rust, 1990b).

It is important to point out what was missing from this reform agenda. VNIK engaged in its preliminary work before serious discussions took place regarding the possibility that the Soviet Union would move to a market economy or even adopt political pluralism. Consequently, educational reform rhetoric was not economics or politics driven. The focus was on the student, the learning child, who was to be self-determining and able to make choices. Of course, there was recognition that each human being is located in the social and economic sphere, and also the recognition that school reform, by its very nature, is a political process, but the concepts on which much of that reform has been based has been lodged in the language of the 1988 educational reform, before any indication that the political and economic structures were going to collapse (Rust, 1990b).

East German Responses

While dramatic changes were taking place in countries such as Poland and Czechoslovakia, East Germany set itself on a course of stability and resistance to change and the East German leaders appeared to retain support from the Soviet Union. In October, 1988, when Helmut Kohl, the West German Chancellor, visited Moscow, Gorbachev had emphasized that the traditional Soviet position concerning German unity had not changed. However, the East German leaders became more and more alarmed at the deterioration of the strong arm of their Soviet protectors and of events in the Soviet Union itself. As in all authoritarian systems there were clear signs of resistance that would manifest itself wherever there was any sign of weakness or compromise. This alarm finally reached a point of action in May, 1989, when the East German regime banned the German-language issue of *Sputnik*, a Soviet periodical that had engaged in open discussion of self-criticism and the need for change (Darnton, 1991, p. 100).

Such events were accompanied by developments in Hungary and Czechoslovakia where thousands of East Germans were taking advantage of a spirit of openness with regard to border crossings into Austria and West Germany. In fact, Hungary began tearing down its barbed-wire fence during the summer of 1989, and on 11 September, Hungary opened its borders completely with Austria and approximately 55,000 East Germans move to the West. A similar process was at work in Czechoslovakia. The situation became so explosive that East Germany closed its border with Czechoslovakia on 3 October, but the hand-writing was already on the wall.

On 2 October a crowd numbering about 20,000 demonstrated in Leipzig in the first of 12 weekly demonstrations. The citizens of Leipzig would meet on each Monday at 5:00 p.m. in four churches in the center of the city, where they would hear speeches by the pastors, pray together, and sing old Lutheran hymns. Then they would walk through the center of the city holding banners and lighted candles. These peaceful demonstrations grew each week. On 9 October more than 70,000 people participated, then 120,000, then 150,000, then 250,000, and on 6 November approximately 300,000, nearly the entire population of Leipzig (Wallach & Francisco, 1992, pp. 39-40). The most crucial of these demonstrations appears to have been 9 October, when Honecker reportedly issued orders for demonstrators to be shot, but through a series of apparent miscommunications, the Secret Police withdrew, which sparked an electrified cry from the peaceful demonstrators: "We are the people."[2] Strikes were taking place in many other cities as well, the largest taking place in East Berlin on 4 November, when 500,000 turned out. Such activities were not restricted to the large cities. Even in the small towns people were taking to the streets demanding that leaders engage in a "dialogue with the people" (Bergner, 1990). Demonstrations were taking place in other cities as well. At Rostock approximately 5,000 people gathered at the Marien Kirche each Thursday, where the min-

---

[2]*Wir sind das Volk.*

ister Gauck gave a thirty minute lecture before they walked through the city in an open demonstration for change. Some teachers were very diligent in attending and they often took their students with them.

The inability of the East German government to take strong action was clearly linked to the growing physical weakness, because of cancer, of Erich Honecker, which left a vacuum in the leadership of the country, but it was most directly linked to statements by Gorbachev when he visited Berlin on 6 and 7 October 1989 to help celebrate the fortieth birthday of the GDR. He warned Honecker that the Soviet Union would not support repressive actions on the part of the East Germans. As the situation deteriorated, Honecker finally resigned on 18 October and was replaced by Egon Krenz, who promised to reorganize the Socialist Unity Party (SED) and the government. The people continued to escalate their demands, and on 4 November nearly a million people rallied in Berlin demanding free elections, a free press, and freedom to travel. The East German government ground to a complete stop. Finally, on 9 November 1989, the Berlin Wall was opened and hundreds of thousands of East Berliners flood into West Berlin in an all-night celebration. The way was finally open to reform fundamentally the government and to establish new working relationships with West Germany. While the above account of developments in East Germany has been elaborated in a number of publications (e.g., Darnton, 1990; Paterson and Smith 1992), the primary interest in this section has to do with the role of educational institutions in the developments leading up to the collapse of East Germany.

Perestroika and East German Education

As has been stressed in Chapter IV, schools in East Germany enjoyed an impressive standard in terms of stability and productivity, albeit within the context of a pervasive command system that dictated every significant activity in the institutions. This command system pervaded every level of education, including universities, whose leaders were particularly resistant to change. Whereas the Soviet Union, which had provided the model by East Germany for four decades, was becoming increasingly receptive to educational reform, the East German educational establishment became increasingly resistant to reform. Recall the heralded 1984 education reform in the Soviet Union, which was actually announced a year before *perestroika*, so it was formulated in the old ideology but it suggested a sense of movement and flexibility on the part of Communist Party leaders and it was strongly supported by three leaders, Andropov, Chernenko and Gorbachev.

In contrast, East German pressures for educational reform were met by resistance to change on the part of leaders. Margot Honecker proclaimed before the conference of Ministers of Education at Erfurt on 15 November 1985, that central control of education would actually be strengthened in order to prevent any ideas about reform and pluralistic thinking from entering into the discussion of education. Of particular concern to her were the teachers who challenged the system, the church leaders, who spawned the initial protests, and artists, who had been historically a subversive group. She wished to insure that the educational program remain unaffected by the winds of change and she challenged the teacher educators to become more vigorous in providing the appropriate ideological foundation for education (Honecker, 1986).

Soviet initiatives had provided cracks in the entire ideological structure in that they allowed not only internal criticism but the possibility that external contacts could be expanded. The East German response to these initiatives was guarded and ultimately negative. East Germans had walled themselves from the West for the past four decades, and now their major ally and socialist model, the Soviet Union, was going in a direction which the education power structure in East Germany deemed unacceptable.

The East German situation had peculiarities that help explain such a strong resistance to openness. Communism in East Germany had grown out of the terrible condition of Naziism in the 1930s and 40s. The East Germans had resorted to ignoring or even scandalizing its own recent past, and its educational system had presented itself in such a way that there was a sense of having no recent history

(*Geschichtslosigkeit*). In the mid-1970s there had been expressions on the part of the regime to overcome some of this void, but it had been largely symbolic in nature and little concrete movement was seen. Openness would surely require the East Germans to face themselves in ways that would be difficult.

On the national level, the most important occasion in 1989 that might have signaled a willingness on the part of education leaders for significant change was the Ninth Pedagogical Congress of the GDR, which took place in June. In preparation of that congress, there was a sense among reform-oriented educators that something must be done to address the deteriorating political, economic, and educational situation. The Ministry of Education had actually invited individuals and groups to submit suggestions for change and improvement (e.g., DLZ, 1988). According to registry accounts of mail received related to the Congress 258 recommendations came directly to the Ministry of Education, 403 on the Congress bureau, and 447 to the Central Office of the Young Pioneers (Kaack, 1992). Of course, most of these were conventional tracts, often illustrated and artistically designed to glorify the positive mission of socialism, but many were critical of the situation and recommended fundamental change.

Heike Kaack, a political functionary for the CDU following the collapse, found approximately 250 of these reports in a filing cabinet of the Ministry, where she was working and her analysis of their contents indicated five major categories of criticism coming from educators, parents, and others. First, by far the greatest number of recommendations for change had to do with reducing the amount of ideological content in the curriculum. The recommendations suggested that school ought to become a place where pupils would learn to resolve conflicts peacefully and learn how to engage in open, free discussion about differences in points of view. There were many specific curricular recommendations, such as the elimination of military training in school and the enhancement of aesthetic, artistic programs, the adoption of courses dealing with ethical and moral issues, and the development of course content related to ecological issues. Significantly, "peace education" took on great significance. Of course, peace education had always had a place within the ideology of Central and Eastern Europe, but it was to take on new and different dimensions as East Germans faced a new reality. Second, schools were condemned for having become sterile, bureaucratic institutions, where the child was seen as an object rather than as a subject. Appeals were made to turn schools again into places where the joy of learning would once again take center stage, where creativity and fantasy would again become a part of the learning process. Third, schools were seen as places where central mandates were expected to be carried out without variance, and both teachers and parents appealed to the central Ministry of Education to create institutions where teachers and parents could become more responsible for their own educational programs. Parents had developed habits of supporting the school, but they had never been given an opportunity to think of "parental rights" or make decisions that carried some critical responsibilities with them. Pupils had been held in a state of submission but they must begin to learn to become responsible for their own learning. They must develop confidence in teacher-pupil relations by having a new, warm relationship with their teachers. Fourth, some small attention was given, in some letters, to the need to revamp the educational system so that differentiation of programs and courses of study would play some role in the POS, so that new subjects could be introduced into the curriculum, so that instructional approaches might be changed. Fifth, a little attention was given to specific issues such as school attendance problems and the introduction of a five-day week.

The hopes of those expecting something to occur at the Ninth Pedagogical Congress were immediately shattered, when Margot Honecker refused to allow any discussion of reform matters to come to the floor. In her major speech before the 3,670 delegates, she made an oblique reference about how "today much is being exaggerated by the enemies who are sowing seeds of doubt about socialism." She stressed that "our time is a time of struggle," to insure that the way East Germany has chosen may be defended (Honecker, 1989, p. 12). In fact, no effort was made to reply to the communications that had come to her, and many of the more critical papers that had been sent by individuals and institutions were referred to the State Security Ministry (*Stasi*) (Kaack, 1992).

A central issue related to education ought to be the state of mind of the children. Prior to the collapse of the German Democratic Republic, there was an outpouring of communications from children and youth in regard to their schools. Dieter Kirchhöfer, then a member of the Academy of Pedagogical Sciences, gained access to hundreds of letters and documents, sent by children to the Ministry of Education and other organs of the state. These letters provide certain insights into the children's expectations about what they wanted to happen. Many letters were written by pupil functionaries to the Central Board of the Free German Youth in conjunction with the Ninth Pedagogical Congress. These pupil leaders had been required to hold meetings with classmates to discuss the Congress and report back ideas and suggestions. This may not have been voluntary; nevertheless, it was something that had never been open to pupils before. Often, however, these letters convey the point of view of school administrators, youth group, and party leaders who used children and youth, as was common in the GDR, to give their opinion. These letters also contained the usual report of achieved goals, the ritual explanation of new activities, self criticism and expected statements of confidence in party leadership. Many, though, did contain true questions and comments that would not have been included in such letters to the Central Board before. The means of realizing these wishes and ideas, however, was left open.

The most popular topics were learning, improvement of teacher-pupil relationships, and self-responsibility and independence. Comments about learning raised fundamental questions of what was being taught and how. Although pupils agreed, in general, with school requirements, they wanted, nevertheless, more classes that were separated into higher and lower levels, courses such as geography and history to be more relevant to the world situation as they were beginning to understand it, and the chance for more discussion and less lecturing. In addition, they asked for more choices in elective courses, more variety and less pressure in required courses, more balance in textbooks--more pros and cons, access to school records, and school-free Saturdays.

> I picture to myself that the Ninth Pedagogical Congress will decide to develop new curriculum; for example, in history since human investigation continues and pupils want to and should learn more (village school, boy, 11).

> It would be better in the subject of Productive Work if we, for example, spent a whole week in the factory twice a year than if we worked there every two weeks for a morning. Are we getting computer instruction (village school, boy, 12)?

Pupils wished their teachers to be more casual and flexible, to take more time for them and their concerns, to give them more voice in decisions, and to treat them as mature people. Surprisingly they asked that teachers devote more attention to weaker pupils, not just to super or model pupils.

> We'd like a good relationship with our teachers so that we can tell our wants and problems to them and can be critical and still be accepted. The teacher should also try to get to know us. If we do something wrong, we shouldn't be criminalized right off. Pupils don't like abusive language, not from the teacher either (small town school).

Inclusion in preparation and carrying out of instruction and activities in youth organizations along with the desire for less regimentation were important themes of pupils' desire for independence and taking responsibility.

> Pupils would like to be accepted as adults and not constantly be led by the nose (small town school).

> Social democracy also encompasses independent, conscious action. At first that is a difficult thing for us because we

were always glad if our teachers pre-digested everything for us... (big city school).

Included in these letters was criticism of Free German Youth work, relatively radical at this time, but not the middle point of discussion by any means.

We don't want tired old topics like May 1 or Thälmann's birthday for our wall newspaper anymore (village school).

The approaching Ninth Pedagogical Congress stimulated pupil communication in other areas, too. Letters were sent in reply to an invitation by the press, especially the Pioneer and Free German Youth publications, for reader opinion and discussion. The publishers carefully selected and shortened letters, but did answer every letter sent in. In addition, letters were often written spontaneously and voluntarily and sent to other publications including state council chairpersons (*Staatsratsvorsitzenden*), resolutions, decisions, and communications written by individuals or put together by schools and sent to central government offices, short-lived school newspapers, suggestion boxes set up in schools, and to school "wall newspapers" (bulletin boards of announcements, pupil creative work, and opinions).

In this time of strong central control of education in the German Democratic Republic as well as resistance to change, many letters had the traditional mark of self-criticism, perhaps a condition of acceptance of their demands. Nevertheless, the tone was not submissive or hypocritical. Letters got right to the point and gave the impression of self-confidence and desire to be part of the solution, an indication that the spirit of Moscow-centered reform was touching East German school children.

We want to have a voice in what becomes of our school and not leave it to the adults alone (village school, boy, 12).

Another means used by East German children and youth to convey their opinions, and one ultimately more influential in realizing democratic procedures were the street demonstrations of fall, 1989. In the Leipzig demonstrations, Kirchhöfer reports that 8-12% of the participants were under 18--in the case of three schools, 80% of the pupils took part. An even greater percentage, 40%, was under 18 in the Berlin demonstrations of 7 and 8 October, when the popular Gorbachev was in attendance. Placards had a youthful tone to them: "Gorbi," "We stay here," and "Now we're coming!"

Children, of course, of the German Democratic Republic were used to demonstrations. On state holidays such as 1 May and 7 October, peace meetings, the honoring of special guests, and other numerous occasions, school children were required to do their part. They had to wear what they were told to wear and carry the symbols that were given to them. They had to rehearse first, then after a short time on stage, so to speak, they had to wait until the boring speeches had ended. Often they stole away or stood around chatting, letting flags and placards lie on the ground.

> It was completely chaotic....We were shoved from one side to the other. Besides that, we couldn't see much of the podium or the speakers. Mostly it was so noisy that we couldn't understand what was being said... I think it went on too long. It wasn't exactly pleasant to be standing in such heat hemmed in among a lot of wild people (girl, 13).

But the character of the children's involvement in the demonstrations of fall, 1989, were different. Kirchhöfer obtained copies of essays children had written in school that indicated a strong personal engagement, opposition, and an element of danger.

> Thirteen times I was in the Monday demonstrations [in Leipzig]. At first we were like a family. Now people are more aggressive and don't listen to each other anymore (boy, 10).

I was always at the demonstrations. I demanded: 'Down with the SED,' 'Free Elections,' 'Expose the Crimes' (boy, 11).

I found it very good that we could bring about a transformation with our demonstrations. I also found it good that the police didn't attack much (besides October 7). I wouldn't have thought that the demonstrations could turn out so peacefully so that no blood bath developed as in Rumania (girl, 12).

When the demonstrations in Leipzig began, I often went demonstrating with my father. Why I did that, I really don't know. Perhaps because my classmates told a lot about their Monday demonstrations. They told about it in such a thrilling way, that it got me excited to go. I liked the way people got angry at the secret police (*Stasi*). Then each time I went and shouted along with them--even things I didn't really understand (girl, 13).

It was a unique chaos. In September [1989] at the demonstrations, everyone yelled something about freedom, etc., but no one knew from his own experience what freedom was. At the first demonstrations everything was still more or less quiet; then as more than 10,000 people stood on the street and made their demands, the cops were already a little bit uneasy. The demonstrators became physical and threw stones, etc. The police attacked brutally. If you experienced that, then you were afraid to set foot in the street on a Monday evening. But we [the people] got someplace (girl, 14).

The transformation [Wende] was the experience of my life. It was the most breath-taking experience for me. Above all, because I was right in the middle of things. Monday after Monday. More and more people. The tension rose more each time. Really nerve-wracking (boy, 13).

As the situation became more and more critical, those people at the center of the educational hierarchy began, reluctantly, to take some action. One section of the Academy of Pedagogical Sciences, for example, wrote an open letter to Margot Honecker, Werner Lorenz, and Gerhart Neuner expressing dismay that they as leaders of the educational establishment had failed to respond to the growing agitation in society. They maintained that the millions of children and youth, parents, and the tens of thousands of teachers, educators, and researchers wait for some expression from their leaders and some willingness to enter into open discussion about the future (Open Letter, 1989). The Academy of Pedagogical Sciences finally produced a small document, labeled, "Proposal for Discussion" which laid out certain problems and responsibilities the academic community faced with regard to the "renewal of the socialist school" (DIPF, 1989c). In the preface of the document members of the research community were reminded that it was their responsibility to respond to the changes taking place in East German society. The entire tone of the document was to continue to defend "democratic foundations, such as Unity, secularism, statism, free service, and equal opportunity," but it was becoming necessary to address aspects of socialism that had apparently failed. This was particularly apparent in the failure of the socialist schools to cultivate the development of individualism and flexibility. The document makes specific reference to the need to restore the sovereignty of the teacher in connection with:

- The freedom to make choices regarding the application and revision of the program of studies;
- The responsibility to deal with the unfolding of each child as an individual, particularly related to marks, promotion from grade to grade, occupational decisions, and protection from the arbitrary intervention of the public and officials over them;
- The ability to take a political stand as a professional and as a teacher, and abolishing the role of the teacher as a 'propagandist of Marxism/Leninism;'

- The opportunity to function with full civil rights, to change work places, to travel (p. 12).

This document appeared on 8 November 1989, one day before the Berlin Wall was to come down. It is a sad testimony that the top of East German's educational hierarchy began to take action far too late for them to have a significant impact on East Germany's ultimate educational destiny.

In spite of the general reactionary moves on the part of the educational power structure, there were those in the East German educational establishment, who remained reform oriented. Even in the most reactionary of educational systems, some level of pluralistic thinking always exists and voices of dissent and agitation for different courses of action are expressed. This was most evident in certain programs at the Institutions of higher education.

Reform Impulses at Institutions of Higher Education

A number of institutions of higher education were involved in internal and general change initiatives. At Humboldt University there was not only passive resistance to the authority structure of the institution and the regime, but critical voices had come to play a strong role in certain departments. German Studies had established close links with the artist community of the German Democratic Republic, including writers, who continually challenged the hard liners. The English Studies faculty and students at Humboldt University were also becoming increasingly active. In fact, the English Studies students organized a protest movement to boycott the 1989 Whitsuntide celebration sponsored by the state. According to Dieter Klein, the Vice-Rector of Humboldt University just prior to the fall of the Berlin Wall, from 50 to 75 of the 1,000 teaching personnel at Humboldt University were actively engaged in meetings, writing papers, and general discussions for fundamental reform of Humboldt University. It has also been estimated that over 4,000 students joined with many faculty to participate in a Berlin demonstration organized by the artist community on 17 October 1989.[3] At Karl-Marx University in Leipzig students and faculty were prominent in the Monday evening demonstrations. The Marxism-Leninism faculty of 150 even began to splinter into factions for and against reform, when the *Sputnik* journal was banned in May, 1989 (Darnton, 1991, p. 100). At the Teacher Training College Halle-Köthen, the faculty and students were actively engaged in "democratic" reform discussions, although these discussions remained in the context of a socialist state. These were coupled with active participation in demonstrations for a peaceful resolution of the crisis (Keßler & Krätzschmar, 1992, p. 142).

The above observations should not be interpreted to mean that university people were on the forefront of the movement for fundamental change. Dirk Philipsen (1993, 97-111) provides a provocative interview with Werner Bramke, chair of the History Department of Karl-Marx University and a middle ranking party official, who had engaged in a mighty internal struggle to reconcile his desire for a purifying "socialist renewal" and his fear of speaking out against the party. He helped to provide a positive outlet for student outrage at events such as the banning of *Sputnik* in 1989, and indicated that there was an openness to voices of dissent within the university itself (p. 105). Recalling the monthly meeting of the department directors, Bramke said, "I was the first to bring up this [*Sputnik* ban] issue, and I said 'I am ashamed of this measure....' No word of criticism was uttered in response to what I had said," which suggests that such statements were indeed considered to have been bold. Bramke finally comes forward to take a leading role in affairs only after the party had effectively collapsed in 1989. Even so, it would be unfair to suggest that universities were completely "aloof from revolutionary initiatives" as some commentators have claimed (Mitter, 1992, p. 45).

Although it is clear that the academy was not on the forefront of activism for change it did provide some inspiration particularly because students were so active in the demonstrations. The academic people did make a definite contribution to the growing demands for change, but this contribution was more conceptual than behavioral.

---

[3]From approximately 20,000 students and 1,000 teaching personnel.

For example, Social Sciences researchers at Humboldt University produced certain position papers in their *Forschungsprojekt Sozialismustheorie* (Research Project on the Theory of Socialism), that had a decisive impact on the generation of ideas and concepts that provided a conceptual foundation for the kinds of changes being discussed. As a part of this project, in July 1989, Social Sciences faculty produced a significant study assessing the social and economic situation of socialism in the world and they attempted to conceptualize how socialism must be transformed, if it was to sustain itself (Land, 1989).

Reform Impulses in the Schools

In the individual schools throughout the country, seeds of discontent and protest were also evident. There had always been some diversity in most schools, particularly those where the leadership had been somewhat benign or where the party had not been overbearing. The voices for change usually restricted their activities to their individual classrooms in that teachers would alter the curriculum or discuss current topics that would clearly be discouraged by higher authorities. However, most schools experienced some general level of stress and growing diversity. In some schools there was a move to relax the dress code for young pioneers, which never materialized. The schools typically devoted an hour of instruction each week to "current political topics." In the past these had usually provided a forum for political indoctrination, but the students began raising questions that required thoughtful, balanced responses. The monthly instructional meetings for indoctrination in socialism, run by the party members at the school, often provided a platform for teachers to challenge the *status quo*, although teachers had learned how to couch their statements in politically acceptable terms. At certain schools, even party members began to speak out in critical terms against the direction the regime had been going and especially the direction Margot Honecker, wife of the President and the woman who had been Minister of Education for a quarter of a century, had taken education.

The impact of the regime to tighten up its control rippled down to the individual schools. At the 12. Polytechnische Oberschule in Marzahn, a district of East Berlin, for example, the action of central school officials was direct and unmistakable. Humboldt University had been using the school as an experimental institution for many years, and it had developed a reputation for not conforming. As the political situation became more tense, a new headmistress was appointed to the POS in the beginning of 1988/89. She was a devoted member of the SED and was relatively inflexible in that she demanded that the school conform to the letter to all the regulations that went out to the schools. Reform-oriented teachers became increasingly restless and agitated as they witnessed a repressive atmosphere coming into their institution. Such repression was, of course, not universal, particularly in the smaller communities. At a POS in Freiberg, the headmistress encouraged the teachers to discuss the emerging situation with each other and with the pupils. Teachers even encouraged the children to attend the demonstrations taking place in the community, as a learning experience. In this school the faculty was able to maintain a sense of collective collegiality throughout the period just prior to the collapse.

After the summer vacation of 1989, when the borders of Hungary had been opened, the situation reached a point of crisis in many schools. The broader political developments led to severe tension in the minds of most teachers, as they struggled between having a sense of loyalty, a desire to maintain harmony and stability in their school, and a sense of criticism and challenge. The summer had witnessed a mass exodus of East Germany through neighboring states, and this became a point of contention among many educators about how to deal with it in the individual schools. In East Germany there was a so-called preparation week just before regular instruction began, and great time was devoted in some schools to the questions of the period. Some teachers and leaders simply wanted to keep a lid of such issues and not even raise them. They argued that young people could not understand what was happening and they should not be exposed to these "negative" events. Others wanted to place the exodus in a bad light. Others wanted the issues to take center stage in their classes.

There was also growing pressure for internal changes. For example, at the 41. POS in Berlin, teachers who were not members of the SED began to argue that they should not be expected to attend the indoctrination meetings held regularly by the Party members in the school. The 63. POS in Rostock was fairly typical of what was going on. Things remained somewhat calm, but there was growing apprehension that something must be done in view of the fact that the economy was plummeting and the educational leadership had long ceased to be competent, but no one knew what to do. A series of meetings was held at which time concerns were voiced, but not much happened in real terms. The consequence was a growing split among teachers and increasing stress and pressure on them.

A school was often thrown into a state of emergency when an event had a direct bearing on it. The 12. POS of Marzahn, mentioned above, was actually a part of a two-school complex and a crisis at the sister school, the 14. POS, developed when one of its teachers failed to appear in the school and several days later it became clear that this teacher had chosen to travel to Hungary and migrate to the West. This situation led to a special meeting of parents and staff members to explain the event and it contributed to a terrible breach between the reform oriented elements and those who wished to maintain the *status quo*. The headmistress of the school had ruled with an iron hand for many years, and her explanation was that the young teacher, who had left and gone west, had been a "traitor" to the children and the school. The party leadership at the school gave impassioned arguments that the school hold firmly to the course set by the leaders of the GDR. On the other hand, many teachers stood and argued that the missing teacher had the right to make whatever choice she thought was in her best interests. The term "traitor" quickly became the label given to any teacher who left the children and went west. However, such events usually allowed parents and teachers to join together in an open discussion about what might be in the best interests of the children.

To the credit of the teachers, schools remained remarkably stable through the growing crisis. Even though there was growing disunity on the part of teachers in calls for action, there appears to have been increased solidarity in terms of care for the youth in the schools. The children were typically provided a secure, stable, environment, though many schools held public meetings and assemblies with the children where questions were invited and open discussions were held.

The *Wende*

There are specific dates in history that take on a unique sense of importance and mystery. Thursday, 9 November 1989, when the Wall came down in Berlin, is surely destined to become such a date in German history. Even though the Berlin Wall was breached in the late evening, most teachers became aware of it before they retired for the night, although a few teachers first heard of it the next morning as they were getting ready for school. The event appears to have been a great shock to almost all teachers, even though in retrospect they probably should have expected it to occur. The old leader of the country and his wife, the Minister of Education, had already resigned their positions and they were so harassed that they would soon escape East Germany, as many teachers were fond of saying, "almost as thieves in the night." and it should have been clear that the *Wende* (turning point or transformation) would come about. When the Wall did come down, the word most often used by teachers to describe their feelings was "euphoria." It was indeed, a time of celebration and release of pent up feelings. In one East Berlin school, the parents and teachers had been meeting at the school to elect a parent council. There had been apprehension about the meeting. School staff had been fearful that parents would attack the school because one of its teachers had deserted the school and had escaped west through Hungary. Surprisingly, the meeting went rather calmly, but toward the end of the agenda a telephone call came in with the announcement, "the Wall is down." The meeting broke up and the entire school faculty left as a group and spent the night in West Berlin, along with hundreds of thousands of other East Germans. In fact, that night a large number of teachers participated in the celebration and in the discovery of the other half of Berlin. The next day school was conducted, as usual, in an orderly fashion. One teacher explains his experience as follows:

> When I heard about the Wall coming down, I realized it was a once-in-a-lifetime opportunity, but I decided to remain in East Berlin and stay with the kids. In the afternoon, after school let out, I went to Warschauer Gate and there was a small door there that was open. Thousands upon thousands went through that door. I went with them and as soon as I had crossed the bridge a man came up to me and asked me if I was an East German. We went to a bar and remained there until six o'clock the next morning, when I had to leave and get back to the school to meet the kids.

Before the weekend was over people from all over East Germany had made the journey into the "West." However, the feelings were usually somewhat mixed. One teacher described her reactions in the following way:

> At first I was filled with a sense of euphoria. I was thinking, 'man, now I can just go over there.' Then slowly, I began to fall into a deep depression. I became filled with fear. I realized the socialist system is over, and everything that is humanitarian in that system is going to die. I won't feel secure in my house. There will be great unemployment. Everything that is bad in the West will come to us. There will be racism and fascism. It was clear that the BRD would take over. It was logical, but I kept asking myself, 'what will happen to our land?'

This teacher was not alone in her fear. The Berlin Wall had actually represented a protective symbol in the lives of great numbers of teachers, who believed it was keeping out the trouble makers, the radicals, the physically dangerous, the exploiters. To these educators, the break in the Wall symbolized the death of something they had devoted themselves to as well as a sense of security. These people trembled in fear of an uncertain future.

Schools are some of the most stable institutions in any society. Those of us who are intentionally working to change institutions often express frustration with this stability; however, the events of November 1989, indicate that this stability reflects an important positive side. When the Berlin Wall came down, the GDR found itself in a state of total disruption. The traditional authority structure, including the educational authority, disappeared almost over night. The directors of the individual schools lost their legitimate role as leaders. There was almost a total vacuum of authority from the Minister of Education down through the school leaders, but it is significant that the schools continued to function as efficiently and as actively as ever. The morning after the Wall came down, almost every teacher in East Germany was at his or her appointed place, ready to conduct school. Many of the children were not there, for they were heading West with their parents, but the teachers, many of whom had spent the entire night in West Berlin, were ready to work. School was conducted in an orderly productive manner. Of course, all the children had to tell what they had experienced, and the teachers wanted to tell of their experiences, their impressions, their hopes and fears, but the classes ran according to schedule, and the planned lessons were given. Those schools that had television sets kept them on throughout the day, so that everyone could keep a running account of what was happening. In spite of this slight variation in the program, school went on almost as usual in the lower grades, while there was a great deal of agitation and excitement in the upper grades. A teacher in Cottbus explained that there was an immediate break in stability when the conventional leadership of the school wavered, but that teacher and his colleagues quickly compensated by tightening up their own routine so that discipline was maintained and the school continued to function as well as ever.

Teachers in the East German schools themselves have various explanations for the sense of order that prevailed in the schools. It was clear that there was chaos and great instability everywhere, but a common thread seems to emerge in teacher's explanations of their behavior. In a situation where formal authority disappears, the teachers fell into reliance on what might be described as a higher humanitarian law: "We are responsible for the kids, and we must be there for them." Of course, there was great frustration about what to do, how to teach, what content to use, what source material to rely on, how to reach to a school leader who represented the old system. But these feelings of inadequacy were accompanied by a sense of life, a feeling of joy. Ideas began to spring up everywhere. East Germany was about to experience a period of enormous freedom and the generation of great creativity.

Chapter VII

Creativity in East German Schooling

Politics into the 1990s

Even after the fall of the Berlin Wall, the grass roots political activities of the populace continued. Large demonstrations continued as people demanded that the Socialist Unity Party's power monopoly end. Resignations came almost daily from key officials, and arrests were made of people who were charged with criminal activity. Television proved a devastating witness of the corruption and private wealth of the leaders, who had exploited public poverty for their own benefit. Honecker's private hunting lodge will remain imbedded in the memory of great masses of people. On 1 December 1989 the constitution was changed so that the SED was eliminated as the leading political party in the country (Fischer, 1992, p. 103). Egon Krenz, who was the new leader of the GDR at the time the Wall came down, was forced to resign on 6 December 1989 and he was replaced by Hans Modrow, who announced that free, secret parliamentary elections would be held on 6 May 1990. However, the real power of the state had been taken over by a so-called "round-table system of consultative government" on 7 December 1989 (Wallach & Francisco, 1992, p. 46). Almost all former opposition groups were included in the Round-Table, including the church. The Round-Table objected to the late election date and certain other factors in the government, including the continued presence of the *Stasi*, the state security police. A crisis ensued and the government almost collapsed; therefore, Modrow accepted the Round-Table as a part of a grand coalition. One of its first acts was to declare that parliamentary elections would be held on 18 March 1990 and local elections on 6 May.

The collapse signaled the death of the old order of things. Within weeks the German Democratic Republic witnessed a broad, diffuse, and confusing array of initiatives. Fischer (1992, p. 105) notes, for example, that by February 35 political parties, 16 citizens initiatives, 12 women's groups and initiatives, 52 youth organizations and initiatives, 6 trade unions, and 42 vocational organizations advocating political programs had been established. Such organizational activities and initiatives were also reflected among educators.

Educators and the New Freedom

As evidence of underhanded activities and illegal processes in the old GDR came to light, those educators, who had committed themselves to its spoken ideals began to feel betrayed by the leaders, the *Stasi*, and the "system." This sense of betrayal soon shifted to guilt, insecurity, and self-doubt. This feeling of self-doubt was exacerbated by the fact that the conventional authority structure on which teachers had come to rely, had disappeared. Margot Honecker, had already departed the Ministry of Education on 2 November 1989, and the Ministry never did recover its influence. Its legitimacy had been stretched beyond the breaking point and it simply collapsed. It could no longer play even a symbolically supportive role in the developmental activities taking place in the schools throughout the land.

Seen from a hierarchical systems standpoint, one might conclude that little educational change occurred in those first months after the collapse. This has led some commentators to conclude that the failure of the political and economic systems of East Germany was accompanied by a collapse of the educational system, and that West Germany needed to intervene to restore it (e.g., Fischer & Schmidt, 1991). Other observers realized some changes were made at the local institutions but had little idea of their magnitude. This led people such as Wolfgang Mitter (1992, p. 45) to conclude that the *Wende* "stimulated innovative activity at the grass-roots level of schools and also at some universities at an early stage, though to a small extent."

It is easy to see why perceptive observers would come to such a conclusion. Educational institutions are what contemporary systems theorists call dissipative social systems, which require extensive external support in order to survive. The assumption could easily be made that the collapse of the Ministry of Education would signal the stagnation and even death of the educational institutions themselves because they were receiving no external support. In fact, many institutions were initially frozen into inaction, and they required dramatic intervention to move them to action. In Halle, for example, the students became so frustrated with the schools that in mid-January of 1990 they went on strike against the teachers demanding that they have a voice in what was happening (Einicke & Boose, 1990, p. 12). By and large, however, because the East German institutions continued to receive financial resources, their continuation was sure enough for them to begin taking action. They were able to draw intellectual and emotional support from universities and other educational centers in East Germany, from West Germans, and from other parts of the world. It is for this reason that Stucke (1990) called those first months after the *Wende* the period of cooperation. A considerable number of East German educators made arrangements to go to West Germany, other Western European states, and even to North America in search of answers to their pedagogical questions. As shall be seen, certain institutions also began assisting them and arranging partnerships with them. The conclusion must be drawn that sufficient support existed for educational institutions to engage heavily in reform.

Even without this support, the total loss of the central authority structure accompanied by feelings of self-doubt on the part of the school community created a condition ideally suited for radical change. It facilitated the release of self-organizing energies that had never been allowed to be expressed. New systems theorists claim that systems will do everything possible for self-preservation (Krohn, Küppers & Nowotny, 1990, p. 7), but that the self-regulation process of a system also includes the possibility that the perturbation may reach a breaking point, where the system simply collapses (Carnairo, 1982). In addition, there appears also to exist a self-organizing capacity of most systems that allows them to adjust to extensive external shifts, so that self-preservation ultimately means the emergence of quite new orientations and configurations of the systems themselves. This latter possibility is precisely what happened in East Germany. Certain aspects of their activities shall be explored, particularly with regard to (1) central initiatives of the Academy of Pedagogical Sciences, (2) higher education developments, (3) vocational education developments, and (4) individual school initiatives throughout East Germany.

The Academy of Pedagogical Sciences[1]

Education in East Germany had been highly centralized, and Margot Honecker, the wife of the President, had ruled education with an iron hand for 25 years. On 18 October 1989, Erich Honecker was ousted from the leadership of the East Germany SED Party and the regime began to unravel. Both Margot and Erich Honecker's safety fell into question and they soon left for Moscow. The Ministry of Education became largely impotent because the entire machinery had become entrenched in the routine of responding only to directives from above. Although the Ministry of Education came to play almost no role in developments taking place, they still remained actively connected to the changing situation at the central Academy of Pedagogical Sciences (APW) located next door to the Ministry of Education in East Berlin.

The Academy of Pedagogical Sciences had been the institution responsible for planning and implementing matters, such as curriculum throughout the GDR. From its inception on 15 September 1970, the APW had represented a type of contradictory institution. It was under the direct supervision of Margot Honecker and the Ministry of Education and, therefore, was expected to satisfy her policy dictates and those of her ministry. However, it also consisted of some of the best qualified experts in the country. Such talent demanded some sense of autonomy and creative independence, though that was held in check by the ideological climate of East Germany.

---

[1]*Akademie der Pädagogischen Wissenschaften.*

By the middle of October 1989, the work assigned to the APW became increasingly intense. Working groups were formed and discussions, research meetings and political forums were held with a single issue before the group: What should be done about the deteriorating situation in education? Their world had already begun to fall apart, and there was intense anxiety concerning appropriate response to developments.

One of the curious developments of that time was the emergence of something colleagues labeled as "wall newspapers" (*Wandzeitungen*), where colleagues could find declarations and personal position papers in the form of "open letters" that dealt with every imaginable aspect of educational reform (APW, 1989). For example, on 31 October 1989, members of the Academy of Pedagogical Sciences in East Berlin found a notice in the form of an "open letter" that colleagues had sent to the Central Committee of the SED demanding that the Committee initiate open discussion with the public, APW members, and school people about curricular changes that might be necessary (DIPF, 1989). Immediately after the *Wende* the APW became actively engaged in deliberations about the "renewal of the socialist school," and on 22 November 1989 a "proposal for discussion" was distributed by 27 of the leaders of the APW explaining that the socialist school of the past had lost its way. It must be redirected and be based on the unfolding of each individual in the context of a "radical democratization of society."

One of the major issues confronting those at the APW had to do with a fundamental revision of those curricular subjects such as political studies, civics *(Staatsbürgerkunde)*, and history, that had been devoted to indoctrination to socialism. For illustrative purposes, some elements of history course revision shall be discussed. Almost immediately after the *Wende* the APW sent invitations to a number of specialists of history instruction in the GDR, who gathered at the APW on 7 December 1989, together with representatives of all political parties and some church leaders to discuss the future of history instruction (DIPF, 1989b). A working group at the APW set about to revise the history curriculum (APW, 1989) to be based on a pluralistic, historical presentation. This working group rejected the idea basic to all Eastern Block countries that Marxist/Leninist history was based on scientifically established fact. By February the basic framework for a completely revised history program of studies for forms 5-10 had been worked out, and it was distributed to a number of people for their reactions. The editor of *Evangelische Monatsschrift*, Günter Wirth, as an example, wrote a letter on 19 February 1990, where he criticized the lack of attention being given in the history program to the Jewish and Christian religions (Wirth, 1990).

Whereas history in the old German Democratic Republic had long been taught in service to the state, the new orientation was to "strengthen the individuality of each pupil" (DIPF, 1990a). On 28 March 1990 the Academy presented the Ministry with an internal report which provided the basic framework for history instruction from forms 5-10. Because the transformation of East Germany was in such a formative stage, the proposed history program reflected the need for differentiation, for pluralistic thinking, and for consideration of different social forces (Ministerium, 1989).

The program represented a radical departure from the old Marxist/Leninist framework. At the ten-year POS a major intention of history had been to help instill in the youth a "love for the socialist Fatherland, educate to socialistic patriotism and international proletarianism, and instill an anti-imperialistic orientation..." (Ministerium, 1988). The core history program had been designed for forms 5-10, and was carried out, although the number of hours increased in latter years. The East German program had great strengths in that it was highly integrated, was articulated between all form (grade level) levels, and had a clear theoretical and conceptual thread running throughout. However, these very strengths were also its major weaknesses in that the program was one-sided and authoritarian; it did not allow for alternative perspectives in any way. The final version of the old history program was published in 1989, and it stipulated that over a six year period the pupils were to be taken through an epochal history of the world, with emphasis on developments in Germany, as framed by Marx and Lenin. According to this framework, mankind has progressed through a series of epochs: original society, slave society, feudal society, early capitalism, imperialistic capitalism, and finally socialism. In each of the epochs, progressive forces were at work to move society to another level of development, while reactionary forces were attempting to prevent its development. Of course, the pupils learned that the forces of progress eventually won out in each epoch. The main emphasis of history instruction was the fight against fascism and the ultimate triumph of socialism.

Unfortunately, the new curriculum of the APW was never published and made available to teachers struggling to determine what they should teach and how they should reorient their instruction. Even so, the report was available to specialists, who were working on their own to develop a program of studies. The most active group known to date were specialists in what later became the state of Saxony. Wendelin Szalai and Renate Kappler from Dresden, who had worked with the Academy on its draft, took the lead in contacting colleagues from the region and as early as 20 February 1990, didactic representatives of the History Sections of Leipzig University, Leipzig Teacher Training College, and the Dresden Teacher Training College were able to submit a proposal to the Regional Ministry of Education and other important bodies to develop a history program for what they anticipated to be the future state of Saxony (DIPF, 1990b). This proposal was accepted and in June a full outline of history for forms 5-12 in Saxony was distributed to approximately 600 history teachers (Sächsisches Staatsministerium, 1990). A year later a second revision was made available, which included updated elements suggested by those teachers using the outline (Sächsisches Staatsministerium, 1991). Both editions pointed clearly in the direction of a "democratic" program of studies.

Higher Education Developments

When the Berlin Wall came down on 9 November 1989, the response of higher education personnel was active and general. The wish of the academic leaders at the time of the *Wende* was typically for the two Germanys to remain separate. The reform documents that were produced in the early 1990s had the orientation of a reformed socialism (e.g., Falk, 1990b). A full confirmation of events is yet to be recorded, but some sense of developments can be gained from efforts at a selected number of institutions. There was an immediate decision to eliminate Marxist/Leninist teachings as a foundation course in higher education, which made approximately 10% of all teaching personnel obsolete. In fact, the issue of the number of teaching personnel in higher education soon came into the discussion. It has been estimated that whereas the student/instructor ratio in West Germany was 14/1, in East Germany it was 4/1. Part of the problem could be rectified by equalizing the number of students in East Germany as compared with West Germany. In 1989, the number of young people who qualified for higher education studies stood at 30.3% of the appropriate age group, whereas in East Germany it stood at 15%. This meant that the number of young people gaining entrance into higher education would likely climb rapidly. The political parties that began presenting themselves appear to have advocated a rapid increase of students. The SPD, for example, exclaimed, "whoever wishes to study and is qualified, has the right to select the subject and the place, as long as the university and higher schools have the capacity to accommodate them" (quoted in Fischer, 1992, p. 117). Klemm and his colleagues (1992, p. 163) estimate that it will take approximately two decades to achieve parity in East and West Germany, but some of the personnel imbalance would naturally be corrected in the short run by admitting greater and greater numbers of students.

In the period right after the *Wende,* some institutions of higher education were particularly vulnerable. The teacher training colleges at Zwickau, Dresden and Halle-Köthen, for example, had been responsible for the preparation of Pioneer leaders. Hundreds of young people at every stage of preparation enrolled in these institutions would find themselves potentially without employment unless programs were changed. At the Teacher Training College of Halle-Köthen, the faculty and students had actually initiated discussion of reform in the early fall. When the collapse came, they were in a position to move toward resolution of many problems. According to members of the staff, there was a general feeling of elation with the new freedom that had come to them and they immediately sought out academic contact with colleagues elsewhere in both East and West Germany. Very quickly the faculty developed a new program of studies for the diploma students in education. They also received money from the West German government to help in the reforming of their teacher education program. Significant in all of this was a feeling on the part of faculty that they and their colleagues in West Germany were working cooperatively toward a joint enterprise of teacher education and pedagogical reform (Keßler & Krätzschmar, 1992, pp. 142-3).

At Zwickau the situation was doubly difficult. The role of this institution had been to train Pioneer leaders, and the major subject of study of most Pioneer leader candidates had been *Staatsbürgerkunde* (civics), a program of study that immediately lost its usefulness. Professors Harald and Elke Gräßler made immediate contact with a number of people in West Germany, including Wolfgang Nahrstedt at Bielefeld, Walter Tokarski in Cologne, and Gisela Wegener-Spöhring in Göttingen, where discussion began concerning redirection of the program toward *Freizeitpädagogik* (free-time pedagogy). Zwickau soon became the major center for this area and received ministerial sanction as a legitimate major field of study.

The guiding institution of higher learning in East Germany was Humboldt University. Among the changes instituted in the first months after the collapse were the following:

- Many contacts were made with West Germans in almost every subject field. These contacts facilitated a general discussion on reorientation and change and helped point all segments of Humboldt University toward an adoption of Western academic practices. The Science council (*Wissenschaftsrat*) of West Germany took some lead in these exchanges, and, interestingly, it insisted that the West

German system be not simply to be transferred to East Germany. Rather, it argued that existing conditions provided an opportunity for both states to engage in a process of self-examination and renewal (Wissenschaftsrat, 1990, p. 10).

- A new Humboldt University constitutional framework was established, which defined the ruling council of the University. The first council was elected in January 1990, barely two months after the collapse, and its representatives consisted of approximately 10% of the university community of 10,000 people, including faculty representatives (35%), research and teaching assistant representatives (25%), student representatives (30%), and others 10%.[2]

- All members of the central administration were newly elected. The most visible figure was the new Rector, Heinrich Fink, Professor of Theology. Fink's election was especially critical because he was a part of the old community but not a central figure. In fact, theologians played a central role in the agitations prior to the collapse. In addition, his personality was such that he gave stability to the community and was able to build a collegial, consensual base for university operations (Spiegel, 1991).

- The principle of the unity of research and teaching was restored, which again gave teaching personnel responsibility to determine the content of lectures. The partnership of teachers and students was stressed also (Falk, 1990b, p. 46; Lemmens, 1990).

- The so-called *Studium generale*, which had formed the core of traditional German higher education, was reintroduced to provide a general education to all students in the future.

- Most programs of study were revised and curricula changed to reflect the new social and political realities. For example,

---

[2]This provision has raised serious questions since the unification, because the West German Higher Education Law (*Hochschulrahmengesetzt*) stipulates that the University Council shall have a majority of professors (Spiegel, 1991, p. 74).

in the Social Sciences Faculty, a general reorientation was initiated even before the Berlin Wall came down. On 3 November 1989, a week before the collapse, the Faculty submitted an open letter to the Academic Senate calling for program reform, and on 14 November 1989, six days after the collapse, the Social Sciences Faculty submitted a proposal for a fundamental revision of curricula and scientific work, including elimination of traditional Marxist-Leninist theory as a compulsory orientation and a declaration of the autonomy of the University from political interference (Falk, 1990a).

- The large Department of Marxism-Leninism, with its 268 member academic staff, was closed in September 1990, even before the two Germanys were officially united, though 122 of these staff members were retained and transferred to other academic programs (Spiegel, 1990, p. 74).[3]
- In conjunction with curriculum revision, degree programs were undergoing revision. Caution was being used with regard to this step because students complained that radical change would result in additional time and work on their part. Even so, activities were moving in a deliberate and constructive direction.
- The University had embarked on a self review process of academic personnel and of programs. It was clear, for example, that the Marxist-Leninist section of Philosophy would be done away with, that the component of Criminal Justice that was affiliated with the *Stasi* would be disbanded, and that certain elements of history would undergo fundamental change.

---

[3]According to Dieter Klein, an attempt had previously been made by the University community to strengthen the academic stature of the Section by appointing a number of scientifically good people to it, and these were the people retained at the time the Section was closed.

There remained important changes to be made. For example, Humboldt University recognized the desperate need to reorganize its teacher education program, and it was making preparations to do so (Falk, 1990, p. 45). Its Educational Studies faculty had been one of the most compliant and ideologically impregnated of Humboldt University's programs during the past. Even as faculty were mobilizing for fundamental change, the Education Studies faculty had tended to downplay the significance of this agitation and even challenge the direction developments were taking. As late as September 1989, party officials conducted open sessions with Education Studies faculty about recent developments, and, according to those who participated in these sessions, the general tone of these meetings reflected disappointment in the direction things were going and romanticized expressions that the good old days be restored. Humboldt leaders were fully confident that they were making the kind of changes that would place it once again among the best German universities.

Vocational Education Developments

Vocational educators took advantage of the *Wende* to inform themselves as fully and as quickly as they could of vocational education programs in West Germany. According to many vocational educators, Western firms were uniformly open and receptive to these visits during that cooperation phase after the collapse. The East Germans became conversant with what was going on in West Germany and recognized that substantial change would be necessary in order to implement the new technology that existed and succeed in the market system that appeared inevitable in the future of East Germany. According to the last director of the Central Institute for Vocational Education,[4] the so-called dual system of West Germany was very attractive to vocational educators, but it appeared at that time to be somewhat incompatible with the traditions of Eastern Europe. The technical school (*Fachschule*) in East Germany was es-

---

[4]*Zentralinstitut für Berufsbildung der DDR.*

pecially problematic because it appeared to have little in common with the vocational and technical schools of West Germany, but discussions were initiated intending to reorganize the technical schools in such a way that greater comparability would be attained.

Those at the Central Institute for Vocational Education played a central role in bringing working groups together to rewrite the more central training programs. By March 1990, the commercial training program, for example, was completely revised, certified as legitimate, published, and disseminated to vocational schools and training centers throughout the country. The revised program was targeted to begin in September 1990, when the new training year would begin.

At individual schools active discussions were underway, and many alterations in the program were effected. In Rostock, for example, the three vocational schools decided to join resources and begin to restructure under a single administration for all schools. They established a School Conference with six representatives from each school and participated in the selection of a revised administrative structure and staff. In fact, the academic aspect of the three schools was combined into a single school, which was intended to provide a broader range of high level course offerings.

Individual School Developments

While certain regional and central activities were important, the most startling events took place in approximately 6,000 individual schools throughout the country. In those first months, there was considerable disorientation in almost every school, including those schools that eventually became models of change and renewal. One such school was the 22. POS in Berlin-Kaulsdorf/Hellersdorf. Michael Tiedtke and Christiane Zschommler (1990) provide a graphic account of the state of great turbulence and disruption in the school because at first nobody knew what to do or how to restore order. The teachers certainly did not feel they possessed the skills to organize the school in a productive manner. Tiedtke and Zschommler explain:

Their free space had grown, but only a few teachers were able to take advantage of the situation to use and experiment with new approaches. Teachers could take deep breaths and act more self-consciously, but a mass breakthrough did not occur. Instead, there reigned powerlessness, resignation, and waiting for higher directives.

Such a situation existed until the next fall, but from the very beginning there was a small cluster of teachers who had decided to establish a working group, which began to take on more and more visibility. Within a short time after the fall of the Berlin Wall, the psychic energies of educators though out East Germany were released and channeled toward change--some of it radical. The next months might be characterized as one of the most energizing periods imaginable. In most of the more than one hundred schools the authors visited in the 1991/92 academic year, evidence was found of efforts to rethink the existing program and to propose a new, more appropriate form and content of education. The only places where little was found to have happened were in certain rural areas where the schools, even before the collapse, tended to have their own way of doing things. In urban areas, there was a sense of urgency toward change.

At first the school changes were inspired by local and individual needs to deal with a chaotic and unstable situation. At the 25. POS in Berlin-Marzahn, two teachers, alarmed that the school might begin to fall apart, sat down and worked out, within days after the collapse, what they thought would be a suitable direction for the school. After completing a brief three page document, they approached the school director, who provided some input and his name to a revised document that was circulated to the school staff on 19 December 1989, less than six weeks after the *Wende* (25. POS, 1989). The document reveals the state of mind of some teachers at the time. Its beginning paragraphs include the following observations:

The schools are currently without any central, unified leadership. Because of the crisis of our state, many school district administrators are not able to take any responsibility, to take a clear position, and to make necessary, clearly thought-out decisions.

The teachers then point out that the unstable situation provides an opportunity for teachers and school leaders to act.

In order to prevent anarchy from taking over our schools, we (teachers) recognize we must become focused on a unified pedagogical leadership, carry out a process of renewal and preserve those things of value. We feel the foundation of our pedagogical work must be the continuation of a high quality instructional process. If that is to be achieved, we must carry through with discipline, order and mutual respect in instruction and other aspects of schooling.

The teachers then make three major recommendations. First, echoing their socialist past, they claim the central objective of their work must be the development of a many-sided, educated personality[5] by maintaining clear standards in all subjects and conveying these to the pupils and parents. Second, competent leadership must be maintained only on the basis of competence in the class collective, the teacher collective, and the various organs of the educational bureaucracy. A process of review must be instituted to determine whether, when, and how the leadership appointments should be changed. Everyone associated with the school must work with one another, for one another, and not against one another. Third, free-time educational activities should no longer be in the hands of outside social agencies but must be conducted with a new quality and must be integrated with the purposes of the renewed school. The teachers then recommend the establishment of a number of committees that

---

[5] *Allseitig gebildete Persönlichkeit.*

will focus on specific aspects of renewal: order and security, instruction, organization and economics, and free-time. Following a full discussion of the proposal with the school staff, the recommendations were forwarded to the local school office for their consideration. The document was likely filed away and the school was left to its own resources to take charge of itself.

Within a short time, buzz words and concepts began to circulate through the schools, in large part through spontaneously organized meetings, large conferences, and the founding of pedagogical societies.[6] For example, a Foreign Language Round-Table was organized by Ernst-Georg Kirschbaum of the *Volk und Wissen* Publishing House with representatives from a wide range of foreign language programs. This group developed recommendations regarding the climate that must exist in foreign language classes, the types of languages that ought to be taught, the competence that ought to be attained by the time pupils arrive at the university, and the types of evaluation processes that could be used to assess language competence (Klapper, 1992, p. 241).

Schools also received considerable input from the Academy of Pedagogical Sciences, where people such as Gisela Weiß, Karin Pingel, and Harald Meixner began to work with individual schools with which they had previous contact. By the spring, Weiß had reached the point where she could propose the establishment of a *Center for School Development/School Consultation* to be located at the APW. Pingel was located at the APW's Center for School Development and School Experimentation and she became actively involved in consultation with schools wishing to engage in change. This effort had a specific thrust, in that it focused on the development of *Gesamtschulen*. By 15 June, schools in Dresden alone, that had been working with the local teacher training college, had contacted Pingel with the intention of working together with her center

---

[6]Such as the *Gesellschaft für Pädagogik, Gesellschaft für Freizeitpädagogik, Berufsverband der pädagogischen Psychologen, Föderverein für arbeitslose Jugendliche*, etc.

(Volstädt, 1990). Meixner (1990) wrote a small article in the *Deutsche Lehrerzeitung* in May requesting schools that were interested in participating in a reform project and he was overwhelmed with requests for participation.

A number of universities, including Humboldt and Leipzig, became directly involved in school development. For example, The Pedagogical Section of the University of Leipzig began discussions regarding general school reform imperatives at the time of the *Wende*. It took a clear position that schools ought to remain comprehensive in nature and attempted to establish close relationships with the *Gesamtschule* experts in West Germany. The faculty set up a so-called Consultation Center for Inner School Reform, that served as an information and support system for many people attempting to develop and implement their own school reform ideas (Faust, 1992, p. 173).

Also of significance was a small photocopied journal called *AD HOC: Information und Diskussion zu Bildungsfragen,* put out by some people at the APW,[7] that appeared almost immediately after the *Wende*. It began as an in-house information newsletter, with 300 copies. This number expanded to 850 in the next issue, then to 1,000 copies in the third issue and continued to grow to several thousand copies.

The initial change process represented a broken front, with some schools hesitating and holding onto their traditions, while other schools stepped out boldly and decisively. In some schools, the entire staff participated in institutional definition and development. In other schools, the efforts were centered on a small cluster of teachers who took the initiative. Some change processes were somewhat formalized. In Rostock, for example, the school office directed schools to form "concept councils" and charged them with responsibility to recommend general changes in their particular schools.

---

[7]Including Rolf Hanisch, Jürgen Langer, Volkhard Peter, Mahael Rannacher, Barbara Rüdiger, and Anita Sachse.

Self-organization theorists would explain the process as one in which far-from-equilibrium conditions facilitated the emergence of auto-catalytic and cross-catalytic processes that resulted in almost run-away developments. This happened because events and changes became known and inspired other changes which accelerated throughout the nation (Jantsch, 1979, p. 31). During these first months after the collapse of East Germany, the schools of there had, by and large, all become heuristic or purpose-seeking, widely open ended and diversified. There was uncertainty, but a high level of self-organizational energy was evident.

A number of schools, such as the 25. POS mentioned above, developed their plans to a point that they actually submitted them to the local school district offices for approval. A smaller number of these proposals were sent to the Central Ministry of Education. So far, more than 240 such proposals have been identified, though almost none was acted on by anyone in the Ministry. Some schools were persistent. The 22. POS in Berlin-Köpenick (22. POS, 1990) was one of the first schools to develop a complete plan of renewal. The school staff and the parent organization came together and by 9 January, two months after the *Wende,* they had made certain fundamental decisions, including the decision to create a school that provided the entire 12/13 years of schooling leading to the *Abitur.* By the end of January the school staff had left the old uniform curriculum of the *Einheitsschule* and had worked out a course plan beginning with form (grade level) nine. This proposal was developed with enough detail that it was sent to the Ministry of Education for consideration and approval. While the school staff waited for some response from the Ministry, they continued to develop and embellish their plan. By 1 March a full program for each form (grade level) had been developed in what was now being described as a *Gesamtschule* model. In other words, the language and concepts of West Germany were already firmly implanted in the reform discussion. Reflecting a growing impatience with the Ministry of Education, the school staff sent a letter on 15 March explaining that they had submitted a proposal but had heard nothing. The next day V.

Abend, representing the Ministry, sent a reply explaining that the Ministry was in no position to do anything and that the Ministry had asked all local school district officers (*Bezirksschulräte*) to take over such responsibility.

The staff of the 22. POS could take solace in the fact that they received a reply of some sort. Almost all of the other proposals submitted to the Ministry of Education were simply filed away with no action taken on them and no response given to them. They are now located in temporary paper storage boxes in the Ministry's archives. At least they provide a rich depository of the creativity of that period. In the next sections certain observations shall be made about local innovations in the POS and in the EOS.

POS Renewal Plans

Almost every developed renewal plan of a POS contained two important dimensions. First, the school plan contained a section outlining the goals that the school would pursue. Second, the school plan usually contained a structural plan that would be appropriate to meet those goals. Each POS had a slightly different story to tell about the process it went through. Because the 12. POS in Marzahn had the good fortune of having been an experimental school for Humboldt University, it already had the reputation of being open to innovation. Experimentation had prepared them to confront the new realities. They had already struggled to develop a new program of studies that remained integrated, yet was useful for all types of students, and provided extra instruction to those who needed it. They had also worked on a differentiation concept that addressed student interests and helped students develop social competence. One of the directions the school took was to experiment with so-called "project-education," which had long been banned as an imperialist invention (Babing, 1990, p. 7).

Because schools had gained the reputation for being very innovative, as the East German regime became more and more reactionary in the later part of the 1980s, efforts were taken to draw schools such as the 12. POS back into line. And so in 1988, the school had been assigned a director, who was clearly a political appointee and who was unable to inspire respect on the part of the faculty. When the Berlin Wall came down, this school leader's authority role crumbled. Because there was no help from the central authorities, some of the school teachers took the initiative to begin organizing themselves. Already in December 1989 staff members had contacted their acquaintances at Humboldt University and together they began to work on complete reformulation of the school program, based on principles that had been developed in experimental work at the school during the past decade. The school director, who had been appointed the year prior to the *Wende* in order to bring the school into line, was resistant when she contacted Dr. Weiß at the APW. Unfortunately, she had her own agenda and she tried to push the school staff in a different direction than they were interested in going, so they stopped working with her. At this time, however, she was released from her job, and in early 1990 one of the teacher leaders, Klaus-Peter Bender, was appointed as the new school leader.

Here is an instance of a school which had worked out a reasonable plan of action several years prior to the collapse and seized the moment to implement its plans as fully as it could. It was defined by the staff as a *European Peace School.* The school leaders decided on this label because they anticipated that Berlin would become a central city in Europe and could become a model for peace activities for the entire continent. They would teach several European languages and focus the curriculum on Germany in a European and global context. The school staff knew that the "European house" has many rooms, but these rooms ought to harmonize with one another and not be the source of conflicts. Consequently, the school program aimed to teach pupils communication skills and help them become competent in resolving conflicts and differences.

The school and Humboldt researchers had recognized the sterility and boredom of a program of studies that emphasized content without taking the interests and developmental process of youth into consideration. Because of their commitment, the teachers complained about imparting a specified content to all children. They said they felt unable within the existing framework to ensure the fullest possible equality of educational opportunity. Therefore, they turned to the Humboldt specialists with whom they had previously worked in attempting to develop a program.

Whereas this Marzahn school had been engaged in several years of experimental work and appears to have been in an ideal position to take advantage of the power vacuum that came from the collapse, the 22. POS in Kaulsdorf/Hellersdorf appears to have been much like most schools of the time. Even before the fall, dramatic changes were under way. Military studies as a school subject had been abolished in the GDR on 5 November 1989 (Fischer, 1992, p. 103). Shortly after the collapse, the 22. POS reacted like most schools in the DDR in that it eliminated its civics studies and reorganized other courses that had been ideologically oriented. It eliminated the Pioneer and FDJ groups, and other aspects of schooling outlined at the beginning of this section; however, it did not have any tradition of innovation and certainly was not in a position suddenly to declare itself capable of school revision. In the next months the administrative position of the school shifted sharply when the school director resigned and the old party secretary left the school. A former teacher, who had been terminated by the previous administration, was then asked to come back and become the new school director. That teacher supported the efforts of the group working for school change. Even so, there were sharp differences about what to do, and the teachers were unable to obtain enough information about possibilities to really build a case for one direction or another. In other words, the school found itself to be in a state of tension and crisis. Teachers were talking past each other, the school discipline began to crumble, and the whole atmosphere was filled with chaos and frustration.

In spite of all this, the working group continued in its efforts to build something, and slowly a new atmosphere began to emerge where relationships were built on trust and closeness. This began to spread even to the students, who also became engaged in improving the campus. They set up a school cafe and began to settle down to a new type of routine. The school actually formed a bond with some actors who lived in the community.

Because all schools were struggling with ways to change themselves, certain institutions became models for other schools. Teachers at Mathias-Thesen POS (1990), for example, gave credit to "colleagues from the *Gesamtschulen* of the BRD and West Berlin, but also to colleagues of the Hellersdorf school in East Berlin." Because of these models, POS reform plans began to take on a common character. No single school, of course, fits the following general outline. We will note examples of the more common variations.

Goals

Among the goals emerging in the POS would be the following:

- The school would help pupils develop a social capacity and provide a supporting social climate for teachers and pupils.
- The school would provide scientific literacy for all pupils.
- The school should not be distorted by some pervasive ideological orientation. It must allow for diversity and encourage people to express their own orientations.
- The school must cultivate the individual potential of every child and keep educational opportunities as open as possible for every student. It must attend to neglected children and those with learning difficulties and also to gifted and talented pupils. None of these pupils should be isolated from the rest of the school community.
- The school would serve as a means for each child to engage in actual life, rather than preparation for life.

Administrative Changes

Even though the central authority structure had collapsed, the school district and regional school officials continued to function as they had prior to the collapse. The school dutifully continued to defer to their authority by requesting that they approve the plans that were being developed. As noted above, for example, the plan of the 25. POS (1990) in Marzahn was forwarded to the local school district office only; the plan of the 12. POS (1990) in Marzahn was presented to the school chief of the Marzahn District, to Berlin School authorities, and also to the Central Ministry, with a request that it be approved as an experimental school (Bender, 1990).[8] In an attempt to restore the authority that had previously existed, the school district officials often acted as a barrier to the reform attempts of the individual schools, resulting in a period of tension between reformists and reactionaries. Two typical administrative developments of the period are to be noted.

Local Autonomy

Because of the vacuum at the top, teachers found it necessary to begin making their own decisions about the content and processes of instruction. This also included drawing in parent groups for discussion and deliberation on future plans of action. It must be emphasized that local autonomy was not seen as a positive aspect of their activities. The experience noted above of 22. POS in Kaulsdorf/Hellersdorf (1990) was very typical. That is, a sense of powerlessness and resignation reigned for several months. Teachers had learned to rely on central directives, and they often found it difficult to fall back on their own ingenuity and resources; it became apparent that many teachers were not prepared to take advantage of the situation in that they often failed to make autonomous decisions and become responsible for their actions. Nevertheless, many teachers broke away from the old party-line pedagogy and began to teach in an experimental manner as they sought new methods and entered into open discussions about pedagogical themes.

---

[8]Local school personnel knew that they technically required the approval of the Ministry of Education in order to be an Experimental school (DLZ, 1990).

School Directors

Because the school director appointments had been made on ideological grounds in the GDR times, this was one of the first items of concern to reform-minded school people. Schools in many areas were informed that the school leader could remain only if that leader had the support of teachers, administrators, and other staff; therefore, the school was directed to conduct an election with members of the so-called *Schulkonferenz* to determine if the director had support. Faced with this situation, many directors resigned rather than subject themselves to such scrutiny. In Rostock, the schools voted in March whether to support the directors or not. It turned out that the vote often had little to do with actual changes made. At the 63. POS, for example, the director was expected to remain, but suddenly in May a change was made. At the 23. POS in Berlin, as another example, the director had always been a "true believer" in the socialist system, but she had a reputation for being tolerant and open, and the staff supported her overwhelmingly. In spite of this, she was taken out of the school.

Party Apparatus

The political party apparatus in the schools disappeared almost overnight. The party secretary no longer had any special position in the school, and the regular political information and indoctrination meetings were terminated. Education in the school was relieved of its one-sided ideological base, and the authorized press that had been directed by the Socialist Unity Party was almost entirely taken out of the picture.

Organizational Features

The centerpiece of the East German school system had been the POS. The idea persisted that certain aspects of this school ought to remain, including its polytechnical character, work experience for pupils, and the close connection between school and work. Essentially every school plan reflected some kind of unified school (*Einheitsschule*) model, in addition it was clear that the school would undergo revision and attain a flexibility that would allow it to provide equal opportunity to all children, regardless of social origins, political orientation, philosophical persuasion and religion. Within weeks these notions were further elaborated to include claims that the renewed school would not be allowed to promote a belief system or narrow world view but focus on the free unfolding of each personality. It would ensure shared responsibility of educators, parents and pupils. It would provide a general education and overcome the pervasive tendency to limit ways of thinking and knowing. It would provide some balance between compulsory and elective subjects. It would address local, regional and pluralistic needs and impulses (e.g., Stöhr, 1990).

Within a short time the language of the West began to creep into the discussion of school reform. Following World War II, the West Germans had rejected the term *Einheitsschule* because it had been identified with the political left; therefore, the term *Gesamtschule* was adopted for West German comprehensive schools. Within weeks the term *Gesamtschule* replaced *Einheitsschule* in the East because it seemingly provided for more differentiation according to achievement levels and a different type of organizational structure. Many schools were open about their debt to West Germany in this regard. For example, the first two sentences of the Mathias-Thesen POS plan reads as follows:

> In the interests of the pupils and the emerging pluralistic society, our school must change. We hope to develop a school type, that replicates many of the features of the *Gesamtschule* model of West Berlin (5. POS, 1990).

In Rostock, where school officials had requested that each school select a "concept council" to work out reform for its individual schools, the general sentiment was that each POS would become a

Gesamtschule, where the child is regarded as a total personality. Organizationally, some schools, such as the 2. POS in Marzahn (1990), opted to continue providing a ten year program, while others, such as the 12. POS in Marzahn (1990) and the Bertolt-Brecht POS (1990) in Schwerin, chose to develop a program that would contain an upper level, leading to the *Abitur*.

Organizational Levels

Typically, the school would be organized around teacher teams serving four sections:

> lower section (forms 1-3),
> middle section (forms 4-6),
> upper section (forms 7-10),
> *Abitur* section (forms 11-12/13).

Each of these sections had three parallel groups conforming to the conventional school types found in West Germany. The pupils in these sections would work together in projects, form-level courses, common free-time activities, etc.

Course Restructuring

One of the marked shifts in all schools was a dramatic change in courses and course content.

Obligatory and Elective Courses: Whereas the POS in the German Democratic Republic provided a uniform set of courses that all children were expected to attend, the new school plans included more elective courses. The 2. POS in Frankfurt/Oder (1990), for example, instituted two art courses, two sport courses, two mathematics/natural science courses, and a social studies course that were elective. The 28. POS (1990) in Berlin designed elective courses as one of its central features. It declared, "even when instruction is at its best, every pupil is not really in a position to be completely successful." Consequently, it would be necessary to institute optional courses that allowed a student to develop his/her unique talents. The main question schools struggled with was when these options would begin. Most schools anticipated a rather standard program at the lower section, where all children would be expected to participate together. Some schools, such as the 37. POS (1990) in Berlin wanted to begin elective courses as soon as the fourth form, but the more typical plan was to begin them during the upper section of the program. There was some variation in that one school began providing electives in form seven, while another chose form eight, and still another chose form nine. This includes so-called compulsory choices, where a pupil must decide from among options including: a second and third foreign language, mathematics, technical drawing, music/art, sport and/or literature.

Ideology and the Curriculum: It was clear that the pervasive ideology in social studies, history, and political education was no longer appropriate. A number of subjects related to this ideology were terminated, including *Staatsbürgerkunde* (civics) and military studies. In the place of civics came new types of courses related to American social studies, which emphasized man in society, economics, anthropology, and political science. A number of related subjects of study were radically revised, including history, which in many cases was built around open discussions of our intellectual and philosophical evolution. The tendency was for teachers to draw inspiration from school books found in the FRG.

Foreign Language Instruction: Schools recognized that the foreign language issue had to be resolved. Whereas Russian had been mandated in all GDR schools, it was clear that other languages, particularly English and French, must become a part of the school curriculum. However, there was almost no preparation for what took place. For example, at the Schule an der Scheffel Berg in Zwickau, the local school district official assembled the entire school and an-

nounced to the children that they didn't have to take Russian anymore, that they could enroll immediately in English or French. This
caused great confusion among staff members about what to do and
who might be prepared to teach these languages. As their plans developed, they decided to begin the program the next fall and to allow
pupils to begin the first foreign language (usually English) as early
as the third form, with an obligatory first foreign language to begin
in form five. This was typical of many school plans. Most school
plans included provisions for English or Russian to begin in form
five with four hours of instruction a week. In form seven the second
foreign language would begin with instruction and would usually include English, Russian, and French. Both the first and second foreign languages were to take three hours a week. The third foreign
language would begin in form nine or ten and also have three hours
of instruction a week.

The Arts and Aesthetics: In arts and aesthetics courses, teachers
rejected the narrow orientation of the previous regime and looked for
alternative and diverse interpretations of the arts. Teachers began
taking responsibility to decide, as was the case in most of the fields
of study, which aspects of this richness to stress.

Instruction

Many school plans included instructional issues. Instructional
plans took a variety of forms, but some consensus existed in certain
respects. Within the German tradition there has always been a tendency for a class to remain together throughout the school day. Of
course, as optional subjects came into the picture, there would be a
slight amount of shifting, but the class remained, as far as possible,
in what is called a *Stammklasse*. The nearest equivalent to this notion
in America would probably be the homeroom. This idea was retained
in almost all plans being developed. In addition, teachers wanted to
have greater autonomy to make decisions in their individual

classrooms. According to Lorenz (1991), Mecklenburg-West Pomeranian teachers wanted the following:

> The excessive content and uniformly cadenced instructional process must be made more interesting, differentiated, and active.

The teachers at the 28. POS (1990) declared that even though "instruction ought to be based on the instructional plan, it would not be dogmatic, as in the past, but based on a general framework, actual life, and science." Those at the 37. POS (1990) in Berlin-Hohenschönhausen even stipulated the type of instruction that would be appropriate for each form level. At the first form, for example, instruction would focus on learning by games, graphics, continual shifting from open to more closed types of processes, smooth transitions from subject to subject, and by appealing to individual needs of pupils. Teachers also tended to prefer instruction based on the principle of student-active learning rather than passive participation, in that instruction included project work and intensive work on specific themes and historical periods. The 2. POS (1990) in Marzahn actually developed a plan that specified which courses were to be taught using "frontal instruction" (teacher centered) and which classes were to be taught using a different instructional approach.

Advancement from Form to Form

Some schools rejected the tradition of extensive retention of students. They concluded that individual problems of youth cannot be resolved by holding them back or by terminating them.

Homogeneous grouping

Most schools anticipated implementing some grouping according to interests and achievement levels. The major question was when this would come into practice. The 1. POS (1990) of Halle Neustadt became an experimental school for the Pedagogical Center of the APW in Halle, and a model was set so that homogeneous grouping would occur at various levels according to the subject. Differentiated classes would begin for the first foreign language in form seven, for mathematics, German and Chemistry in form eight, and for Physics in form nine. These differentiated classes would continue through the rest of schooling.

Production Work

Schools remained committed to the tradition that pupils would continue to be exposed to the world of work as a part of regular instruction. Schools usually continued to stress the idea of schooling as preparation for work, but courses such as "Introduction to Socialist Production" underwent fundamental revision or were eliminated in favor of some other designation that would be more acceptable to the international community. These new courses often began to stress preparation for work in a free market economy. Those in forms nine and ten would continue to participate in a two week off-campus work experience.

Marks

Many schools decided that no marks, usually known as grades in the United States, would be issued for the lower forms. One school chose to eliminate marks in the first two forms. Another school had no marks in the entire lower level. Marks would usually continue to be based on a five point scale.

EOS Renewal Plans

Even though the focus of change was on the POS, other types of institutions were also undergoing radical change in their own way. At the EOS, a different set of issues was often raised. The Ernst Schneller Grimma EOS (1990) in Berlin could trace its origins back to

1550, and it declared in clear, direct terms that its greatest desire was to restore that distinguished classical humanistic tradition. Discussions took place as to the appropriateness of such a narrow avenue to the *Abitur* and higher education. The EOS was expected to redirect itself and begin to serve a broader public, rather than restrict itself to the small elite cadre of pupils it had served in the past.

School Leaving Certificates

The leaving certificates must provide the possibility for the widest range of further development, including vocational and higher education studies. All schools made provision for certificates of completion both at the end of forms 10 and 12/13, culminated in the secondary school leaving certificate (*Abitur*). One school chose to provide a certificate of completion after form eight as well.

Free-time Programs

The Pioneer groups and FDJ organizations disappeared almost overnight in most cases without any consultation with the children or the parents. Many schools went so far as to forbid their existence. However, most schools anticipated that a rich free-time program would eventually be available, usually for children in the upper three sections of the school, with the provision that the teachers not be compelled to participate. The 2. POS in Frankfurt/Oder (1990), for example anticipated the establishment of a youth club that would be open to pupils throughout each afternoon. Activities might include model trains, puppet theater, gymnastics, environmental studies, photography, painting, drawing, and sports of many types.

Day-Care

After school, provisions would be made to take care of the pupils until 4:00 or 5:00 p.m. when parents returned from work.

Compensatory Education

Provision would be made to assist children who were having difficulty with their courses.

Five Day Week

Even though plans had been under way in the GDR for some time to create a five day school week, its introduction had not been universal. Within two days after the collapse, however, the Central Committee of the GDR announced that the five day week would become standard (Anweiler, 1992). Such a move was supported by parents and teachers who acted in concert to provide time and space for themselves and their children to visit the West and to begin a new life.

So far in this chapter East German responses to the initial period following the collapse of East Germany have been described. Dramatic educational changes came out of these first months following the collapse. The clear message that comes out of this analysis is that East Germany was extremely active in responding to the new situation and that West Germany served as an important source of inspiration, support, and ideas in these developments. It is significant to ask what changes the West Germans underwent in response to the events of 1989.

Private Schooling

Almost immediately after the collapse, private schooling became a part of the general discussion of the educational overview. In fact, the one theoretical orientation that began to replace the old Marxist/Leninist ideology came out of efforts to stress human potential, ecology, independent peace education, aesthetics, and music. This was part of the German Reform Pedagogy that belonged to the more general Progressive Education movement inspired by educators such as John Dewey, Ellen Key and Maria Montessori, and included certain Eastern European Progressive educators such as Blonsky. These people stressed that the main function of education must be to foster the modernization and democratization of the school, while ensuring such things as equality of educational opportunity in urban and rural areas. For the humanists, education is not intended to enlighten people as much as to help develop the full potential of human beings-- people who are independent, self-reliant, and able to free themselves from the present contradictions and constraints that have led to the crisis in society. The main mechanism for delivering this type of schooling lies in the private sector. The largest association of private schooling in the old states of Germany has been the Federal Association of German Private Schools (VDP). By November 1992, at least 186 schools in the new states had joined together with approximately 1,000 schools in the old states (DLZ, 1992). In the first stages of development, schools for adults and older youth were financially possible, but the prospects for private schooling for children of all ages still lies in the horizon.

In any other context, such universal changes would have been termed monumental. In the context of the unstable situation of East Germany, they were seen as natural consequences of the larger instability. Little accord was given to the dynamics of change involved, in large part because they were locally decided and did not represent a formal change of the entire system.

Section III

The Unification of the Two Germanys

Chapter VIII

Toward a West German Education Model

Introduction

The political underpinnings of education were revealed by the political posturing for power as East Germany faced its first free, secret parliamentary elections. The Socialist Unity Party (SED) had already been greatly weakened because its role as the political leader of the country had been eliminated from the constitution. Even though it had attempted to define itself as the party of "democratic socialism" at its convention in December 1990, and it changed its name to the Party for Democratic Socialism (PDS) on 25 February 1990, its strength continued to decline (Fischer, 1992, 104). The heroic opposition groups, that had led the efforts to overthrow the establishment in 1989, were not prepared to compete with seasoned political groups coming into East Germany from the West, at least in an election to be held so soon after the collapse. It would go too far beyond the central focus of this volume to recount the entrance of West German political parties into East Germany, but the political dynamics must surely be understood in the context of a frontal attack on the integrity and political sophistication of the East Germans.

The integrity of the people was discredited in that they were systematically connected with the terrible events in Germany's recent past, including its Nazi past. One heard the recurrent comment: "They haven't learned anything," as comparisons were drawn between the twelve year period of Nazi barbarism and the forty year socialist dictatorship. Indeed, the East German communist leaders had avoided taking any responsibility for East Germany's Nazi involvement. They had argued that the Nazis had tried to annihilate not just Jews but communists as well; consequently, the communist leaders in East Germany could hardly be held responsible for the crimes of Naziism. With the collapse of the East German regime, the West Germans expected them to confront their own past, to admit their complicity, to undergo the same cleansing process they claimed to have engaged in.

But the ghost of totalitarianism was best exploited by implicating the entire GDR with the state security system (*Stasi*). It had indeed been ubiquitous in the GDR and had infected every aspect of East German life. Anyone who had wanted a career dealing with policy matters, academics, or other major responsibility had little choice but to be associated in some way with the *Stasi*. All of the major political candidates from East Germany were accused of some connection, and they all initially denied such charges. Enough charges held firmly, however, to bring down people such as Democratic Awakening candidate Wolfgang Schnur and afflict SPD leader, Ibrahim Böhme and CDU leader, Lothar de Maiziere.

All major parties entered into the election process. The Social Democratic Party (SPD), the Free Democratic Party (FDP), and the Christian Democratic Union (CDU) quickly established a base of operations in East Germany, working in alliance with existing parties in East Germany. From its beginning, the GDR had maintained political parties having names similar to those in West Germany, but they had actually been front organizations that were intended to symbolize a pluralistic political scene in East Germany. In fact, these parties had held no power and had supported the SED in almost all of its actions.

The election on 18 March was astonishing. More than 93% of the electorate turned out to vote. The CDU won more than 40% of the vote and smaller parties with which it had worked closely won additional votes. The SPD fared poorly as it gained less than 22% of the votes. The PDS gained a surprising 16% of the vote. Post-election analysis indicates the voters divided into two distinct groups, those who were voting as a "citizen of a united Germany" and those who were voting as a "citizen of the GDR" (Wallach & Francisco, 1992, p. 55). Those voting for the CDU identified with being German. The CDU had communicated clearly that it stood for unification of the two states and the adoption of a single German currency. Those voting for the PDS were East Germans who favored a separate Germany. As is the case in many revolutions, those who actually inspired the East German revolution, such as New Forum, Democracy Now, and Democratic Awakening, also received almost no support from the electorate, in this case because they resisted unification. The difficulty with the SPD was that it appeared to fall between the two groups and had not communicated a clear-cut message about where it stood. It was neither East German in its party base nor was it predisposed toward an all German unity. The outcome was that the CDU and its allies won a breathtaking victory. East Germany would be unified with West Germany to form a single state. It took less than a month for a new coalition government to be organized under the formal leadership of Lothar de Maiziere, the new head of East Germany's CDU.

The new parliament got off to a unique start. Darnton (1991, p. 284) notes that when Americans made a revolution they issued a declaration of independence. The East Germans issued a declaration of guilt, in that one of its first actions was to "admit...its share of responsibility for the humiliation, persecution, and murder of Jewish men, women, and children."

While the political situation was taking form, the economy of East Germany continued to deteriorate. In the first year after the Berlin Wall fell, the economy declined by over 50%, a rate that did not diminish in the next two years. By 1991 the new states, which contained 20% of the population, was contributing but 7% of the economic output (Koch, 1992, p. 6). Unemployment, which had previously been unknown in East Germany, rose rapidly. While official unemployment rates in the first year had risen to an alarming 12%, that did not reflect the real situation. All together, more than 30% of the labor force were in some type of unemployment by December 1990, and the figure continued to rise. By the end of 1991 the situation was catastrophic. Data related to unemployment is found on *Table 1*. Even though the official unemployment statistics stood at 13.8% at the end of 1991, a total of 51.3% actually exited the workforce after the collapse.

The first major task the new government tackled was to work out an agreement with West Germany for a single currency. On 18 May such a treaty was signed that would bring about a single currency on 1 July 1990. Kohl held true to his campaign promise that the people would be able to convert their money on a one-to-one basis.[1]

	Millions
Table 1	
The unemployment profile in East Germany at the end of 1991.	
Those in the labor force in November 1989:	9.700
Those who left the labor force after 1989:	
and exited East Germany (approximate)	1.000
and went back and forth between the two Germanys	.500
and were officially unemployed	.343
and were in temporary work	.519
and were in government sponsored temporary employment	.393
and were retraining programs	.445
and were in early retirement	.525
Total	4.725

The negotiations for economic unity were paralleled by negotiations for political unity. On 12 April the new government agreed to pursue unification under Article 23 of the West German Basic Law, which stipulates that the states falling under the Basic Law are pro-

---

[1]There was a sliding scale of exchange. People born after 1 July 1976 could exchange only 2,000 East German marks. Those born between 1931 and 1976 could exchange 4,000 German marks, and those born prior to 1931 could exchange 6,000 German marks. Any additional exchanges would be made at a 2:1 exchange rate. (Wallach & Francisco, 1992, p. 67).

visional and can be expanded at any time.[2] The framers of the Basic Law believed that the document was temporary and that one day a full constitution would come into effect (Article 146). The time had come for such a process to be initiated, but the urgency of unification was so great in the minds of those negotiating unification, that the decision was made to incorporate East Germany into the Federal Republic of Germany under the existing Basic Law. On 14 May the first steps were taken toward federation as the states of Brandenburg, Mecklenburg-West Pomerania, Saxony, Saxony-Anhalt, and Thuringia were defined. East Berlin was to become a part of West Berlin. On 31 August the Unification Treaty was signed, and actual unification took place on 3 October 1990.

The Politics of Educational Reform

Along with political and economic unification, negotiations began concerning educational unification. Thus, the second major educational phase of the post-*Wende* period began in the spring of 1990 and continued through the formal unification of East and West Germany. This second phase lasted until sometime near the end of 1991. However, the transformation began almost as soon as the Berlin Wall came down. Two days after the collapse of the Berlin Wall, the Central Committee of the SED declared itself prepared:

> to transform civics, history, and German instruction, social science instruction in vocational education, and Marxist/Leninist foundation studies, to establish the basis for a rapid transition to a five day instructional week in the education system, for a solid higher education preparation, including the early entrance to education at the extended secondary

---

[2]Article 23 reads: For the time being, this Basic Law applies in the territory of the *Länder* Baden, Bavaria, Bremen, Berlin, Hamburg, Hesse, Lower-Saxony, North-Rhine-Westphalia, Rhineland-Palatinate, Schleswig-Holstein, Württemberg-Baden, and Württemberg-Hohenzollern. It is to be put into force in other parts of Germany on their accession.

school (*erweiterte Oberschule*), to ensure new vocational possibilities for students who leave the polytechnical secondary school (*polytechnische Oberschule*) early (quoted in Anweiler, 1990, p. 99).

In the same declaration the Central Committee also stressed the need to develop new instructional plans, alter the examination structure to be based on achievement, and change administrative regulations that restricted the independence and responsibility of teachers and that inhibited and restricted students. Even during the brief reign of President Modrow and his Minister of Education, Hans-Heinz Emons, some general changes were being instituted in the education system, the most dramatic being the adoption of a policy on 28 February 1990, in which differentiated classes would be organized beginning in the ninth grade, signaling the end of a uniform educational program through ten years of schooling (Fischer, 1992, p. 107).

The results of the elections in March made people aware that the GDR would soon be part of Germany's past history, and preparations began for a highly centralized school system that had been structured by the state to be replaced by a federated school structure. In order to bring about a smooth transition, a so-called Educational Commission consisting of representatives of both the GDR and the FRG was set up. The FRG Commission was led by the president of the Standing Conference of Ministers and the state secretary of the Federal Ministry for Education and Science. These people demanded that the schools and institutions of higher learning be brought as quickly as possible into the "network of European and other international exchange and cooperation relationships" (Standing Conference of Ministers, 1990a). This meant, of course, that East Germany would fall under the umbrella of the West German educational tradition. The articles related to education in the Basic Law would form the legal basis for the new states of the Federal Republic; however, the most important legal provisions had nothing to do with the Basic Law. The West Germans demanded that treaties the old states of the Federal Republic had previously entered into also apply to the new states.

The most critical among these treaties, in regard to schooling, was the 1964 Hamburg Treaty (discussed in some detail in Chapter 3), but in three formal meetings of the Education Commission and other meetings of subcommittees of the Commission related to general schooling, vocational education, higher education/science, and further education, all of the significant agreements of the Standing Conference of Ministers of Education were included in packages of recommendations that for all practical purposes determined the nature of education in the former East Germany. The first formal meeting of the Education Commission took place on 16 May 1990. The then Minister of Education and Science, Professor Hans Joachim Meyer, greeted the participants, reminding them that a "spirit of cooperation and mutual tolerance" will be necessary to accomplish the main tasks of the Commission (Standing Conference of Ministers, 1990a). For illustrative purposes, we shall note agreements related to schooling that East Germany would be expected to follow.

As mentioned above, the most important agreement the old states of Germany had entered into had been the Hamburg Treaty, which defined the beginning and ending of the school year, the beginning of compulsory education, the completion of full-time compulsory education, the terms of school holidays, the foreign language arrangements, the school leaving certificates, and the grading policy. The most critical part of this agreement was the definition of the types of schools that would be allowed, the most important being the *Grundschule* (primary school), the *Hauptschule* (main school), the *Realschule* (secondary general school), the *Gymnasium*, and the *Gesamtschule* (comprehensive school), discussed fully in Chapter 3. However, supplementary to the Hamburg Agreement were a long list of other agreements that would be in force. These included the following Standing Conference of Ministers of Education (1990b, p. 4) agreements:

- Recommendations Regarding Work in the Primary School (2 July 1970)

- Agreement Concerning the Orientation Phase (Classes 5 and 6) (28 Feb. 1974)
- Recommendations Regarding the Main School (3 July 1969)
- Agreement Concerning the Instructional Framework for Pupils in School Classes 7 to 10 in the Secondary General Schools (16 June 1978)
- The Place of the Middle School in the School Structure (17 Dec. 1953)
- Guidelines and Recommendations Regarding the Structuring of Instruction in Grades 5 to 11 of the *Gymnasium* (14/15 June 1966)
- Skeletal Agreements Regarding the Mutual Recognition of Leaving Certificates from the Integrated *Gesamtschulen* (27/28 May 1982)
- Agreement Regarding the Restructuring of the Upper Level of the *Gymnasium* (11 April 1988)
- Recommendation Regarding Regulations of Special Education (16 March 1972)
- Common Examination Requirements in the *Abitur* Examination (1 Dec. 1989).
- Foundational Agreements of the Standing Conference Concerning Foreign Language Instruction (11 Dec. 1989).

By the spring of 1990, it was already clear that extensive provisions would be required of the new states. These agreements set in motion a number of psychological forces that have had lasting negative effects in the relationship between the new and old states. When the Unification Treaty was drawn up, Article 37, nr. 4 stipulated that "the Hamburg Treaty and other pertinent agreements of the Standing Conference of Ministers of Education" would be in force in the new states of Germany.

A number of additional stress points of this phase could be identified relating to central and individual institutions, ideological and professional qualifications, and programs. A major stress point was the decision to abolish all institutions that were a part of the centralized educational machine, including the Ministry of Education and its Academy of Pedagogical Sciences, the organs overseeing vocational training, and the State Secretariat for Higher and Technical Education responsible for planning and control of universities, colleges and technical schools. For illustrative purposes, we shall comment on the Academy of Pedagogical Sciences.

Academy of Pedagogical Sciences is Abolished

On 31 December 1990, the APW was abolished and its 600 members sent home. It is not entirely clear where the decision was made, but even in the early summer those working at the APW recognized that it could not serve as a centralized academy in a decentralized system. In spite of this, those at the APW tried to work out ways to perpetuate itself. In fact, on 9 July 1990, it formally reconstituted itself into an "Institute for Educational Research and Sciences,"[3] but it was obvious that if certain parts of the Academy of Pedagogical Sciences were to survive, they would have to be taken over by some other entity, and the most likely candidate would be a ministry of education in one of the new states. Various sections of the APW worked vigorously to define a role that some state ministry might find useful, and members of these sections engaged in extended and detailed planning sessions. In October and November of 1990 various representatives of state education offices discussed the possibility of at least some sections joining with state pedagogical institutes or other educational programs. While this was going on, the APW received official notice that it would be abolished. Finally, on 20 December members of the APW were sent a "friendly" letter from Dr. Reiher, representing the various bodies engaged in disestablishment, explaining what conditions colleagues of the APW faced when the institute closed. They would not be given the rights nor be subject to the responsibilities typically awarded those being placed out of work. Instead the following conditions would prevail:

---

[3] *Institut für Bildungsforschung und Erziehungswissenschaften.*

- Those under 55 would receive 6 months and those over 55 would receive 9 months compensation.
- All were advised to register at the employment office and seek new employment.
- All would be eligible to apply for participation in programs for retraining or alternative qualifications (Kossakowski, 1991, p. 98).

Subsequent to the closing of the APW, the Berlin city-state Senate Education Office issued a directive that former members of the East German Ministry of Education, the APW, and district school offices were, as a rule, not eligible to function in the educational system. In other words, the leading figures in East German education would only find employment, if they found it at all, outside the education system.

The disestablishment (*Abwicklung*) of central educational institutions such as the APW can easily be rationalized on the basis of the federative direction East Germany had decided to take. However, a process of disestablishment was also carried out throughout the educational system, particularly in institutions of higher learning.

Higher Education Institutions Cleansed

Higher Education Institutions experienced two major stress points. On the one hand, specific departments were targeted to be abolished or drastically reoriented. This process was not uniform throughout East Germany because various new state governments applied slightly different procedures and priorities. On the other hand, all faculty members at all of the universities and other institutions of higher learning were informed that a special clause in the Unification Treaty stipulated that their tenure rights had been abolished, and that they were required to fill out questionnaires related to their professional training and qualifications, their past political party affiliations, and their past political opinions and activities. West

German law prohibits such invasive inquiry, but faculty members were informed that they would be subject to dismissal if they refused to provide complete information about themselves.

So-called evaluation commissions were set up to judge the ideological and professional qualifications of university instructional employees.[4] If any employee failed to qualify, that person would be terminated. Some cynicism has been expressed about the process. Dorothy Rosenberg (1991), for example, maintains that West Germans attempted to carry out a denazification process that they feel was never carried out in East Germany. She maintains also that the West Germans never completed a denazification process on themselves and that their collective guilt about this scandal is now being poured out on the East Germans. To provide some detail concerning the way the review process functioned, we shall look at the case of Humboldt University in Berlin.

The Unification Treaty between East and West Germany had placed East Berlin under the control of the West Berlin city-state, but the treaty implied that a three year transition period would be in effect. Consequently, Rector Fink maintained that Humboldt University ought to be free of formal West Berlin control for that three year period, so that it could engage in an internal review and reform (Bollag, 1990b). However, within three months (18 and 22 December 1990) the Berlin Science Ministry, which was responsible for higher education, issued a strong policy statement that entire sections of Humboldt University would be disestablished (*abgewickelt*) (Volksmund, 1992, p. 81). The grounds for such a decision was Article 13 of the Unification Treaty, which allowed institutions in East Germany to be dissolved. The announcement indicated that a number of specific fields of study would be completely closed, including Criminal Justice, where five faculty members had already been dismissed because of their involvement with State Security officials (*Stasi*), Library Science, and Scientific Theory and Organization. These were relatively

---

[4]The process was carried out with regard to those in the judiciary, the civil service and education.

minor areas and they were systematically closed down without fanfare, but five major programs were also chosen to be eliminated: law, economics, history, education studies, and philosophy. These were judged to have been the location of ideologically based studies; therefore, they were deemed to be inappropriate. The announcement represented a shocking blow to the Humboldt University community in that the very heart of the university was to be eliminated.

While the discussion here is on Humboldt University, it is important to note that a similar process was taking place at all universities in East Germany. The striking difference between Humboldt University and the others was that officials at Humboldt responded sharply against the disestablishment announcement. Rector Fink, brought legal action to prevent the Berlin government from interfering with the autonomy of Humboldt University (Will, 1992). Indeed, a number of questionable procedures had been followed leading up to the December announcement. The Berlin Science Minister had not consulted Humboldt University officials prior to the announcement. No attention had been given to formal regulations regarding disestablishment in either East or West German universities. No evidence had been presented to indicate why these particular university programs were unsuitable. Only a unilateral decision had been made by a West German government office, that had assumed fault on the part of Humboldt University and had given itself the right to correct some perceived malpractice occurring at that institution. Rector Fink maintained that formal disestablishment procedure had not been followed, and that the procedure used was invalid.

The city-state of Berlin eased up on its decree. Present students in all areas were ensured that they would be able to complete their studies--disestablishment of the five major programs pertained to the elimination of teaching and scientific personnel. Even here, the city went on, no mass dismissal would occur but a only a selective letting-go of personnel who were deemed unfit to represent a legitimate German university. It was necessary for all personnel to remain until their suitability was determined and replacements were found for those dismissed. To accomplish this, all personnel, from the academic deans down to the secretaries, were released from their positions and either given temporary appointments or suspensions from their positions until a final decision could be made.

As has been mentioned, the Unification Treaty between the two Germanys had made provision for disestablishment of a number of public institutions, which would no longer be appropriate. Consequently, educational institutions such as the Academy of Pedagogical Sciences and the Central Institute for Higher Education were closed because they had served a highly centralized state and no longer had a place in a federated system. Fink claimed disestablishment agreements were never intended for university programs such as law, economics, history, education studies and philosophy, which were deemed essential to a university. In addition, he claimed the procedure for the release of personnel had been twisted. Even though the University was already embarking on a process of personnel review to assess the involvement of academic personnel with the *Stasi* and to review academic competence, the new mandate went far beyond reviewing personnel for ideological and professional suitability. Each position was thrown open and existing personnel were being required to reapply for these open positions in competition with all other applicants. Fink's legal action was strongly supported by the Humboldt University Council and the students in general.

The action taken by Humboldt University set off a major legal battle about disestablishment. University officials argued that the Berlin Science Ministry had no authority to disestablish basic units of Humboldt University. In fact, they argued that since the Science Ministry had no intention of disestablishing the five major fields of study in question, then Humboldt University ought to be protected from such action. On 12 February 1991, the suit of Humboldt University was rejected. In anticipation of appeals, the judge also ruled that an appeal would likely not overturn the decision and that action to disestablish the units in question proceed (Will, 1992, p. 22). The judge mandated that the process forward.

A part of the process was the appointment of a series of so-called *Structure and Appointments Commissions* for each unit being disestablished. Each commission consisted of three academic persons from West German universities, designated by the Berlin Science Minister, three academic persons from Humboldt University, designated by the University Council, one non-academic appointee and a student. Their task was to define the new unit organization, including the academic personnel to be put into place, and to begin the process of finding appropriate academic personnel to fill these positions (Will, 1992).

In the meantime, the University appealed the judge's decision to the Berlin *Oberverwaltungsgericht* (Higher Administrative Court). The case against the announcement of the Berlin Science Ministry weighed heavily on the meaning of the term "disestablishment of an organization." Legal precedence and the German Basic Law had long held that "disestablishment of an organization" meant that an organization unity was to be abolished, liquidated, or come to an end.[5] It could not mean that the functions of this unity were being transferred somewhere else. In decisions in April and June of 1990, this court agreed that the closure of the Department of Marxism-Leninism along with certain other units and dismissal of its members was legal because they qualified under the disestablishment rules, but that the disestablishment of the five major fields of study was irregular. These programs had continued to exist under revised names, so all personnel were to be reinstated with back pay (Rosenberg, 1991, p. 26). However, they then fell under new regulations related to East German personnel, which had reduced all personnel essentially to the beginning of their careers (so-called C1 and C2 status), and they were given 60% of the salaries of West German colleagues (Volksmund, 1992, p. 82).

While the court process was being decided, the West German Government was putting into place a Supplementary Higher Education Law. Article 8 of the Law stipulates that in cases where university decisions are made requiring professorial action, only those professors who have been appointed according to state law, in this

---

[5]A number of legal references cited by Will (1992).

case Berlin state law, were eligible to take part in the decision-making process. Of course, at that time there were no such professors at Humboldt University, and Article 9 of the Law stipulated that the *Structure and Appointments Commissions* would take over responsibilities reserved for professors. Here is another case where the law stands in contradiction to the entitlements of the Basic Law (Article 5 (3)) related to freedom of teaching and research--these freedoms are spelled out as basic rights and are not open to restriction or legal manipulation. However, that is precisely what was happening to Humboldt University. The legal battles were not fought just in the courtroom. During this time, the public media waged a highly negative campaign against Humboldt University and its supposed role in the German Democratic Republic (e.g., Spiegel, 1991).

It is useful to review what happened to personnel in East Germany as a consequence of this cleansing. First, the number of East German university personnel have been dramatically reduced, in some cases the number of academic personnel has been cut in half. For example, at Jena only 47% of the 354 professorships have been retained. There has also been a marked influx of teachers from West Germany. In 1992 there remained approximately 6,000 East German academic personnel, while more than 1,200 West German academics had taken positions at institutions of higher learning (Schattenfroh, 1993).

Balancing the University Landscape

One of the critical issues with regard to higher education has been bringing balance into the various states. Because East Germany was a highly centralized nation, little consideration had been given to geographical balance as institutions of higher learning were established. Of course, the main concentration of institutions of higher learning was in the larger cities. Berlin made claim to Humboldt University, a school of economics, a music conservatory, an art academy, a theatrical academy, and two engineering schools. Leipzig had a university, a technical university, an economics academy, a teacher training college, and a theater academy. A university, a technical university, a medical academy, a teacher training college, and a music academy were in Dresden (Rytlewski, 1990, p. 422). There was not a single university in what became the state of Brandenburg. In the interests of equity, a number of institutions were to be shut down and a number opened. The most dramatic of these changes was in Brandenburg. It was decided to upgrade the teacher training college in Potsdam to a general university, to establish a second general university in Frankfurt/Oder and a technical university in Cottbus. The state of Thuringia is also making plans for a new university in Erfurt.

Each of the Brandenburg universities was given a special charge. At Potsdam, where a teacher training college had existed, special attention is to be given to teacher education. At Cottbus, special emphasis is to be given to environmental issues, particularly related to industries and other sites of production. At Frankfurt/Oder an innovative institution was conceived focusing on law, economics and culture. Because the European University Viadrina at Frankfurt/Oder is the most innovative of the new universities, we shall give some attention to it.

A distinguished university had actually existed in the city from 1506 to 1811, before its charter was moved to Breslau in Silesia, now a part of Poland, so the city had been without a university for almost two centuries. The decision was made to restore such an institution in Frankfurt/Oder having the old name. In 1991, a planning commission composed of international scholars was named. They worked so efficiently, that one year later the law and economics schools were opened to 400 students. In the fall of 1993, the school of culture studies (*Kulturwissenschaften*) was added.

According to its first Rector, Hans Weiler, the university has been based on two fundamentally innovative concepts: internationality and interdisiplinarity. Internationality is related to being European in orientation and particularly to having a special relationship with Poland, which is just across the Oder River. Internationality has four components. First, it would have a truly international student body, and approximately one third of its places would be allocated to Polish students. Second, special efforts would be made to recruit faculty members from outside Germany. Third, its curriculum and graduation requirements would include a significant amount of international and comparative content. Fourth, special emphasis would be given to foreign language training. In its first two years of existence, the university moved dramatically toward this goal, as 40% of its students came from Poland and almost 25% of its faculty came from outside Germany. Interdisciplinarity was to be achieved in at least two ways. First, the three new schools of law, economics, and culture studies are developing a set of teaching and research relationships that will be reflected in jointly taught courses, school-wide graduation requirements, interdisiplinary research projects, etc. Second, the school of culture studies is replacing the long German tradition of compartmentalized social science and humanities faculties. Strictly defined discipline boundaries are being replaced by a single department with faculty representing social sciences, history, linguistics, comparative literature, philosophy, and geography, which will offer a single diploma called culture studies.

European University Viadrina has encountered a number of difficult problems, many of which are connected with its intention to be something other than a conventional West German institution. For example, West Germany has a 6% restriction on the number of foreign students who can be admitted into programs such as law and economics because they are subject to *numerus clausus*. Another problem has to do with the German *Beamte* or civil servant status awarded to German professors. Foreign scholars are threatened with the possibility of being given a second class status. Presently, extrordinary measures must be taken to obtain an exception for the scholar. The regulation that new states pay only a percentage of the salary of their West German counterpart, regardless of their quality, is particularly troublesome. These and other problems suggest that the imposition of West German regulations on all institutions of the new states act as a brake on any innovation attempts being undertaken. In this case, the argument cannot be used that the East Germans are incompetent and require the guiding hand of the more sophisticated West Germans because the main innovators happen to be international scholars of some repute.

To summarize, the institutional outcomes of recent changes have been significant. Whereas there were 54 institutions of higher education in the GDR, the new states of the FRG now have 13 universities, 12 art and music academies, and 21 new *Fachhochschulen* (unknown in the former GDR). The 17 medical, economic, law, and engineering academies of the old GDR have been closed or transformed into other types of institutions.

Teacher Education Westernized

The West Germans insisted that teacher education be brought in line with the West German tradition. East German teacher training institutions came under special criticism as seed-beds of communist indoctrination, dogmatism, and centralism. All that had to be given up in favor of a more progressive, Western tradition. The agreement of the Education Commission specifies the following:

> Teacher education in the new states should conform to the regulations concerning teacher training of 18.9.1990 that hold for the Federal Republic as stipulated:
> - A precondition for every teacher education program is that the teacher candidate qualifies for higher education study.
> - Every teacher education program is divided into two phases:
>   1. Study at a university or comparable institution
>   2. A preparatory assignment to seminars or other arrangements under the supervision of the school administration
> - Each phase will be concluded with a state examination (Standing Conference of Ministers, 1990d, p. 5).

Vocational Training Disintegrates

Even before formal unification in October 1990, vocational training had been incorporated into the West German system on 1

July 1990 as a part of the economic, currency and social unity treaty. This meant that the vocational program, including those aspects of the West German system that are out of date, were imposed on East Germany. While such an observation holds for all aspects of West German education, it is particularly troublesome regarding vocational training. While the system of the old states excels in its ability to maintain high standards, it suffers in its ability to change the training programs. The trade unions, government, and employer partnership necessitates a long and tedious process of consensus building that slows down innovation and impedes the ability of individual companies to strike out on their own and break new ground. In addition, once these standards are in place, they tend to hinder growth and change. For example, by 1978 it had long been recognized that the training of metal industry workers was no longer appropriate, and so the employers' organization of the metal industry and the metal worker's union began to negotiate new goals with vocational schools. Principles for the new system were jointly established, particularly that the future skilled worker would be able to perform a wide variety of tasks independently and mediate effectively between planning, execution and control processes (Verordnungen, 1987, p. 274). Over an eight year period job descriptions were completely restructured. And they replaced regulations that had existed since the 1940s and the 1950s. In fact, these old regulations were so outdated that no company in Germany trained in accordance with them. Thus, a variety of curricula grew in the different companies. In the new regulations, the 37 metal-work occupations that had existed in the FRG were clustered into six new and more general metal-work occupations, which were further divided into a total of seventeen different profiles. A similar process was taking place in other sectors of the work world. By 1988, the 600 recognized occupations that had previously existed had been reduced to 382 (Bundesminister 1984, 1987, 1988). Even so, much remains to be done.

East Germany also had training programs under development both before and after the collapse. As noted in the last chapter, commercial training in East Germany had been completely revised in

March 1990, but the West Germans did not look into what the East Germans had done. They simply mandated a program that itself was in need of being updated, and many East German vocational educators have complained that this program they have taken on has represented a step backwards for them. Arguments about training program structure are always present. The major difficulty to befall vocational training in the new states of Germany had to do with the disappearance of training places. Recall that training in the GDR occurred mainly in the large combines, firms and cooperatives. Small firms and handicraft businesses were almost non-existent, so there were no training possibilities with them. When the large industries began to disappear, the training places disappeared as well. Even those firms that were privatized tended to reduce or eliminate training, mainly because they inevitably became smaller. Of course, training options existed for the young East Germans, but large numbers of these were in the old states. In 1991, for example, more than 20,000 young people traveled to the old states to begin training because only 65,000 training places were available in the new states (BW, 1993, p. 21). The prospects for an improvement appear to be good, but it will take years to rectify the situation.

The Schools Cleansed

The teachers of the schools also went through an evaluation process to determine professional and ideological suitability. At the professional level, many teachers did not have a formal qualification that was equivalent to the West German standard. The major difficulty had to do with those who had obtained their training at one of the 25 Institutes for Teacher Training (*Institute für Lehrerbildung*), which had the status of a technical school and admitted candidates right out of the POS. The initial decision was to accept teachers in the new states having all types of qualifications, but the long-term professional future of large numbers of teachers was cast in doubt.

In terms of ideological qualifications, teachers were also required to subject themselves to a survey that inquired into their previous partcipation in political activities and the potential abuse of their power as teachers. At the school level, it has been widely believed that a ranking system existed regarding people who would probably be terminated. The school directors were at the top of the list, and as has been noted, the overwhelming number of them were terminated even though many of them were rehired as directors or more often as assistants in a school administration, where they could help the new directors who were usually   inexperienced in the position. If they were not rehired as administrators, most of the former school directors became ordinary teachers, so the number of school directors who left the profession was relatively small. Next in line came those who had served as secretaries to the SED party organization in the school. It was quickly decided that membership alone in the SED did not constitute grounds for dismissal. Finally, the ordinary teacher came in question. The major criteria for suitability in reference to ideological background was whether the teacher had wrongly used his or her professional position to disadvantage or discriminating against someone on ideological grounds. Few teachers were dismissed although there were enough cases to send shock waves among teachers.

One of the great fears teachers expressed in personal interviews was the possibility of loosing their jobs because of cutbacks in the numbers of teachers, and they feared that any blemish on their records would constitute grounds for dismissal. Rosenberg (1992, p. 26) once again expresses a more cynical point of view about the teacher evaluation process. It was noted in Chapter 5 that a great surplus of qualified teachers exists in West Germany, and she feels the removal of East German teachers could serve the economic interests of West Germany in that mass dismissals of East German teachers could create a pool of new jobs for unemployed West Germans.

The 1990/91 School Year

The unstable situation in the schools was to continue for the 1990/91 school year. The new school structure would begin in the next school year, at least in four new states and East Berlin. Only

Saxony decided to postpone the introduction of the new school system until the 1992/93 school year and by doing this, remained unstable for a longer period than the other states. The time before the new structure came into effect would allow for new school laws to be established in each state and for decision-making on such basic questions as whether a school building would serve as a primary school, a main school or a *Gymnasium*.

This period was also characterized by clashes between the officials, who were attempting to define education through political-administrative declarations (reform from above), and the school people, who had already begun to redefine their schools (reform from below). In those first months after the *Wende,* local school officials had tolerated a good deal of variance although they were in no position to cultivate or support change endeavors at the school level (Lorenz, 1991, p. 31).

By the spring time, however, these same school officials initiated attempts to establish a tight management structure over the schools. Formal administrative structures and role responsibilities and chains of command for school officials were defined. From the beginning of the 1990/91 school year, individual schools were run by directors, who had been approved and elected by so-called school conferences (parents and staff). Each school organized formal groups for parents, teachers and pupils, which had democratically elected representatives to speak for them.

As has been discussed, the main initial reform activities had to do with the reorganization of various fields of study. The struggle to redefine the content of fields of study took place outside the public forum and was usually not even clear to the teachers themselves. In addition, the general conditions for pedagogical work were continually changed. For example, the school leaders were repeatedly subjected to elections, and it was rarely clear how individual schools would be redefined to correspond to one of the West German school types. As the new states attempted to assert themselves, the ongoing school experiments were interrupted and disbanded. Social insecurity and feelings of resignation became prevalent on the part of teachers. The period was characterized by uncertainty and disappointment.

Partnerships in Change

The election of 18 March 1990, had been a referendum on unification. The East Germans voted that they wished to join together with the old Federal Republic. Once it was established that new federal states would be formed, questions were raised as to how this might best be accomplished. One strategy had already been adopted: state partnerships. Soon after the *Wende* various states began working informally with sections of East Germany. These partnerships worked well, and Germans had great hope that such relationships would facilitate the transition of the new states to a federated form. The initial partnerships were based on geography and political sentiment. The southern states of East Germany gravitated naturally toward the southern states of West Germany. A state usually worked closely with one sharing a border. For example, Thuringia had a common border with Hessen in the West and contacts were quickly made. Mecklenburg-West Pomerania had a common border with Lower Saxony in the West and it was also near Hamburg, so close working relationships were soon established with both. Even though these relationships were based on humanitarian motives and goodwill on the part of West Germans, there was an imbalance in the relationship. For example, Christian Wagner was the CDU Minister of Education for Hessen at the time of the *Wende*, and he immediately set out to convert those in Thuringia to the West German three-division school structure. He even proclaimed a sort of social-class argument for such a system. The *Hauptschule* was intended for the socially weak and the immigrant children. The *Realschule* was for the children of the middle-classes and the dull children of the higher classes. The *Gymnasium* was intended for the gifted children from the middle-class and the children of the higher classes (Peter, 1990). Under such a system justice would reign. Thus, Wagner established groups in Thuringia to work out programs of instruction for each of the three schools.

When state representatives were elected, some shifting in terms of partnerships with West Germany because of political affiliation. Because four of the five new states had voted CDU, the representatives chose to associate with strong CDU states in the West. These associations were important in that the partner state usually served as the major model for the new state as it began developing its school law and deciding on the specifics of its school system. The major partnerships were as follows:

East Berlin	West Berlin (CDU)
Thuringia	Baden-Württemberg (CDU)
Saxony	Bavaria (CSU)
Saxony-Anhalt	Lower Saxony (CDU)
Brandenburg	North-Rhine-Westphalia (SPD)
Mecklenburg-West Pomerania	Schleswig Holstein (CDU)

Besides the importance of these connections regarding the ultimate school law and system models, there were additional noteworthy aspects. First, a good deal of financial support came from the various partner states during those early months after the collapse. Second, consultation support was plentiful and came largely from state partnership arrangements. Third, a growing number of West German functionaries entering the police, cultural organizations, institutions of higher education, and political positions began to come on the scene in East Germany and they often came from the partner state. As might be expected, the encounter of East and West Germans was often dramatic and mystifying. Even the motives of those coming East covered the full range of possibilities. There were the dedicated, the sympathetic, the high minded, as well as the shocked and alarmed. Karlheinz Dürr, from Baden-Württemberg, typifies this last orientation:

Since the *Wende*...I have helped develop new courses for the retraining of teachers in such subjects as economics, politics, and sociology. Arriving in the East with an open mind, I was stunned at the situation I found: the facades of the buildings--schools as well as universities--were in many cases literally crumbling, and the teachers, professors, and administrative staff seemed to be paralyzed by a combination of indignation, indecision, frantic attempts at self-preservation, and finally, resignation....November 1989 left all too many of them helpless and without the drive or courage to take the initiative (1992, p. 391).

Mr. Dürr then proceeds to condemn the East Germans for their unwillingness to change. He felt it would be necessary to force them to change if anything constructive was to happen. Many East Germans were, indeed, guilty of failing to recognize their own worth and strengths. Dieter Vaupel (1990) went to Dresden in Saxony to provide inservice training of teachers, and at first he began his presentations with the comment: "We are also here to learn something from you." However, he soon gave up after he found responses to be something like, "what could you possibly learn from us?"

The manner in which partnerships evolved was somewhat varied. Berlin presents the most direct connecting of East and West in that it consisted of joining two halves of one city. Two people involved in the whole planning process for integration, Hermann Budde and Harald Meergans (1991), provide a graphic account of developments in joining the two Berlins.

Budde and Meergans point out that long before formal unification occurred, the city governments of the two Berlins had collapsed into a single working entity. As early as May 1990, the West German education senator and the East Berlin education councilman agreed that the 1990/91 school year would be the last a divided city would experience. In other words the city had approximately 15 months to prepare for educational unification. This was the desire of most parents, children, and the general public. It is critical to note that even though unification implies accommodation on the part of two entities, in actuality it did not even occur to those in West Berlin that they might be expected to accommodate their educational system in some way. It was the East Berliners, who were expected to change.

The heads of education in the two Berlins organized an Advisory Commission to work with the education councils of both East and West Berlin. It consisted of a balanced representation from both parts of Berlin, its membership being made up of representatives from institutions of higher education and research institutes. Such membership was deemed appropriate because it was originally thought that time would be available for critical reflection and consideration of various alternatives regarding unification. However, the process quickly evolved toward concrete proposals for certain structural reforms of the East Berlin schools. For example, the East Berliners adopted the West Berlin private school law in July 1990 (Krzyweck, 1991, p. 291). Adoption of the West Berlin six-year primary school structure was also recommended by the Advisory Commission. There was also sentiment in the Advisory Commission for the borrowing of a *Gesamtschule* structure on top of the primary school. The *Gesamtschule* would possess both a lower and an upper secondary section, so it would be able to award the *Abitur*. Some consideration was given to a relatively small number of *Gymnasien* (total of 25) serving as a complementary secondary school. The Advisory Commission also began to detail arrangements for inservice teacher training and recertification. The intention of the Advisory Commission had been to put forward certain recommendations and have public discussions about possibilities and adjustments, but both political and professional developments upset the entire process so that little came out of the deliberations.

While the Advisory Commission was working out policy recommendations, an educational management process was also being established whereby working groups from East and West Berlin would design the management system of East Berlin education. At the time the working groups were being set up, the assumption on the part of East Berliners was that the management system would reflect the style and needs of those in East Berlin. In fact, it soon became apparent that the East Berlin school system was expected to conform to the West Berlin school system.

The above activities were going on in the spring and early summer of 1990, so by October, when formal unification took place, it had already been decided that East Berlin would adopt the West Berlin educational system. In the beginning of October, the City Council of Berlin declared officially that on 1 August 1991 the School Law of West Berlin would become the School Law of the whole of Berlin. This meant that the East German school structure would disappear and that the West German structure of a six-year common primary school followed by a lower secondary structure of *Hauptschule, Realschule, Gymnasium,* and *Gesamtschule* would be used, followed by an upper secondary academic program leading to the *Abitur.* The 13 year school program leading to qualification for university study would, therefore, be adopted.

The decision meant that every school in East Berlin would become something new and different the next fall. Staff at any given school in East Berlin had no idea whether their school would be a primary school or a specific type of secondary school. Many factors would have to be calculated into the decision, including the facilities available in each school, the interests shown by parents, as well as the competence and interests of the school staff. The ultimate responsibility for determining what a school would become, would fall on the shoulders of each of the 23 various districts (*Stadtbezirke*) in Berlin (Krzyweck, 1991).

Before much could be done in working out arrangements, local elections were held in Berlin in December 1990. The old liberal coalition government was voted out and a conservative CDU government came into power. This meant that the highest levels of the school office would also shift toward a conservative orientation. Delays were also experienced because school type preferences of parents had not been determined. In February, 1991, parents were informed that they would have an opportunity to attend a number of informational meetings to learn of their options. A survey was developed and circulated to all parents having children who would attend lower secondary schools the next year, approximately 50,000 pupils, asking them what type of school they would like their children to attend. The outcome of this survey is reflected in the first column of *Table 2*, under "expressed preferences." These figures might be compared with the actual enrollments in West Berlin at the time, found in the last column of Table 2. Parents were also informed that they would be required to register their child for a specific type of school by the end of April 1991. In the middle column the actual choices parents made are indicated.

Table 2

Percentage of parents wishing their child to attend a particular school in East Berlin, and the percentage of children actually attending various types of lower secondary schools in West Berlin in 1990/91.

	East Berlin %		% West Berlin
	Expressed Preferences	Actual Registrations	Actual Enrollments
Hauptschule	2.2	1.3	9.6
Realschule	16.5	12.8	21.5
Gymnasium	36.6	37.6	41.2
Gesamtschule	44.7	48.3	27.7
Source: Budde & Meergans, 1991			

In comparing the preferences expressed by East Berlin parents with the actual attendance figures in West Berlin, two major differences stand out. Almost no East Berlin parents wanted their children to attend a *Hauptschule*, while almost 10% of the children in West Berlin attended such an institution. The most popular preference in East Berlin was the *Gesamtschule*, whereas the *Gymnasium* was the clear preference in West Berlin.

It is appropriate to emphasize that the surveys and actual registrations most likely did not reflect the attitudes of parents about the nature of the school system they would have preferred. The options in the system had been decided prior to the survey, and parents were asked to state their preferences from among West Berlin school types. If the decision had been whether East Berlin ought to be characterized by the *Gesamtschule* or the three-school type structure, informal interview data indicate that parents would likely have voted overwhelmingly for the *Gesamtschule*. However, since the decision had already been made to provide for four types of lower secondary schools, it is easy to see why many parents would want to advantage their individual child by sending him or her to the *Gymnasium*. Even so, when it came to actually deciding where their child would be placed almost half the parents decided on the *Gesamtschule*.

One of the shocking outcomes of these decisions was the leaning of parents toward the *Gymnasium* and the *Abitur*. At the time of the *Wende* only 14% of an age group was obtaining such an academic distinction. Suddenly 36.9% of several age groups in Berlin were enrolled in the *Gymnasium*. The number of enrollees in the *Gymnasium* was not so high outside of Berlin in the five new states; nevertheless, it was nearly one third of the age groups in question. In one year then, East Germany had achieved with this one big jump in numbers what had taken the West Germans thirty years to accomplish. No one could predict the consequence of such a sudden increase.

At the local school level, teachers and administrators   intently debated what they would like their school to become. From our discussion in the last chapter, it should be remembered that most schools had begun to develop a type of *Gesamtschule* proposal. However, because the six year primary school would be separated from the lower secondary school, POS teachers knew that some of them were destined for the primary school and others for the secondary school. Two decisions confronted all POS staffs. Should the school apply to be a primary or a secondary school? If it would apply to be a secondary school, what type of school would it want to be? This was not easy; many schools entered into extended debates about their future. Even after they had made a decision, it was unclear whether the school district office would honor that decision because it had to coordinate plans for the entire district. By the end of March, 1991, the school districts had put together a tentative plan for schools, but it was necessary to wait until the parental registrations at the end of April to make a firm decision about what would happen to each individual school.

While Berlin was integrated into an existing system, the educational systems of the five new states of East Germany were reorganized. The most important aspect of this transformation was the establishment of a legal basis for the educational systems in the various states. In the next chapter, aspects of those school laws shall be elaborated.

Chapter IX

School Laws in the New States of Germany

Introduction

The new states were expected to establish their separate school laws in less than half a year. These laws were to be seen as "provisional" in anticipation that they would be adjusted once the basic school systems were in place.[1] Already, newly formulated laws are beginning to appear. At the time of this writing, Saxony-Anhalt had already produced its "New Formulation of the School Law of the State of Saxony-Anhalt." This has been translated by the authors and placed in the back of this volume so that the reader can see the entire scope of such undertakings.

Saxony chose to begin its school reform program at the beginning of the 1992/93 school year, so it was one year behind the four other states and East Berlin, which began their new systems at the beginning of the 1991/92 school year. The school laws represented a remarkable achievement, but the time constraints inevitably led to the adoption of many provisions from the partner states of the old Federal Republic. For illustrative purposes, certain aspects of the transformation process are outlined here for one state: Mecklenburg-West Pomerania.

According to Lorenz (1991) Mecklenburg-West Pomerania engaged in a number of innovative activities during those first months

---

[1]The dates the various provisional laws came into effect were as follows *Erstes Schulreformgesetz des Landes Mecklenburg-Vorpommern, 26 April 1991; Erstes Schulreformgesetz für das Land Brandenburg, 28 Ma 1991; Schulreformgesetz für das Land Sachsen-Anhalt, 24. Mai 1991 Schulgesetz für den Freistaat Sachsen, 3. Juli 1991; Vorläufige, Bildungsgesetz des Landes Thüringen, 25. März 1991.*

following the *Wende*. Educators were quick to take advantage of the chaotic situation to begin a process of democratization by ensuring that parents, students, and teachers would play some role in school governance. They began to stress pluralism and tolerance for different viewpoints. They also began to move away from group instruction toward individualized instruction and attention to the specific needs of each pupil (p. 31). Even though differentiated instruction and homogeneous grouping had not been allowed to be put into general practice during most of the prior forty years, large numbers of schools in Mecklenburg-West Pomerania were quite familiar with a program that had been ongoing at a local teacher training college in Güstrow that had experimented with differentiated instruction and homogeneous grouping techniques for more than 20 years. Consequently, they were able to begin their own experiments with differentiated instruction and homogeneous grouping almost immediately following the *Wende*.

Mecklenburg-West Pomerania voted CDU in its 1990 election, and the state Ministry of Education was taken over by a conservative West German, who had come from Schleswig Holstein. He intended to bring a traditional German school system with him. During the Weimar period in the 1920s a four year primary school was instituted, after which the children were given a rigorous examination to determine which of three school types they would enter: *Hauptschule, Realschule*, and *Gymnasium*. The Minister of Education in Mecklenburg-West Pomerania intended to restore this basic framework, even though it had long been superseded in West Germany. In the old states, for example, transfer to a lower secondary school was no longer based on an examination but on a joint decision of parents and teachers. In addition, the lower secondary school types had adopted a two-year observation period, during which time it was easy to rectify wrong decisions by transferring pupils from one school type to another.

On 20 December 1990, Mecklenburg-West Pomerania Minister of Education circulated a letter to all teachers in the state informing them that he was going to hold public discussions explaining how he would transform the *Einheitsschule* into the above-mentioned system of a four-year primary school and three types of lower secondary schools, with the possibility that, through petition, a *Gesamtschule* might be allowed. The very next day, he sent the state legislature an outline of what he would like in the new school law. A major move to begin closing down locally inspired school initiatives that were already under way came with the circulation of a notice to parents of lower secondary pupils on 8 January 1991 requesting them to return a form indicating what type of school they would like to place their child in. The notice indicated that parents of children in the lower secondary level would have the option to place their child in one of the three conventional West German schools. Thus, it became clear that the *Gesamtschule* was not even in the plans of the state Ministry of Education. The extensive work parents and teachers had done to develop a *Gesamtschule* concept in the individual schools came to naught.

On 27 February 1991, the first draft of the new state school law was presented to the state legislature. The draft went through a difficult review process and was changed significantly. The original plan anticipated that children would be placed in the lower secondary school on the basis of an examination but the revised plan gave parents the right to choose which type of school their child would attend. The original plan did not included an "orientation phase" at the beginning of lower secondary school to allow adjustments from one school-type to another, in spite of the fact that the Standing Conference of Ministers of Education in West Germany had come to an agreement concerning such a phase in 1974.[2] The original plan did not foresee the existence of a *Gesamtschule*, but the school law was altered to incorporate that possibility into the plan (Lorenz, 1991, p. 32). These and other changes represent significant advances; however, the original proposal was much more regressive than what existed in West Germany and the adjustments were little more than ac-

---

[2]*Vereinbarung über die Orientierungsstufe (Klasse 5 und 6). Beschluß der KMK vom 28.02.1974.*

commodations that meant bringing the school system in line with existing school law in most of West Germany. There remained great resistance to this regressive school law proposal and on 25 April 1991 it barely passed into law with a 33:31 vote margin.

All of the new states were writing a school law similar to that of Mecklenburg-West Pomerania. Even though the models for the new states came from the old states, new forms of schooling did appear, however, which were outcomes of the struggle between those who wished to impose regressive ideas on the new states and East Germans who favored renewal. Here we shall compare some of the more important dimensions of the various school laws in the new states of Germany, particularly related to aims, structure, governance, sponsorship, and content.

Aims

Even though the language may vary somewhat, there is a common humanistic tone to the provisional aims in all the five state education laws. The states guarantee the right to an education for every individual. The states stipulate that a person receive the type of education appropriate to that individual's accomplishments and interests. The states also make explicit that education reflects the values of a free, democratic state based on law, and that education is directed to the development of a free, democratic consciousness.

Certain states make explicit certain provisions that might be implied in the tone of all states. Brandenburg and Saxony-Anhalt stress the rights of parents to help decide the type of education appropriate for their children, although some restrictions exist that inhibit the full exercise of these rights. Saxony and Saxony-Anhalt state that the legal foundation for education is the Basic Law of the Federal Republic of Germany. Thuringia and Mecklenburg-West Pomerania state that social origins play no role in defining the educational possibilities of youth, that all have equal educational opportunities. Brandenburg and Thuringia also make explicit that the ideological view and religious orientation of the parents be respected.

Certain peculiar aims exist in the laws, the most striking being the provisions in Brandenburg and Saxony that German Sorbs, a minority group numbering approximately 60,000 people who speak a particular language related to Polish, have the opportunity to learn the Sorb language and be instructed in the Sorb language.

Döbert and Manning (1994) provide a useful summary of the basic aims of the school laws. They conclude that the mission statements are variously worded, but there is a high degree of consensus about the general intent, in that they all reflect a strong European humanistic tradition, including the following:

- the student is to be educated toward freedom, tolerance, individuality and responsibility;
- the student is to be encouraged to think and act independently, in order to take personal responsibility in life, and to act responsibly with regard to society and the environment;
- the student ought to be socially engaged and socially active, in order to recognize the foundations of mankind, the value of the rule of law and democracy, and the importance of peaceful coexistence of all peoples;
- the student must learn to be willing to achieve and maintain a free, democratic orientation;
- each student's abilities and interests must be recognized and be given an opportunity to develop them.

Sponsorship

While states stipulate the kinds of public sponsorship that are available, all states make provision for private sponsorship of schools. These private schools will be under state control, but cooperation between the public and the private sectors is to be aided and encouraged. All states allow for states to provide financial aid to cover day-to-day and personnel costs of private schools. Brandenburg allows 100% of personnel costs to be covered by the state. Saxony-Anhalt allows up to 90% of such costs to be carried by the state, while Mecklenburg-West Pomerania place both a minimum (60%) and a maximum (90%) support allowed.

School Administration

Each school law defines the role of administrators in running schools, but it also makes clear the broader role of representative groups, including the so-called school conferences, teacher conferences, subject conferences, class conferences and parent representatives. The school conference has the broadest representation and requires collaboration on the part of administrators, teachers, parents and pupils in shared governance. The spheres in which shared governance are specified is usually detailed and explicit. In Saxony-Anhalt, for example, the school conference is responsible for a whole range of activities, including general rules of behavior in school, standards for education, adoption of texts, procurement and distribution of instructional materials, equipping the school, principles of evaluation and judgment, and the regulation of school events. Mecklenburg-West Pomerania mandates that the school conference be included in the selection process of school directors.

Structure

The structural reform in East German education has probably been the most extensively discussed and debated. The East German response to the West German model has taken various forms. It is yet to be seen what the new articulated system in East Germany will bring, at least in terms of social development and individuality. The tension between adoption and renewal manifests itself in East Germany through the primary and secondary school levels. The primary school in four of the new states is four years in length, while in Brandenburg it is six years. Brandenburg is the state where the city-state of Berlin is located, and it has oriented itself to that West German state. In the new states, then, young children attend a primary school for four or six years, after which they are channeled into different secondary school types. Therefore, a decision must be made between ages nine to twelve as to the appropriate educational experience for the child.

The lower secondary level is marked by great differences with regard to each other and with regard to the old West German states. This level begins with form five in all states except Brandenburg and East Berlin and lasts until form ten. It has been pointed out many times that the West German intention was to replace the East German unified or comprehensive school by the West German tripartite school system (*Gymnasium, Realschule, and Hauptschule*), where these different secondary school types stand next to each other and cater to quite different student populations. Even so, it is important to note that only Mecklenburg-West Pomerania adopted this tri-partite system without modification, and it was noted above that the adoption process in that state was highly controversial. As previously stated, East Berliners had essentially rejected the *Hauptschule* as a school type. Such a sentiment is also reflected in the four other new states, where a two school articulated lower secondary school system has been adopted. The *Gymnasium* has become the elite school in all states while the *Hauptschule* and *Realschule* have been collapsed into a single institution. The other systems have tended to stress a two school articulated system. Saxony-Anhalt adopted a "secondary school" (*Sekundarschule*) and a *Gymnasium*, Thuringia a "standard school" (*Regelschule*) and a *Gymnasium*, Saxony a "Middle school" (*Mittelschule*) and a *Gymnasium*, Brandenburg a "comprehensive school" (*Gesamtschule*) and a *Gymnasium*, although in this latter state, the *Realschule* has been added mainly in the rural areas. Döbert and Manning (1994) describe these new institutions as "schools for the majority" of the children implying that the *Gymnasium* remains an elite school or a "school of the minority." They also suggest that one could designate the new institutions in a negative manner, in that they be labeled "remainder schools" or schools for those who are unable or not interested in attending the *Gymnasium*.

Special provisions are related to the comprehensive school. In contrast to all other new states, Brandenburg has adopted the comprehensive school as its standard school. Where it exists, it is expected to provide the three West German school-types under one roof. Generally the school laws tend to exclude this form of education in spite of the fact that many school faculties and parent groups wish some form of the comprehensive school as a basic educational principle. Because of this, Mecklenburg-West Pomerania opened eight *Gesamtschulen* and Saxony-Anhalt opened a single school. That school was opened, for example, on the initiative of a West German, who became its headmaster. A *Gesamtschule* in Rostock is one of a large five-school complex. Saxony and Thuringia chose not include it as an option in their first school laws. There has been wide criticism of the West German tradition of separating children at the young age of ten years, and the new states have tempered this tradition by adopting some form of transition process during the first two years of lower secondary school. Forms five and six in Mecklenburg-West Pomerania are designated as orientation forms (*Orientierungs-klassen*). In the secondary school of Saxony-Anhalt these forms are known as promotion classes (*Föderstufen*), but also function as orientation forms. The *Gymnasium* also considers the first two years as "observation forms." In Saxony forms five and six are also designated as having an "observation function" to make certain children are in the appropriate track and school. Thuringia is the only state that does not have some special designation in its school law for the first two years of lower secondary school.

The upper secondary level is modeled closely after that of the old federal states. There are a number of issues concerning this level. The standard for admission into upper secondary school at the end of form ten is unclear. Thuringia has provision for those who have completed the *Realschule* to be admitted into upper secondary school, although this requires an additional year at the upper level. Saxony has a similar provision. In Saxony-Anhalt, students who have completed a ten-year *Hauptschule* or *Realschule* program with unusual performance are able to gain admission to the eleventh form of the *Gymnasium*. Because in Brandenburg comprehensive schools usually have an upper secondary program, arrangements are available for students to gain access. *Realschule* finishers who show special performance have the right to transfer to the upper secondary school.

The debate continues about whether the upper secondary school should be two or three years. That is, should the time required to obtain the *Abitur* be twelve or thirteen years? The new states have declared that it should be 12 years, which challenges the 13 year West German tradition. Saxony-Anhalt hedges its position in that it states only that it must take at least twelve years, opening the way for it to be extended another year. Brandenburg does not define the time required for the *Abitur*.

With regard to vocational education, the various school laws make provisions for a full array of vocational preparation institutions commonly found in West Germany. Brandenburg, Saxony, and Mecklenburg-West Pomerania make provision for the vocational school (*Berufsschule*), which is the basic school. As in West Germany, this provides vocational theory and general education to vocational students. The vocational-technical school (*Berufsfachschule*) is the school providing full-time vocational training. The technical School (*Fachschule*) provides in-depth further vocational training. The Advanced Technical school (*Fachoberschule*) provides education sufficient to attain admission to the higher education technical training. In addition, Saxony and Thuringia provide for a *Berufsgymnasium* and Mecklenburg-West Pomerania offers a *Fachgymnasium*, which allows pupils to qualify for higher education studies in specific technical subjects. This usually requires an additional (thirteenth) year for the *Abitur*. Saxony-Anhalt and Thuringia offer a promotional vocational school (*Berufsaufbauschule*) that offers training beyond the vocational school.

Curriculum and Instruction

One of the major changes taking place in the schools has to do with the introduction of various new subjects of study and revisions of content in other subjects. In spite of this, the new school laws were curiously silent concerning specific courses and the content of these courses. They typically specify that only the highest school officials shall be responsible for the definition of subjects and fields of study. The specific references to curriculum have to do with religious instruction and sex education.

One of the most hotly debated issues has been the reintroduction of religious studies. The old states of Germany have shown a strong commitment to religious studies. Efforts were even made to include a clause in the Unification Treaty specifying that religious instruction would be mandated in the East. In fact, great attention was give to religious instruction by the Education Commission of the FRG and the GDR at its 17 July meeting (Standing Conference of Ministers, 1991). However, compulsory religious instruction was eventually eliminated (Völschow, 1992). Certain supporters of religion sounded an alarm by claiming that more than 90% of the youth of the GDR had become atheists and that the old Christian traditions had been systematically distorted (e.g., Meier, 1990). Following the collapse those committed to religious instruction began a campaign to have it restored in the East, but others have been just as vigorous in resisting its introduction. The matter has been so difficult in Brandenburg, that the school law simply suspends final decision on religious instruction. There have been great efforts to adopt a program of "ethics studies" or "life formation" to provide a substitute for religious studies, but that has also not been easily accomplished (Eggers, 1992). In contrast, Saxony, Mecklenburg-West Pomerania, Thuringia, and Saxony-Anhalt mandate that religious instruction is a subject of study. However, only Mecklenburg-West Pomerania mandates attendance to religious instruction, although in the other states those pupils choosing not to participate in religious instruction must enroll in ethics or life formation courses at least until they are 14 years of age.

Brandenburg also stipulates that sex education must be a part of the general school curriculum and it must deal with biological, ethical, and cultural elements related to sex. The law notes parental responsibility regarding sex education. They must be informed of the sex education provisions in the schools. In Saxony these guidelines are to be made at the school level.

In all states new plans have been revised regarding political education, solid fields of study, and work education (*Arbeitslehre*).

Out-Of-School Programs

Day-care is one of the few structural issues where a certain continuity of the old GDR school can be seen. However, day-care is being accentuated to different degrees in the various new states. All states mandate that every primary school provide day-care for all parents wishing such a service, and Saxony and Saxony-Anhalt make provision for every lower secondary school to establish such a service, if it has the resources to do so. Brandenburg mandates day-care for both primary and lower secondary schools. Thuringia and Mecklenburg-West Pomerania make provision for day-care in all special-education institutions. Even though different political parties stress quite different policies, they all appear to support, to some degree at the state level, the retention of day-care facilities. Because of the extreme financial difficulties that presently exist in Germany, it is likely that day-care will be severely reduced, so that neither the interests of parents nor children will be satisfied.

The first steps toward a reorganization of the East German school system were taken in great haste which precluded the involvement of parents, pupils, and teachers in the process. If the East German school is to be built on a new and solid foundation, then the broad support of parents, pupils, and teachers is necessary. The next steps must also be in harmony with agreements concerning German education in the European Community, including the relationship between formal and nonformal education, multicultural and intercultural education, the growing tendency for parents and students to participate, and the role of the school as a socializing and educating institution.

The future will show if the school developments of the East German states are able to fulfill the aims laid down by the various school laws and if they are also open to reform discussions taking place among West Germans concerning reform in the old German states. In spite of all the particulars of the East German developments, two aspects ought to be of general interest. First, insight might be gained as to how school reforms might be translated into school practice. School reform always stands as a middle ground between educational-political demands and its school-practice capacity. The process that has been under way in East Germany ought to provide insight into the national and international scientific community and into the political and administrative planners attempting to implement practical change. Second, wisdom might be gained by using the differing East German state developments as a means of understanding how better to cope with the regional differences regarding European integration.

Chapter X

Transformed Education in the New States

Introduction

Having just experienced the disruption and disorganization that prevailed in the 1990/91 school year, the schools again faced an alarming adjustment as the new system went into effect at the beginning of the 1991/92 school year. It was not clear whether a given school would be a primary or a type of secondary school until the end of the 1990/91 school year. Then once those decisions were made, it became necessary to define which pupils would be assigned to which school, to select the administration and the teachers for the school, and to prepare the entire program for the opening of the fall term. Each of these tasks alone was daunting.

The pupil selection process was especially difficult at the secondary level, where parents had usually been given the choice of which type of schooling to enroll their child in. This had to be monitored and corrected in some cases where the choice had not been consistent with past performance. In addition, many neighboring parents had joined together in an effort to retain a semblance of the old POS their children had attended. Consequently, the school district office could not simply assign the pupils according to their own formula or interests.

The administrative structure of each school was unclear until very late in the year. The case of a new *Gymnasium* in Rostock will help illustrate the sequence of events a school went through. Herr R. was an active Russian and geography teacher at an EOS in Rostock. After the *Wende* he had been instrumental in organizing ways of keeping pupils on track for their *Abitur*. Consequently, he decided to apply to be a school leader. On 1 May 1991 he presented himself in Schwerin, the capital of Mecklenburg-West Pomerania, as a candidate for a position. He was not certain what kind of school he would be appointed to, but was confident that some type of appointment would be made. Finally, on 5 July he received notice that he would be the school leader of a *Gymnasium* in a suburb of Rostock and that students had already been assigned to his school. R. went immediately to the school and found it to be unchanged from the year before when it had been a POS with classrooms furnished for grades one through ten. Moreover, he was expected to begin school in six weeks time with a staff that had not been designated. He worked frantically getting furniture, textbooks, files and all else exchanged with other schools that had need for what he had and to bring in proper desks, computer equipment, laboratory equipment, etc., that belonged to a *Gymnasium*.

On 5 August R. was finally informed that 41 teachers (34 women and 7 men) had been assigned to his school, and that they had been invited to come to the school the next day. On 6 August 1991 38 teachers showed up. The other three were out of the country and had not received notice of their assignment. The teachers came from throughout the region. Few knew one another; it turned out that the local school district office had made that arrangement intentionally. The next days were spent trying to discern pupil needs and create a suitable program, given the staff and the physical space that existed.

On 19 August the entire school staff finally assembled at school for their final week of preparation time. On 26 August school began for a staff that was physically exhausted. On that day they encountered not only their pupils, but large numbers of parents and a camera crew from a television station that wished to record the first day of this historic event. That is but one example of the stories told by teachers and school leaders of 5,239 schools in the new German states that opened in the fall of 1991.

Successes and Failures of Schools

Some individual schools and types of schools required fewer adjustments than others. The situation at individual schools varied greatly from school to school, but some general observations can be made with regard to different school types. The primary schools appear to have had the least trauma. They usually represented the lower divisions of the old polytechnical schools, and the staff of these lower sections were often kept intact or combined with other POS school staffs to make up a single primary school teaching body; therefore, their personnel were the least affected by the structural changes. The primary programs also did not require such dramatic changes in the way teachers taught. Interviews with teachers at this level suggest that the teaching style had always been warm and humane, with the welfare of little children as the primary aim. This atmosphere continued, though teachers confronted new problems. The East's unemployment rate was nearing 55% if all casualties were taken into account, causing unsettled home situations which had inevitable consequences for the children, who brought their family problems with them into the school. Teachers themselves felt stress about being terminated, even though hindsight indicates they need not have worried. In one East Berlin school, for example, only one teacher was terminated, and that because she did not have the required teaching credentials; nevertheless, this sent shock waves through the school that remained for months. Teachers were also growing uneasy about salaries and benefits. The teaching salary was 60% of West German teachers, and tenure had been abolished, which meant that all teachers were at the lower end of the salary scale, which placed great financial hardship on teachers. The new curricular programs had not yet been worked out and teachers were expected to make do until they had clear guidelines. The textbooks were usually those which came through generous contributions from West Germany, which had committed 30 million German marks for school-book relief as a part of the Unification Treaty (Standing Conference of Ministers, 1990a, p. 3), but these books were also inadequate in that they were written prior to the *Wende* and reflected the ideological tensions and images of the former divided Germany.

In spite of the disruptions, some aspects of education had clearly improved. The authors talked with several parents, who felt that some type of discrimination had previously been leveled against their child because they had been involved in religious activities or because the parents were private entrepreneurs or had some other type of bourgeois background. This kind of treatment from schools ceased completely with the collapse.

A major task the primary teachers faced was to feel some ownership in the institution where they taught. Some efforts were initiated to accomplish this. In Brandenburg, for example, the teachers themselves, with the support of the Ministry of Education, started a movement toward so-called "inner reform" of their schools. The Ministry helped teachers organize regional groups for teachers to reflect on their situation and lay out what they wished to accomplish. This would lead to recommendations to the state organization regarding basic aims and concepts that teachers could agree to. This also included the organization of public hearings and ultimately the development of general guidelines for primary schools in the entire state (Resch, 1992).

The *Gymnasium* also appears to have generally made a smooth transition. For one thing, the better pupils were admitted to this institution, and so the new staff of each school was able to attend mainly to academic problems rather than social and emotional difficulties. In addition, many of the *Gymnasium* teachers had previously worked at the rather exclusive upper secondary school (EOS) or even at some institution of higher learning, and they felt at home in an academic atmosphere. Finally, the East Germans were quite familiar with the German educational tradition, and they knew what the *Gymnasium* represented in this tradition. In other words, teachers generally had a clear picture of what they were to do, even though that picture may have been several decades out of date.

However, the existence of the *Gymnasium* brought with it other social justice problems particularly related to young people who live some distance from such a school. For example, in the Saxony area near the Czech border, Altenberg is the *Gymnasium's* location. The little villages of Geising and Hermsdorf, located 12 to 15 kilometers away from Altenberg, must get the young boys and girls, some of whom are 10 years of age, to Altenberg to school. There are no school bus provisions for such travel, so private arrangements must be made. Consequently, many village youth are being denied opportunities taken for granted in the towns and cities.

Even though other types of schools experienced problems of one kind or another, the institution with the greatest range of difficulties was the *Gesamtschule* (comprehensive school). One of the difficulties was that the *Gesamtschule* represented, in some respects, the closest type of school to the old polytechnical school (POS). This ought to have been an advantage, but in reality it contributed to great confusion and organizational dissonance because some teachers and parents wanted it to be patterned after the POS, while others wanted it to replicate the West German model of essentially three schools under one roof, and others wanted something quite new. In fact, it was almost impossible to implement either the West German or the old POS models. A POS model would not satisfy the Unification Treaty, with its three different school leaving certificates nor would it replicate the West German model where three tracks are enclosed in one school, because most of the children enrolling in the *Gesamtschule* would only qualify for the lowest track. Because few restraints were put on enrolling in the *Gymnasium*, a significant percentage of young people opted for that program, which created a situation where the *Gesamtschule* became little more than a dumping ground for those who did not get into the elite school. In other words, the academic track was not well represented in the school; moreover, up to 60% of the students usually consisted of youth who would have typically been assigned to the *Hauptschule* in West Germany. Such a large concentration often overwhelmed the school.

Finally an organizational situation further complicated matters at the *Gesamtschule*. Because almost all of the experienced administrators had been terminated, schools were being run by neophyte administrators. That is not so serious if there is consensus about a school's purpose and role, which was the case for the *Gymnasium*, the primary school, and even the *Hauptschule* and *Realschule*. That was not the case with the *Gesamtschule*. It took weeks to sort out organizational hitches, and by then the reputation of the *Gesamtschule* had been irreparably damaged. It appears that the comprehensive school in the new states has a future as dubious as in West Germany.

Actually, the only state where the comprehensive school became the pervasive model was in Brandenburg, the only state that did not elect a Christian Democrat government in the first election. Of the 460 schools at the lower secondary level, 300 were designated as comprehensive schools. At the end of the first year of their existence, Hans-Jürgen Kuhn (1992), of the Ministry of Education, suggested five reasons why it would be premature to pass judgment on the comprehensive school. First, in contrast to the experience of West Germans, who established comprehensive schools as a part of a modern-day *pädagogische Bewegung*, the comprehensive schools of the new states was a direct outgrowth of a political decision to restructure the entire school system. Parents and pupils often did not select the comprehensive school out of conviction, but because they were cast into the unfortunate position of making a quick decision about where their children would go to school. Second, the designation of teachers for a particular school took many different forms. In some areas the teachers generally remained together as a group in the same school, while in others the teaching bodies were broken up and assigned to new schools Third, the assignment of children to a particular school also took different forms. In some cases, the children from an old POS remained together, while in other cases they were mixed with pupils that they had not known in the past. Fourth, depending on the decision of local political officials, comprehensive schools provided the only option for pupils in a particular catchment area, while in many other areas this school was thrown into competition with other school types, and pupils and their families were required to choose from among them. Fifth, the characteristic of a comprehensive school had not been completely formulated, so variations of that school type existed from school to school.

Of course, there are exceptions to these general observations. The Blenheim Street School in Marzahn, discussed so often when it was the 12. POS could be counted as one of the exceptions. Administratively, the school leaders had a clear perception of what they wanted, and they commitment themselves to reducing the disruptions that have characterized education during this period of great change. Organizationally, the school had been somewhat innovative and had moved quickly to establish a new format shortly after the *Wende*. Although it has been required to organize itself according to the West German definition of a comprehensive school, it has maintained a commitment to a clear set of goals. This includes the notion of differentiated instruction, which allows different types of students to seek different levels of achievement. In subjects of German, English, math, physics, chemistry, and biology students are grouped homogeneously. The typical format is to take two classes and divide them into three homogeneous groups, so that these core subjects are much smaller than the ordinary classes. Each of the groups has a somewhat different content and depth of coverage. Pupils in the more accelerated courses are given more points (credits) than those in the slower groups. The school allows teachers to stress different things. For example, one English class may focus on oral competence while another may focus on grammatical competence. The school was able to maintain continuity in faculty composition. Most teachers in the upper level of the old POS requested that they remain at the school.

Blenheim Street School continues to suffer some significant stresses. For example, the school building is too small for it to offer an upper secondary school program. This means that all young students who finish grade ten must transfer to another school if they wish to continue their formal schooling. This acts as an emotional drain and a constant barrier to enrollments. Further, when the decision was made public that Blenheim Street School would be comprehensive, only about half of the eligible students chose to return. Most of the others chose to enroll in a *Gymnasium*, which means that about 55% of the students are now of *Hauptschule* quality. It has been estimated that up to half of the students in the seventh grade may have to repeat, if they declare that they want to continue to the upper secondary level.

Instructional Innovation

An important step toward content/pedagogical renewal in the school system has been the establishment of general guidelines, which make the teachers responsible for their own pedagogical planning and carrying out of instruction. These guidelines have shifted the instructional orientation away from that which existed at the time of the GDR, where tight instructional rules existed that were intended to serve the interests of the state and its ideology. Currently, quite a different position exists. The instructional guidelines usually stress that top-down regulations are not consistent with a living democracy and an open society. They usually emphasize the need of instructing pupils to be "mature, self-assured, and enlightened citizens." The instructional guidelines from Brandenburg, for example, point out that such an approach requires the participation of the pupils in the organization of the instructional process and an opportunity for them to engage in independent planning and evaluating of instruction. It requires interdisciplinary and integrated instruction, including projects. It requires group work, partnerships, independent and individualized work, as substitutes for teacher-centered instruction (Ministry for Education, Youth, and Sport, 1991).

The format for the development of instructional materials has typically been sound. Usually, teachers and researchers from higher education institutes and universities, together with experts from the old federal states, have worked to frame the new instructional plans. In the first stages of development, this has required rapid decisions and quick production of materials. In fact, the first materials were usually completed in less than six months. As remarkable as this accomplishment was, the quality of the product remains just as questionable. The short preparation time meant that the new general plans were not subjected to a broad discussion among educators nor were they subjected to research analysis and pilot testing. Their evaluation comes almost exclusively through a "great experiment" within the school itself. In addition, teachers are often insecure about how to use the new instructional formats in their classrooms. Fortunately, great stress has been put on inservice training, but that also has had flaws.

East German Teachers

Teachers had invested, both physically and emotionally, in the development of school plans immediately after the collapse. This investment came to nothing, and many of the teachers had little energy to give to the new school forms they were to work in. The first year of the new schooling programs in East Germany represented, in certain respects, a return to a rigidly controlled and deterministic school format. That is, the new schools where teachers were assigned to teach were often an alien place to them. They had no sense of personal ownership of the changes being made. They were assigned a specific role in a school that had been defined by a nebulous "political decision" somewhere, that teachers perceived, rightly or wrongly, to have come from West Germany. Teachers perceived their role as one of learning how to adjust to the new system that had been imposed on them. Fortunately or unfortunately, the teachers had learned well how to adjust to the demands of a totalitarian hierarchy where they had adjusted to the imperatives or had risked elimination from the system. Seemingly they were to do this again for the new regime.

The teachers that the authors of this book visited explained time and again the problems they were facing. One of the most difficult facing them was the psychological trauma they were experiencing. There was the technical dilemma of having been trained in a system that was not consistent with the certification requirements of the new system. Probably the most serious technical complication was that the East German teaching system required a single major field of study for certification, while the West German system requires two fields of study. The professional status teachers in West Germany aspire to is that of civil service (*Beamte*) recognition. Almost no teachers in East Germany have met these required certification requirements, so they have the lower status of "employee" (*Ange-*

stellte). Of course, they could return to university study and acquire the necessary requirements, but that is a long and difficult road to travel.

One could dismiss this as a temporary problem that will be resolved as new teachers come into the profession, but because of the continuing cuts in the number of teachers there are almost no prospects of new teachers at the present time. In addition, the low birthrate in the new states suggests that the number of children entering the schools there will begin to decline dramatically in the years to come. Already school districts are making preparations for this decline. Consequently, few new teachers will be added to the teaching ranks for several years.

Teacher's instructional time has increased since unification, while their salary has not kept pace with the rapid increases in housing, eating, and commuting costs. The educators explained they were in what Americans describe as a catch-22 situation. They have felt they must behave appropriately or face an uncertain professional future in teaching, and so they try to conform to what they perceive to be the expectations of the West Germans; yet that very attitude prevents them from becoming self-reliant and independent as the West Germans also demand.

The East German teachers found themselves in a complicated situation. They were understandably insecure with regard to curricular and didactic questions taken for granted by West German colleagues. This often led to a tendency to revert to "proven" behaviors and to "fall back on" their old instructional practices, based exclusively on achievement. In spite of this, the tendency toward a "learning school" orientation appears to be growing, but this has accentuated difficulties between the old and the new teacher. In the GDR teachers played a special role in ideologically homogenizing the society, and now these same teachers are expected to play a significant part in bringing about the school reforms presently under way. Among the East German teachers one finds a mixture of liberation and joy about the new directions but one also finds a tendency toward reserve and resignation.

The hundreds of teachers with whom the authors spoke generally claimed to have come into teaching for the simple reason that they enjoyed working with children and youth and they loved learning. Ideology was always there, but it certainly was not the driving force in most of their lives. One teacher and former school director of the Heinrich-Heine Oberschule in Berlin describes her experience in the following way:

> ...a great number of teachers in the former GDR had given their entire strength to the end that our children would become people who loved life, possessed a high self-esteem, were smart. These teachers were always ready to provide theoretical guidance and practical advice, to reflect continually about how they could stimulate the children to take joy in learning, and develop their own individual way of learning, to help them expand their mental and social activities (Luckmann, 1991, p. 23).

That description applies to a good teacher anywhere, but those attributes were marginalized and largely invalidated in the transformation process. Negative feelings were further accentuated by the general social insecurity about employment in the GDR. Approximately 21% of 189,770 teachers in the five new states had been terminated by the end of 1992/93, because of political and economic reasons. From a teacher's perspective, a number of problems have manifested themselves.

Teachers have felt the pressures of time to redefine the educational situation. In their eyes, state control of education has not changed. In spite of a dramatic difference in language and ideology, their direct experience has been that one centralized and authoritarian system has simply replaced another. It has been impossible for the individual teacher to think through and discuss changes with politicians. They see themselves simply as workers in an alien system. Teachers point out that the external structural school reform must be quickly and effectively supported by internal reforms. This is especially the case with regard to the quality of instruction, the pedagogical atmosphere at the school, the effective and democratic organization of school life, including the opportunity to have a voice in decisions.

Figure 1

Teacher releases in 1990/91, 1991/92 and 1992/93 in the five new states of Germany.

	1990/91	1991/92	1992/93
Brandenburg	42,270	34,500	28,000*
Mecklenburg- West Pomerania	25,000	20,730	21,000
Saxony-Anhalt	38,000	32,000	32,000**
Saxony	53,000	45,500	42,250
Thuringia	31,500	29,200***	27,000
Total	189,770	161,930	150,250

*Actually 34,500 fill these positions because teachers
 have chosen to work 80% of the time to prevent mass layoffs.
**Plans are already firm to reduce this number by at least 2,000.
***2,000 of these are working part-time.

The reality of the school system in the new states of Germany cannot be reduced to the level of educational politics. Further steps in changing the educational landscape of the new states must include attitude changes in teachers. This should happen through programs that help teachers to be autonomous professionals. So far this has included massive numbers of courses designed to bring teachers up to par with their colleagues in the West.

Since unification, East German teachers have participated in a reorientation program intended to bring them into full participation as teachers of a unified Germany. This started out somewhat sporadically but quickly escalated into a far-reaching program. In Berlin, for example, only 28 of the 540 inservice courses given to teachers in the Winter of 1991 by the state Ministry of Education specifically targeted the teachers of East Berlin. Most of these courses focused on introducing teachers of East Berlin to the school system and instructional traditions and legal rulings related to education in West Berlin and the Federal Republic of Germany. The instructors were inevitably from the West and the courses were also taught in West Berlin rather than in some East Berlin location (Berlin Ministry, 1991). By the next fall the total number of courses had been expanded to 750, with 200 specifically targeted to the East Berlin teachers.

These courses were intended to introduce teachers to the types of schools in the differentiated German school system, to the content and instructional approaches of different subjects of study, and to the main pedagogical issues of West German education. The introduction in the Berlin catalogue stresses the hope of "getting acquainted with each other and exchanging experiences" between teachers of East and West Berlin (Berlin Ministry, 1991). Curiously, this was to be accomplished by arranging for East Berlin teachers to visit West Berlin teachers and by having almost all inservice courses taught in West Berlin.

Similar efforts were under way in the five new states of the Federal Republic. The framework of courses, the instructors, and the orientation often came from the partner state of the old West German Republic. One of the impressive efforts came from *Land* Brandenburg, which opened a residential center in Ludwigsfelde as well as three regional centers in Potsdam, Frankfurt/Oder, and Cottbus. The Ludwigsfelde center, known as the Pedagogical State Institute of Brandenburg, or more commonly as PLIB (*Pädagogisches Landesinstitut Brandenburg*), opened its doors on 5 August 1991 with the intention of providing a full array of inservice courses to all of the teachers of the state. The state of North-Rhine-Westphalia provided extensive assistance, both in personnel and material resources to the center, and in its first semester it offered approximately 600 different courses. Participants were allowed to sleep over if their course lasted more than one day. The costs for individuals was to be carried by the local school district, thus all costs, including housing, meals, materials, and travel were covered for all participants.

In spite of the Herculean efforts to help teachers and school people update themselves, the programs quickly came under heavy fire. On the one hand, West German teachers often complained that the East Germans were not interested in learning what they had to offer. On the other hand, East Germans became hostile toward their instructors. In a September 1991 newspaper article in the *Berliner Zeitung*, teachers complained that the West Germans have required them to participate in in-service programs only to treat them like little children in that they assume, usually without investigation, that the teachers are not quite competent. There has often been little sense of collegial equity, and the situation has appeared to deteriorate over time.

Overcoming a Sense of Alienation

Objectively seen, the West German schools are much more open than most East Germans perceive them to be. Some institutions are beginning to believe that the play-room of the schools can be significant. One school in Rostock has a marvelous director, who has given great energy to beautifying the school surroundings. Potted plants stand in the offices and hallways, attractive paintings hang on corridor walls, rugs lie on office floors. Most of this has come from teachers and parent groups, who demand that they and the children have an aesthetic quality to their environment. A school in Potsdam and also in Magdeburg have obtained libraries that at one time belonged to classical schools, and that now serve as a rallying point for teacher pride and a depository for valuable documents used by researchers and scholars. The Blenheim Street School, often mentioned above, has taken initiatives that schools must undertake if they are to develop a unique identity. Many of these initiatives have involved students and parents. Without additional resources the school has established a student-run school newspaper and an informal library where pupils can lounge and engage in casual reading. The school relies on pupils, parents and teachers for book and journal donations.[1] School leaders have developed a questionnaire, which they distribute from time to time to find out from pupils and parents what they think the school ought to undertake. Regular sporting events are scheduled which may involve teachers against pupils, parents against teachers, or parents against pupils. The pupils have initiated a "Ninth Hallway" club to beautify and keep up the hallways of the school. One of the critical needs of all schools in East Germany has been to obtain resources to maintain themselves because almost no funds are available from regular sources. The club has taken a major step toward self-organized responsibility to do this. A second club has also been organized and initiated by pupils, the "Green Turtles" club, which is dedicated to improving the general campus by planting grass, maintaining flower beds, and keeping the school yard clean. As a part of this, they have planned and built their own watering system under the supervision of the janitor and principal. A number of initiatives are clearly teacher-oriented. For example, pupil free retreats away from the school are occasionally scheduled so that teachers can join together and build collegial unity.

The most important insight teachers can gain from this is that a system imposed from outside still provides space for their own instructional freedom and initiative. Too many teachers and schools have failed to recognize the potential that exists for molding the curriculum and instructional processes to fit their own local interests and intentions. Alienation can only be overcome if teachers take charge of their professional lives and become owners of the schools where they work.

---

[1]There is no tradition in Germany for schools maintaining libraries, so no resources are allocated for such institutions.

East German Youth

The end of the German Democratic Republic has introduced un-anticipated and fundamental changes into the lives of its youth. Many of these changes might be considered positive and constructive, such as increases in freedom, opportunities to travel, and the right to choose one's own way of life, but even these changes have contributed to a crisis among the youth of East Germany. The right to participate more fully in constructing one's own way of life carries with it great personal burdens, including the potential of failure (Heitmeyer, 1991). In East Germany, the options a young person faced had been restricted and limited, but their life situation also provided a net of security, self-esteem, and identity.

The current situation has, in many respects, overwhelmed the youth. Their home, school, and work training failed to prepared them to deal with an open, capitalistic society. Family training patterns in the GDR were toward conformity, obedience, shared responsibility, politeness, and order. East German parents gave attention to child-rearing activities that created feelings of dependence, conformity, and conventional solutions to problems (Sturzbecher and Kalb, 1993).

The schools also stressed discipline, security and other aspects of an authoritarian instructional tradition. Because schools focused so much on uniformity and collective interests, they did not attend to individual needs. They emphasized standard knowledge and collective behavior to the detriment of independence, creativity, and uniqueness. Because the focus was on reproductive performance, many young people were not taught to develop self-initiative, communication skills, and the ability to solve problems (Schmidt, 1991; Schaarschmidt, 1991).

The norms of the old regime have been abolished but few new norms have emerged to provide guidelines for the youth. In the current situation the youth have begun to question everything. The only measuring rod for them to make judgments on is the degree to which an experience is interesting or not. This has created a difficult situation in the schools because many youth recognize no legitimate authority. The typical response to subjects being studied in school is: "That isn't interesting to us." Some teachers try to get cooperation by asking the pupils to help decide what to study. The following account of one such attempt typifies all too many experiences teachers have had:

> I asked the students in my tenth grade literature class whether they would like to deal with contemporary literature or with the classics. The students decided to read classical literature. We began by reading Schiller, but they quickly explained: 'Shit, this stuff doesn't interest us at all, what does Schiller have to do with us?' I explained to them that they were the ones who had decided not to deal with contemporary literature, and their response was: 'Shit on modern literature, why should we deal with that stuff?' So it went.

A political studies teacher had a similar experience:

> The students wanted to discuss the present social situation, but as we began to get down to what that meant, they resisted strenuously. I suggested that we deal with the meaning of a social group, including what groups expect, how they resolve conflicts, how they make decisions, but it was immediately clear they had no interest in that. One student explained: 'That doesn't interest us at all. I mean, we are in a sports group and when we have problems our trainer takes care of it and so we don't have any more conflicts.' I worry that the kids are not prepared to deal with a democracy.

One of the basic principles of a working democracy is the degree to which people are able to work in groups and make group decisions. Teachers have heard such principles and have attempted to incorporate group activities into the instruction. Conversations with teachers suggest this has been a discouraging experience. In fact, many teachers report that the young people appear to be excited by the old drill and regurgitation method of instruction. The young have probably learned to function in that situation and now that they are given room to use more critical thinking and make more decisions on their own, they don't know quite what to do. One consequence is an unusually large failure rate on the part of the youth in their school subjects.

The lack of worker training and employment have also been destabilizing factors among the youth. In the GDR, vocational training was state supported and guaranteed to each young person. These training places may not always have been the first preference, but they provided security and stability and a change to remain near home. A young person was rarely failed in these apprenticeships. This contributed to a certain residential stability and an inclination toward security and against risk.

In contrast to the situation of the past, the current system places youth under great stress. Families are relatively unstable, schools are in a state of transition, and work-training places are scarce or require travel to an alien city. The youth of the new states of Germany are responding to this in various ways. Sturzbecher (1994) maintains that almost all youth share certain similar desires. Even the radical youth express a wish to return to a state of normality. They would like to have a specific work place, a family, their own flat, an automobile, and above all the prospect of a secure future. West German survey research confirms these conclusions. The so-called Socio-Economic Panel has begun surveying East Germany and has found that employment and income are the primary factors that determine feelings of well-being in the new states. It is therefore predictable that as the economy deteriorated and the labor market shut down, attitudes about life also become pessimistic. The youth have generally been negative in their overall judgment of living conditions. Only ten percent of respondents to the Socio-Economic Panel could make positive judgments concerning the material quality of life in East Germany. Such levels of dissatisfaction have never been found in the old states of Germany (German Research Service, 1992).

Some youth have been reacting to the situation in deviant or even radical ways. Growing numbers of young people yearn to return to the previous socialist conditions, which gave great social recognition to youth. The attitude of growing numbers have shifted from one of high expectations of the market economy to skepticism and resignation. The old economy was once the target of laughter and jokes, but there is a growing positive sentiment that its accomplishments were significant. Sturzbecher (1994) finds that more than half the youth in his surveys challenge the value of a free economy, and females are more inclined than males to question it because they see they are more disadvantaged by the current system than males.

In the school, teachers increasingly complain about discipline problems. Reasons for these problems have been the rapid reorganization of schools; changes in the norms, values and educational concepts; changes in the meaning of education for teachers; and the insecurity that new legal provisions and subjective behavioral expectations have brought for teachers and pupils.

Optimistic projections are that, given time, youth will adjust and the difficulties will disappear. Our findings must temper such optimism because the young generation is very unsure of the limited occupational prospects available. Personal deficiencies are less to blame for the inability to find work than the market economy and the new political system, particularly its personified representatives, the so-called "Wessies." The tendency today, in the face of limited personal chances for development on the part of youth, is for the youth to deny the important role previous security played in their lives, even though there was rampant "hidden unemployment" in the system.

The failure of so many youth to establish a sense of personal worth, comes largely from their sense of being closed out of the employment structure. This psychological sense of deficiency is reinforced by their inability to participate as consumers, and their experience that the attractive positions in the economy, research and politics, are going to applicants out of West Germany. Given this background, observers are finding that the youth have shifted in their attitudes about the market economy from one of high expectations to one of skepticism and resignation. While the so-called "socialist economy" and its "social accomplishments" were once the subject of many jokes, these notions have begun to win a nostalgic new meaning and prestige.

In general, one must conclude that the youth of today in the former German Democratic Republic resist the direction current society is moving. This may be the consequence of the former social welfare policy which put youth at an advantage over other age groups such as the elderly. The situation today appears to have dramatically reversed those advantages. Consequently, the youth are being given labels reflecting their disadvantaged position. Labels such as the "transformation generation" (*Wendegeneration*), and "losers of the transformation" (*Wendeverlierer*) have begun to appear (Friedrich & Schubarth) to describe the youth, who are now being identified as the "lost generation," because they have lost their ideals, have unrealistic wishes, possess no useful occupational skills, and at the same time have no access to programs that will help them work through these loses (Kühn, 1992). In contrast, the older generation is being given the time and resources to retrain itself toward useful social competence, and it is making the necessary adjustment to engage successfully in social and occupational pursuits.

Section IV

Some Special Cases

Chapter XI

Gender Issues Related to Work and Education

Introduction

Traditionally, the woman's place in German society was relegated to the three K's (*Kinder, Küche, Kirche*). As in all mature industrialized societies, the role of the woman has changed dramatically in both East and West Germany. In this brief discussion, only certain indicators of these changes, particularly relative to the emancipation of females can be dealt with: women and work, and educational attainment. Issues related to women in the two Germanys are so inextricably bound with each other that they have not been treated separately.

Women in the Two Germanys

One of the greatest success stories to be told about the former GDR is the degree to which women were able to achieve economic equity with men. Even in the time of the Soviet zone of occupation women in East Germany were given full legal equality and integrated rapidly into the labor force. Actually, women throughout Germany had gained importance during World War II as they participated actively as industrial workers in the war effort. The war had catastrophic consequences for the male/female ratio, and at the end of that conflict there were 167 women for every 100 men between the ages of 20 to 30, and 151 women for every 100 men between the ages of 30 to 40 (Baumert and Hunniger, 1954).[1] After the war the contribution of women remained critical as they helped remove the

---

[1] These figures come from West Germany, but it can be assumed that similar figures held for East Germany.

rubble of the destroyed cities and began rebuilding the roads, parks, and buildings. However, the occupation zones also played a major role in the divergent directions women took. Hanna Schissler (1993, pp. 120-23) claims the cold-war climate of the time allowed the West Germans to dismiss the equity measures taking place in East Germany by describing them as "forced emancipation." At the same time they proclaimed the virtues of traditional female roles. They were, thus, able to argue against a similar course of action on the part of West German women and demand that they return to their homes and devote themselves to the care of their husbands and children.

Such a course of action is curious because the Basic Law of the Federal Republic guaranteed equal rights to all men and women. Basic rights of women existed, but they were interpreted to mean that the sexual division of labor of women was to be protected. It was taken for granted, for example, that if a woman were to marry, she could be relieved of her job so that she could better fulfill her role in the home. A woman was required by law to obtain permission from her husband to work, and she was required to turn over all her property to the man at the time of marriage. Thus, there was little assurance that equality existed in the workplace, the family, the school, and society. It was 1957 before that family law was amended to give women the right to work and to control her own property (*Gleichberechtigungsgesetz*).

Necessity required that women continue to work. The blossoming West German economy required workers, and families often required additional income, so the percentage of the labor force shifted dramatically. In 1950, one quarter of all workers were women but this percentage increased constantly until it had reached 42% by 1982. The figure was much higher for those of the working class. Approximately 90% of the wives of industrial workers were in the workforce (Schissler, 1993, p. 124). This phenomenon created great internal tensions in women. On the one hand, their role as a homemaker did little to contribute to their feelings of self worth, because they were seen as just a housewife. On the other hand, if they went to work they were accused of being irresponsible and negligent as wives and mothers. These tensions led to a variety of choices among women. Some attempted to satisfy the dual role of homemaker and career person. Some avoided having a family and dedicated themselves to career. Some avoided the workplace and remained at home. Each of these choices carried with it negative consequences and difficult dilemmas in the self-definition of women.

The East German women also faced dilemmas, but these were not so severe as in West Germany. The relationships between men and women, at least in the work world, were strictly defined by Marxist philosophy that placed great value on work--the worker's positive contribution to society being the highest ideal. So it followed that women, as well as men, were expected to be contributing members of the workforce. As shall be seen in the next chapter, the entire social welfare infrastructure was built to insure that this could occur, as work became almost as commonplace for women as for men. Over 92% of adult females and 98.3% of mothers were in the workforce, as opposed to approximately 40% in the FRG (Sturzbecher, 1992, p. 7).

It would be a mistake to suggest that women had gained professional equality with men in terms of status in society. One of the paradoxes in East Germany is that women made great progress in the world of work, but they continued to suffer in social status and political participation. East Germany remained, for all intents and purposes, a patriarchal society. This is nowhere better illustrated than in the educational bureaucracy. The Minister of Education was a woman, the wife of the head of government, but she surrounded herself exclusively with men. Even in the work world complete equality did not exist. East German women were more often found in the lower wage groups, in socially secure positions, and in the least competitive industries such as textiles. There were subtle indications of discrimination in hiring and promotion. Women were required, for example, to accept lower wages if they worked part-time because of family obligations. They generally contributed approximately 40% of a household income while men contributed 60% (Lemke, 1993, p. 151).[2]

Even though East German women had not achieved full equality, their relative progress in the workplace was much better than women in West Germany. It is not surprising, therefore, to find an active women's movement emerge in West Germany while a women's movement in East Germany has only recently developed. In the late sixties, spurred by the student movement, West German women's groups began to take an active role in the political arena. Their sentiments were typically that of socialists, who talked about social class divisions and relied on Marxist-based thought to demand liberation from a male dominated society. In 1971 a different type of women's movement took form, which increasingly focused on specific women's issues such as rape prevention measures, abortion, paid leaves for child-rearing, child-care centers, and therapy for battered women. The past two decades have seen an uneven development of the women's movement, but it has evolved into a potent political force in West German society.

In East Germany, in part because of the increasingly repressive moves on the part of the regime in the 1980s, East German women began to take a more activist role in the public forum. At first, they did not take initiative as women but simply as individuals concerned that things were not going well in their country. The issue that first brought women together as women was a new conscription law passed in 1982, that for the first time allowed women to be drafted into the military. Bärbel Bohley took issue with this law and wrote a petition to the government, which failed to respond, but she began to organize other women who were also concerned. Soon about 150 women were involved in what they called "Women for Peace."[3] She subsequently became active in other issues and was eventually arrested in 1988 and deported to Great Britain where she spent six

---

[2]This is significantly higher than West Germany, however, where the woman typically contributes but 18% of the household income.
[3]*Frauen für den Frieden.*

months. As soon as she was allowed to, she came back "where she accepted the daily life of police surveillance and harassment" and became a symbol around which the population was soon to rally (Philipsen, 1993, p. 70). Bohley was one of the critical founders of New Forum. She has been called the "mother of the underground," or the "mother of the revolution" in East Germany. Certain other women began to identify themselves separately from the male dominated groups in East Germany. Cornelia Matzke was also active within the New Forum and she was a dedicated opposition activist in Leipzig. She recognized that all the activities she was involved in were male dominated. Women were usually more quiet or they came to the meetings "with their husbands" and she resolved to do something about it, so she set up meetings, distributed literature, and contributed to the foundation of the Independent Women's Alliance. There was no great fanfare about what she did, as she explains:

> ...I convinced some of my female friends, and so we got a small group together. The first thing we did was to write a proposal for a program and to publicize the fact that we existed. We just wanted people to know that we were out there, and give them some ideas as to what we wanted to do (Philipsen, 1993, p. 131).

Thus, an identifiable "women's movement" was under way in the final stages of the German Democratic Republic. One of the issues that did not receive initial consideration from women's groups was that of education, but it also eventually took center stage.

Equity of Education in the Two Germanys

Female participation in general education is equal to that of males. Some claim it has contributed more than any other avenue of social participation to equal opportunities (Kolinsky, 1989). In both Germanys essentially every female attended school to the conclusion of the compulsory school period although in the first decades of West

Germany they were channeled systematically into the *Hauptschule*, while young boys were expected to attend the more prestigious *Realschule* and *Gymnasium*. However, great progress has been made in extended schooling and higher education studies. As can be seen from Table 1, in the fifties 72% of the 13-year-olds of West Germany were in the *Hauptschule*, but by the eighties the figure had dropped to 37%. In the same period the number of girls attending the *Gymnasium* had doubled, while those attending the *Realschule* had tripled (Kolinsky, 1989, p. 103). By 1990, 45.3% of those receiving the *Abitur* were females. The gender gap was disappearing in terms of formal schooling.

Table 1

Educational participation (in percentages) of 13-year-olds in the *Hauptschule*, *Realschule*, and *Gymnasium* in 1955, 1965, 1975, and 1985.

	1955	1965	1975	1985
Hauptschule	72	66	46	37
Realschule	8	13	21	26
Gymnasium	15	16	24	28

Because East Germany maintained a single ten year common school, essentially all girls and boys attended the same school through the primary and lower secondary levels. Even in the early years of the GDR more than 40% of the *Abiturienten* were females, and by the early 1970s they had attained parity with the males (Helwig, 1982, p. 15), so the progress of female opportunities in secondary school moved much faster in the GDR than in the FRG.

Even though a certain parity had been reached in West German schools, this was not the case with regard to higher education studies. In 1987 only 38% of all students in West Germany were females, while 51.9% of all students in East Germany were females. The figures are even more alarming in terms of those completing their studies. In 1987 only 35.9% of all West German students passing their examinations were women. In East Germany in the same year 52.6% of all students passing their examinations were women The percentage of West German students passing the doctoral examination was but 26.3% (Köhler & Schreier, 1990, pp. 140-43).

However important the above data are, some attention must be given to the internal workings of the school and the messages they have sent to their students concerning equity and role models. In early modern Germany, girls and boys were educated separately and assigned quite different roles. After World War II, West German schools have gradually moved toward a co-educational format, and there has been some expectation that these stereotyped roles would not be perpetuated as strongly as in the past. However, even though co-education had already become the norm in the 1960s, the curriculum appears not to have changed significantly in terms of role stereotypes. In a 1969 study, for example, 85 school readers were analyzed. Only 10% of the females represented in these readers were shown to be active in an occupation. As would be expected, the woman's role was pervasively pictured to be motherhood, friendliness, and service. A decade later a *Bundestag* commission on the woman and society concluded that school books in social studies, history, and science ignore the fact that the great majority of women work (Helwig, 1982, p. 16). Textbook analyses in the 1980s indicate that little had changed in the stereotypes that were being portrayed (Bruce, 1984).

Even though there were certain constants in East German schooling messages concerning the role of the female, over time they also took a revisionist tone. In 1970, Erna Scharnhorst engaged in an analysis of more the readers for the first four grades of school, and she found the woman was dominantly depicted in the workplace, which has been a constant in GDR policies. However, she also assessed more than 60 stories and essays related to the home and family and consistently found the mother or grandmother to be the cen-

tral figure. Only 10 stories and essays included the father and in all
of them he appeared to be somewhat marginal (Scharnhorst, 1970d).

Figure 2

The percentages of female students in various fields of study in East
and West Germany in 1987.

	FRG	GDR
Language and Culture Studies	61.6	62.2
Economics	33.0	79.0
Law	42.9	66.2
Mathematics, Natural Sciences	31.3	50.8
Theology	42.4	48.6
Art	58.3	47.8
Medicine	42.1	56.1
Agronomy	46.4	48.7
Engineering	11.9	29.3
Teaching and Pedagogy	62.5	72.6

Source: Köhler & Schreier, 1990, pp. 140-41

One of the telling aspects of gender stereotypes has to do with
occupational choice and fields of study. In Figure 2 a comparison is
given of the relative choices students made at institutions of higher
learning in the two Germanys in 1987. There are some significant
differences in terms of the fields of study females chose in the two
Germanys. Large percentages of East German female students were
in economics, law, mathematics, natural sciences, and medicine,
which suggests they were successful in invading fields that have
traditionally been the preserve of males. These fields remain largely
the preserve of males in West Germany. Even in engineering, where
almost no females are found in West Germany, almost 30% of all
East German students were female. One must conclude that East
Germany was much more successful in breaking down the gender

stereotypes in various fields of study in higher education than West Germany has been.

Vocational education is also telling; however, the categories used in the two states do not allow for a complete comparison. In crafts training, the level of participation of women in both East and West Germany was approximately 21%. In East Germany that percentage held constant until the collapse. In the West a gradual increase took place until it was almost 28% by 1987. This suggests that some vocations remained largely the domain of men in East Germany, while others have become almost completely feminized. Teaching is a prime example of such a dramatic shift. In 1987, 72.6% of all teacher candidates in East Germany were female. The number was 62.5% in West Germany.

Women in a Unified Germany

Great shifts took place in both Germanys during the second half of this century so that the role of women came to be seen in quite different ways. Unification will also have consequences for women. At the time of formal unification, some gender equity provisions were included in the Unification Treaty of 3 October 1990. Article 31 (1) stipulates that the "all-German legislature [shall] further develop legislation on equal rights for men and women." Article 31 (2) notes that the starting positions are quite different in the two Germanys regarding employment of mothers and fathers, and it mandates the "all-German legislature to shape the legal situation in such a way as to allow a reconciliation of family and occupational life." Despite this optimistic beginning, serious stress points remain. West German women rightly complain that those in the new states do not have a history of being politically active in the women's movement; however, their own history does not suggest that they are models worthy of emulation. On the other hand, East German women are finding that the freedoms they have ostensibly won by the 1989 revolution and by unification with West Germany have resulted in fewer rights for women (Mushaben, 1993, p. 51). They no longer have the same access to abortion, child-care facilities, jobs, pay, occupational advancement, job-training, and so forth. In addition, they are discovering they do not have the political sophistication necessary to mobilize themselves and deal adequately with the new realities confronting them. Unemployment has been particularly cruel to women. An estimated two-thirds of all those who have left the workforce since the collapse have been women. The old German adage, "women are for children, kitchen and church," appears to have become the informal policy of unified Germany, at least as it pertains to the new states. The generous provisions for maternity leave and child-care which East German women took for granted are being dramatically reduced. Women have few prospects for employment, and they feel pressure to decide either for a profession or a family. Those who choose a profession are being forced to make decisions that could permanently disrupt their lives. Increasing numbers are resorting to sterilization as a means of demonstrating to prospective employers that they have chosen a profession over a family. While some of these decisions are made from personal choice, the media report "instances in which young, childless women have been made to feel that, in the region's present economic depression, sterilization is the price of a job" (Marshall, 1993, p. A9). That is a disturbing commentary on the emerging discriminatory practices of a united Germany. With this brief assessment of gender issues, we turn now to family issues in the two Germanys.

Chapter XII

Family Education

Introduction

One of the striking differences between East and West Germany was radically divergent points of view about the role of the family in the educational process. The evolution of family education policies, or the lack thereof, in the FRG and the GDR, are discussed, followed by a brief analysis of the dilemmas this presents to those in the new states of Germany.

Family Policy in the Federal Republic

The family plays a central role in German tradition. Even in the middle of the nineteenth century it had been identified as the primary cell or "germ cell" of society and the state (Rhiel, 1855). It represented the repository of the German people and the social organ most responsible for passing on the German culture (Ehrenberg, 1916). With the establishment of the Federal Republic of Germany, the West Germans insisted that the family retain this traditional role and responsibility. It was seen as one of the few institutions that had not been overly contaminated by National Socialism. The Basic Law (Article 6) insured that the family would hold a special place in West German society. It even spelled out that "the care and upbringing of the children are the natural right of parents, and their duty, incumbent upon them primarily." The role of the state was to protect this "natural" right although provision existed for the state to step in if children were "in danger of falling into neglect." Even as pre-schooling came to play a greater role in West Germany, this was seen only as a "support and compensatory activity" for parents whose time was being increasingly taken up with work, study, and other activities outside the home. The whole atmosphere of these support institutions was to replicate in important ways the kind of life the child would experience at home. It is for this reason that the state had been reluctant to sponsor pre-schooling directly. Rather, it had relied on churches with the idea that their sponsorship would provide the child with a form of life that was in harmony with that found in the family (Liegle, 1990, pp. 157-8).

The family has been so central in the education of children, that as West Germany became a welfare state, it was seen as a support institution for the family. Only when the family fell short in its responsibilities did the state seek to play a compensatory role. Social welfare policies related to the family centered on such issues as providing leaves of absence, not only for the mother but also the father, in the early stages of the child's life, so the young child could receive the attention it required. The state has, however, never told parents what values and behaviors to impart, beyond certain universal concepts. In the years following World War II, these concepts tended to reinforce a conventional family where the father was the head of the household and the mother and children were supported by him in a dependent relationship. The entire press of "democratization" after the war tended to stress relationships based on partnerships and negotiation in all but the family. The basic hierarchically structured family was encouraged by both church and political leaders. The family was expected to transmit the basic values of German society, including order and cleanliness, moral and sexual norms, love, emotional security, honesty, and faith. It was expected to provide a haven where familiarity and intimacy would reign. It would provide a location where occasions such as holidays, birthdays, religious events, and births would be celebrated. It would provide boys with a leadership model and girls with the focus of their personal lives.

The West German family began to evolve away from an institution which provided a standard in life toward one which reflected an increasing individualization and diversification of life situations and life styles. In the process, German family life became increasingly "destandardized." Even legislation reinforced this tendency as it emphasized and defined children's, women's, and parents' rights. Family norms began to be interpreted in such a way that they reflected individualization. The goals of child-rearing became "rearing toward independence," "learning how to deal with conflicts," or "receiving the stimulus necessary to maximize intellectual competence" (Gräfin von Bethusy-Huc, 1987, p. 125). The work-world also appeared to contribute to a breakdown in community interests of families in that it drew the young away from the family to broader community interests (Beck, 1987). Leisure life also drew the young away from the family and into the world of the mass market. Even school came to occupy increasing amounts of a young person's time and deprived the family from playing a central role in the lives of the young. This means that the family has become more marginal in West German society.

The concept "family education" (*Familienerziehung*) does not even exist in the former West German social science and political literature. However, a large number of ongoing activities could fall into what East Germans designated as family education. Childhood and child-rearing appear in most adult education curricula. This has been particularly so in Protestant and Catholic adult education centers, but also in the more neutral *Volkshochschulen*, which provided courses for 720,000 people in 1987 alone (Baumert and Others, 1990, p. 423). Family counseling and therapy has also become a major professional activity for West Germans who are seeking to improve their child-rearing skills and reduce the stress of parenthood. The family role took center stage in much of the programming of the public media in West Germany, not only for entertainment but for serious educational broadcasting. Television has played a major role in the lives of almost everyone in the FRG, and programs such as Sesame Street have been broadcast for many years. Advertising is still another way in which parents were given pervasive messages about what they should and should not do in child-rearing although these messages were always intended to sell products and create feelings of need and deprivation on the part of children and parents alike.

One might conclude that West Germany has given great attention to family education activities; however, these activities were never a part of a centralized, uniform state policy. Policies often conveyed contradictory messages and biased perspectives that characterize most open and pluralist societies. This contrasts sharply to the approach taken by the German Democratic Republic in its prime.

Family Education in the GDR

Just as individuals shift priorities during their growing up years, so do countries. The German Democratic Republic was no exception. From the Republic's start in the late 1940s until its demise in 1990, its reliance on the family as an important child rearing institution altered dramatically. In the immediate post-World War II years, Soviet-occupied Germany, the area which became the German Democratic Republic in 1949, saw as one of its major tasks the reeducation of a population that had been indoctrinated with National Socialist values and ideals. The state assumed direct responsibility for the inculcation of its own Marxist philosophy, modeled after the socialism of the Soviet Union. Schools, youth groups, adult education institutions, and workers unions provided several hours weekly of political education which people were expected to attend. Promotions and favorable relationships with colleagues and those in authority depended on regular participation in such events. Child-care institutions, the *Kinderkrippe* (up to 3 years old), the *Kindergarten* (3 to 6) and *Hort* impressed socialist values into their young charges.

Thus, until the mid-sixties when a generation who had grown up under socialism began to have children of their own, when socialist principles had had time to settle into the minds of people, the state gradually gave over to the family more control in child upbringing. Prior to this time, the state recognized the great influence of the family on their children's value formation, but it did not trust families with the important task of helping their children form values.

In the mid-1960s, at the time when the state was beginning to recognize the family as a partner rather than an impediment in socialist education, the German Democratic Republic adopted a comprehensive law on the integrated socialist educational system, which mandated the desirable achievement level and personality characteristics of its citizens (School Law, 1965). The first article of that law stated that the aim of the educational system was "a high education of the entire people, the education and training of all-round and harmoniously developed socialist personalities, who consciously shape social life, change nature and lead a full, happy life worthy of human beings."[1] The inculcation of these desirable goals and traits became the focus for those active in the upbringing and education of children, which included teachers, child care workers, youth group leaders, and, now, parents.

At this time, then, the family was openly recognized for the influence it had upon children and was no longer discounted nor totally replaced by state institutions; indeed, the state granted that without the support of the family, it could not advance effectively to full socialism, the objective that schools and youth organizations had been working toward (APW, 1983, pp. 283-7). To put this policy into practice, the APW established a special center that was given the charge of preparing materials to help parents with the successful upbringing of their children. These materials explained what the 1965 mandate meant by "the achievement of a high level of development" and what it termed a socialistic personality and practical ways parents should bring this about in their children. Therefore, these books and pamphlets described methods and styles of child rearing that were consistent with socialist ideals (Ansorg, 1969; Erlebach, 1969; Scharnhorst, 1970b; Böttcher, 1965).

These earlier child rearing materials have a heavy patriarchal, political tone. For illustrative purposes, we shall describe a book, published in 1970, which served as an introduction to socialist family education for parents, teachers, and particularly volunteer family counselors (*Jugendhilfe*) (Mannschatz, 1970). In the book, heavy emphasis is placed on raising children in such a way that they will

---

[1] The idea of changing nature to work for mankind was originally meant in terms of rerouting rivers to better serve agricultural areas, building dams, reforesting, and so on. Later the idea was seen as faulty because of the devastating effect on the environment caused by the injudicious application of this idea.

further the socialist system. The author states that "traditional ideas are not appropriate nor sufficient to reach the potential of the family in rearing socialistic personalities. New relationships among people have developed in the GDR. This is represented in our socialistic community. The socialistic way of life is carried through within all areas of societal life. That also applies to the family "which is developing into a community of socialistic people whose relationships are imbued with socialist thinking and who are organized according to socialist principles" (Mannschatz, 1970, pp. 5-6). Thus, the family is to function as a miniature socialist community. Within the family, individuals learn and practice the principles of collective living.

The tone of the above book is not a trusting one. The author reprimands readers lest they think personality characteristics are inherited and not a product of upbringing and environment. He says that when the family fails, then complications come up in the personality development of the child and in extreme cases of failure, children may be removed from the family and put with foster parents or in a state home.

The book implies many times that schools, youth organizations, child-care services, and public agencies do not err in their child-rearing responsibilities. It is the parents who make mistakes. Smaller family errors in upbringing can be made up for by schools, youth organizations, and so forth; however, large errors cannot always be equalized. The goal, then, is for parents to be aware of their task and, from the beginning, avoid errors in raising their children.

The four main premises of the 1970 book deal mainly with the position of the family within society as a child rearing organization, its responsibilities and duties. Underlying all premises, however, is the belief that personality is formed not inborn. We shall outline these premises in the next sections.

Two anecdotes are given in the book to support the premise that personality is a product of upbringing: that of Jürgen and Petra. Jürgen is always asserting himself and showing off. This is so because at home he is spoiled and is the center of attention. Thus, he thinks he is more important than others and that he should have his way over them. Petra, on the other hand, is a leader whose political authority is already influential. Readers are reminded that she did not come to the world as a little socialist, but attended a socialist school, was active in the Pioneer organization, and was supported in these activities by parents who themselves are active in the community. Politics play an important role in her home where political events are discussed and evaluated from the standpoint of an informed GDR citizen. Thus, her behavior is influenced in a positive manner by the family whereas Jürgen's is not.

The second premise is that the family is at fault in developmental problems. Practices such as extreme over-challenging and under-challenging, inconsistency, spoiling, providing an overabundance of material things, forcing a child to grow up too fast, encouraging emotional dependence, overprotecting, allowing passivity, fostering repression, allowing permissiveness, and providing too much or too little security can all lead to difficulties in the development of the per-sonality, more specifically, the socialistic personality. If problems are not too severe, much can be done to correct them within the Young Pioneers, Free German Youth, and at school, but serious problems cannot always be remedied in this way. In extreme cases of improper child rearing or neglect, the *Jugendhilfe,* a state children's aid organi-zation, must step in.

The third premise is that the family is a mini-collective, and as a mini-collective the family is considered on par with the school, workplace, and youth organizations; however, the family is special in that it is a permanent and "natural" collective where the basic needs of a child are satisfied and where the most important decisions about a child's life are made. Therefore, families are urged to drop tradi-tional configurations that are no longer useful; for example, the role of the wife as housewife and underling and the role of the man as breadwinner and authority figure. Just as there are no longer classes within socialist society, there are no longer classes within the family. Man and wife are partners.

The final premise is that successful child rearing is an obligation parents have toward the perfection of socialist society. This is a big order, but parents are not left out on a limb. They are entitled to get the help they need to fulfill this task from social institutions such as the school, youth organizations, *Jugendhilfe*, and from publications.

From the above book, one might gain the impression that the state permeated the lives of East German families; however, that was not always the case. Family M. was a family where it did not. They did not feel any hostility toward the intrusive character of their government. They never ran into trouble for their aloofness. Yet, in spite of their independence, their family life-style fit socialist principles very well. Herr and Frau M. were born near Berlin during World War II and were brought up in the tightly-controlled, post-war socialist environment. Until the transformation, they and their three daughters knew no other system of schooling or government and had rarely left their home in East Berlin even to travel to other parts of the GDR. Like most East German children, the daughters were active in youth organizations such as the Young Pioneers. Yet, the parents regarded themselves as being politically independent. They were not active, for example, in parent groups at school beyond the minimum required of them or in the SED. They did help out occasionally with the afternoon activities of the Young Pioneers or as chaperones on class trips.

Frau M. did not particularly pay attention to what the state had to say about child rearing. She could not name the child rearing goals of the GDR, but she thought that the Young Pioneers did a good job with young people and, perhaps, would exemplify the best of socialist ideas and practice. She said the organization offered many worthwhile activities; for example, old paper collections, the decorating of school classrooms, cleaning up public grounds, arts and crafts, and parties. It promoted working and planning together, cooperation, and sensible use of free time. She thought this was all to the good, but felt that at times the collective spirit was exaggerated to the detriment of the individual. When her daughters were young, school children were required to enter the building by pairs instead of alone. This practice was monitored by older children who often became enamored of their authority. Once her youngest daughter J. entered the building without

a partner and as punishment was required to pick up paper handker-
chiefs and other rubbish from the school yard. Frau M. felt this was
unreasonable and complained to the school.

Most Berlin families lived in apartments. But family M. had acquired some property and for years they labored to build a home on
it. Suitable building materials were always in short supply. Nevertheless, they persisted, and eventually finished the house, planted fruit
trees, cultivated a garden, and bought some animals. It was as much
a farm as one could have in the city.

Herr M. worked at his job as an engineer but Frau M., unlike
92% of East German women, did not have outside employment and
stayed at home. The lives of this family revolved around their property. There was always much to do--animals to care for, fruit and
vegetables to can, a garden to keep up, improvements to make on the
house, and room ovens to clean and fill with coal.

Frau M. does not find any ready words to describe their own
child rearing goals, but honesty and independence are traits she said
they encouraged. Also they wanted their children to be able to make
the best out of everyday life. She believes it was good for her children to work at home. They learned to appreciate the value of work
and of money, too, by earning their spending money instead of it
having it handed to them. "And orderliness--" she began, having
thought of something more, but daughter J. finished her sentence for
her, "is half of life." J. said it with a smile but perhaps it was a
slightly rueful smile. Other things that were important to them in
raising their family came to Frau M.: working together, having a
tightly-knit family, and helping their children find a profession in
which they can work with a full heart. "Joy in work is more important than salary," said Frau M. with feeling.

In evaluating her parents' style of upbringing, J., 16, felt she has
enjoyed a close relationship with nature and with animals that most
children in Berlin have not experienced and because of this, she is
now more aware than most of environmental problems. She expressed a responsibility to help solve them. She did miss vacations
away from home, though. Perhaps their dedication to their home,

land, and animals had been carried somewhat too far. She felt, however, that it was no disadvantage to any of them that the family had not been involved politically. Governments don't mean much in her life. She will leave school after the tenth grade, as most pupils do, and go to work. Like her older sister, she would prefer being a salesperson, perhaps in a shoe store or a drugstore.

Even though materials published in the late sixties and during the seventies often contained extensive political instruction along with child rearing methods, they were, nonetheless, targeted for parents having socialist leanings (Makarenko, 1971). In time, however, the targeted audience for such books was broadened to include Christian parents and those of other minority groups. Perhaps politically independent families like Family M. were forerunners. They remained separate from political coaching while adhering to more universal, but socialist-acceptable, child-rearing principles. Later manuals and books which were often not printed by *Volk und Wissen*, began to emphasize the individuality and personal development of a child. The well-known Soviet educator A.S. Makarenko maintained that the collective can only be as strong as the individuals that make it up (Scharnhorst & Schille, 1989). Thus, such a reversal in emphasis could be regarded as consistent with socialist principles.

This change of direction continued and grew more pronounced. In the later years of the GDR, it was becoming evident that another force, the thinkers and writers--even those loyal to the tenets of East German socialism--were far outpacing the state in recognizing more progressive applications of these principles. Helga Königsdorf, physicist and mathematician turned writer and former member of the SED, echoed the sentiments of Makarenko at the Tenth Writers' Conference of the GDR, November 24, 1987:

> In such times as these, the point comes without fail, when one has to say "I". It can happen, then, that one finds out one has never learned to do this. Courage is in short supply. Yes, it is easier to feel oneself a representative of an institution, an organization, or even a country than to say "I". Yet saying

"I" doesn't necessarily need to contradict these things. We, however, who took in dialectics along with mother's milk, are more than willing to forget the dialectical. I consider the double "I's" that we have spoken about today to be a dialectical process. Experience is not acquired without pain. It is enticing to relinquish one's own identity and dive into a collective. But what is a collective identity without an identity that brings "I" into it.

In spite of the conservatism of the state, this demand for a less authoritarian, more democratic way of doing things--one in which the individual was as important as the group--expressed itself in many ways. One way was literature that appeared and books that were published. One such book, *Von Authorität bis Zärtlichkeit* (Scharnhorst & Schille, 1989), a child-rearing book targeted for families, appeared shortly before the Wall came down and is an example of this forward thinking. The editors were professors in good standing at the APW in Berlin, but the book was not published by the state press, *Volk und Wissen*. It is democratic in tone and entices parents to adopt its principles and try its methods by promising a more fulfilling family life rather than commanding them to follow out of fear of reprisal or from a sense of duty. The title translated is *From Authority to Tenderness* (or Affection) and mirrors what it teaches. An authoritarian tone is absent from this book and an empathetic, almost affectionate or tender tone prevails. The principles are universal in character. With the exception of specific references to holidays, organizations, and laws of the GDR, the book could have been written for parents in any Western country.

Following the principles of Soviet educational theorist Makarenko, it maintains that the family is the agency best suited to rear children and that there can be no successful socialist state without strong family units which help children develop responsibility for the well-being of others as well as for themselves. Child rearing is still carried out in view of a better state. What is different, however, between this 1989 book and those printed two decades earlier is the emphasis on individual development.

Weltanschauung, a fine old word in German philosophy, is used in this book to refer to the guided many-sided development of a person which comprises moral values, norms, and principles. Among values discussed are humanitarianism, freedom for all, loving relationships between family members, understanding between young and old, empathy for the sick, helpfulness toward the weak, tact, courtesy, modesty, comradeship, strength of will, respect for work, thirst for knowledge, respect for other peoples, acting for peace, and, in contrast to earlier statements about changing nature to further the socialistic way of life, an emphasis on protection of nature.

In full accord with the respected and politically correct yet universally acceptable principles of Makarenko, this book furthers teaching by example rather than through motto and prescription. That is, parents are encouraged to educate by what they do rather than solely by what they say. Parents reflect the values they wish their children to acquire. Parents are encouraged to assess themselves as individuals now and again and to strive constantly toward further growth. Parents are constantly improving themselves as they act as partners in their children's development.

Children learn by sharing in daily household chores. They learn through work. By participating in daily tasks, positive characteristics such as taking responsibility, thoroughness, and self-respect are acquired naturally.

Families are encouraged to engage in stimulating activities which may include sports, recreation, and cultural events. Within the family children are given impetus to develop physically and intellectually. The family is also a place where children can get things sorted out and talk with their parents about matters that come up in the course of life. All this demands that parents have reached a high plane of development, that they have acquired the same characteristics that they wish their children to have, and that they are aware of the goals they wish their children to attain. Instruction to their children happens primarily by example and always pointing to the goal that would be realized, rather than to the characteristic that must be eradicated.

Von Authorität bis Zärtlichkeit consistently uses this positive approach, emphasizing the family goals and positive parent attitudes rather than the errors to avoid. The reader is shown many times over that children are an important part of life and happiness, that they are wealth, joy, and comfort, as well as partners and teachers. However, there are two child rearing concepts (termed pre-Marxian by the author) that parents are exhorted to avoid. The first is to regard the child as material that can be formed to the particular advantage of the parents. The second is to attempt to isolate the child from all negative influences in life and let him develop as he will. The latter is found in the pedagogy of Rousseau where the essence of a child is seen as perfect and capable of developing as such if the environment is untroubled. The first might be exemplified by a bourgeois son who was expected to continue the family business despite other, perhaps more humanitarian inclinations, or a daughter whose marriage was arranged with the hope of bringing the parents position and wealth.

There were certain contradictions to the second point in GDR governmental policy. Western television was discouraged if not forbidden outright, inconsistencies were often covered up, the extent of criminality was often kept secret to protect people's sensibilities, and the positive was constantly emphasized. In socialist upbringing, according to the writers, these negatives would not be hidden from the child. Parents would discuss the child's perceptions with him and help him evaluate and come to a deeper understanding of the matter at hand in terms of his own ideals and upbringing. "Upbringing that leaves experiences out of consideration is not only unrealistic but inhumane because the child is let alone with his life problems and contradictions" (Scharnhorst & Schille, 1989, p. 130). Furthermore, parents are advised to give a child opportunities to gather experiences according to his age and maturity level. The family, according to the book, is irreplaceable in helping children gather tools for use in confronting the multiple experiences of later life.

In spite of the relative openness in Scharnhorst and Schille's book, still it only hints at serious family problems that existed in the

GDR. To have spoken of them directly would have meant that the book would not have appeared in print, according to Erna Scharnhorst. Of the 330 pages in *Von Authorität bis Zärtlichkeit,* less that 70 pages, dealt specifically with problems. Of these, 45 pages dealt with the typical psychomotor disorders, diseases and physical problems of childhood like measles, cavities, being under- and overweight, parasites, diarrhea, dyslexia, speech problems, enuresis, and so on. That left 25 pages devoted to behavioral problems like egoism, lying, rudeness, stealing, excessive holding back, disorderliness, and showing off.

While the above book seems to put forth a radical shift in orientation, it actually mirrors the change many East Germans were undergoing in their child-rearing commitments precisely at the time of the *Wende.*

East German Families in a Unified Germany

The collapse of the GDR has brought with it added responsibilities for the family. It can no longer rely on the state to satisfy a major share of the child-rearing functions. Increasingly, the parents are expected to take over many of these functions, yet the situation with unemployment or with both parents working without adequate child care, works against their ability to provide a healthy family environment for their children. For example, Sturzbecher (1992, p. 10) interviewed 76 Magdeburger children in mid-1989 and again six months after the *Wende.* He found that children received less sympathy and support from parents after the collapse. Children reporting little parental involvement in their problems, and conflicts doubled from 30% to 60% in that one year. A high correlation existed between these incidences and unemployment in the family.

Claims are made that East German parents gave so much child-rearing responsibility over to the state that they are no longer competent to cope adequately. While this may be the case with some parents, there is strong anecdotal evidence that others possess unusual skills. We shall provide an account of Frau R., to provide some fla-

vor of this in East Germany, both before and after the *Wende*. Frau
R. was a member of the SED, a successful textile designer heading
her division, and part of a circle of artists and writers. She has been
divorced several years and at the time of the interview her daughter,
A., was 16 years old. After the Wall fell, her firm was dissolved by
order of Treuhand, an agency commissioned by the Federal Republic
to either liquidate or sell East German factories and other work-
places. Suddenly unemployed, an almost unimaginable state for her,
she took advantage of a managerial training program, a type of "re-
schooling" set up by the Federal Republic to retrain East Germans
whose jobs had become obsolete or, in Frau R.'s case, few and far
between. She claimed that the training had not been on a very stimulating level and had been taught in a somewhat patronizing manner.
She had discovered, too, that she did not like straight managerial
work. Her heart was still in textile design.

She was, however, far luckier than most because she would soon
begin a new job related to design that promised to be not only toler-
able but interesting--one in which her considerable talents could be
put to some use. The difficulty was, she said, that she and her
daughter would have to move to Stuttgart, a large city in the West,
which meant to them that they would be living, working, or attending
school in what she considered a foreign country. But she had spent a
long time thinking it over and decided that she could learn the rules of
"this new game" which were quite different than those she had
learned for work in the GDR. Most important, she believed that she
could do this without losing her own identity. She had the same faith
in her daughter, who would attend the *Gymnasium* there. She said
she could not go so far as giving up her apartment in Berlin. It could
be that she might wish to return home someday or that her daughter
would live there while she attends a university in Berlin.

After the collapse, Frau R. had had a long period of grieving--not
so much for herself but for the lost opportunities that arose so briefly
and poignantly during the bloodless revolution of 1989. For a brief
time the GDR stood on the brink of becoming the country that she
had long wished it to become: a nation cleansed of political graft, a

democratic nation open to change, and one past the need to pressure the individual to conform to the survival needs of the state. When this did not come about, she said that she grieved for its unrealized potential and for what it had given away so cheaply to the economically superior Federal Republic. In the state of unification as it was then, she saw much talent and intelligence of her people going to waste.

The two-bedroom apartment that she shared with her daughter had a distinct Bohemian feel. The walls were covered with bookshelves and hung with decorations and pictures picked by a designer's eye. There were things on the walls and on the shelves that might have been bought on short journeys to the West. The style was not exactly German--certainly not the functional socialist style. An old cat sat in a patch of sunlight. Seat cushions were covered by washable terry cloth because of his slobbering. Even though he smelled bad at times, he was not only tolerated but revered.

She and her daughter have had an open relationship of mutual respect. That and the fact that A. always remained true to herself and would not bend to the interest of the collective was more important to Frau R. than anything else. Frau R. had believed that in an atmosphere of trust, A. would unfold in the way that was right for her. Frau R. said that she often had to remind herself to honor the choices that A. made even though they differed from what she would have chosen for her daughter.

A. was a thoughtful, self-disciplined young woman, giving the impression of knowing what she wanted but not in a rebellious or obstinate way. A. had never been kept in her room or deprived of privileges for childish misdeeds. If Frau R. had ever slapped her in a burst of temper, then she had excused herself for it. Even though A.'s parents separated when she was eleven, she has kept a positive relationship to both of them, had equal regard for both, and did not play one against the other.

The serious conflicts had come in school. After three weeks as a first grader, she had begun to hate going to school even though she was intelligent and the work came easy. The teacher (A. thought of her as a "dumb cow") did not recognize individual needs and differences but thought only in terms of the collective. A. did not fit. Double-facedness became necessary for the first time in her life. A. figured out what was expected of her--what she must say and do to stay out of trouble--and did it. Important was that her parents often spoke to her about the necessities, pains, and hurdles of this double life. They helped her recognize the difference between her public self and private self and encouraged her to stay true to the person she really was and not incorporate into that part of her, things she did not believe in. Yet they emphasized the necessity of not ruining her own future by being outspoken or rebellious.

A. had learned to distinguish what she could and could not change and how to cope with the kind of double-sidedness that existed in society. Frau R. said it had been a delicate matter to teach her the difference between lies that were morally wrong and lies that were necessary to survive in a repressive situation. This fine art of constant compromise was something that she wished A. did not have to master, but she believed A.'s future would be bleak if she did not become skillful at it.

School had only complicated child rearing for Frau R. and required delicate countermeasures. Much of her energy, she said, was spent ironing out difficulties A. ran into when she began school. Frau R. had done volunteer work at the school in the way she felt she could contribute best. Since she was a designer and had particular interest in art and other cultural activities, she provided costumes for plays, for example, and arranged trips to exhibitions and museums.

Frau R. and her daughter represented a dramatic shift from the family being regarded by the state as little more than a birthing group at best and a subversive influence at worst to one that is more self-governing and child-centered. That is not to say that the newer family openly defied the state or even wished for its demise, only that it began to recognize its own supreme importance in the development of its child members. Frau R. and other parents face a difficult future. Only time will determine the degree of success they will experience with their family situations.

Chapter XIII

Free-time and Education

Introduction

Free-time education is becoming recognized as an important aspect in the development of young people. By any standard young people in industrialized societies have a great deal of discretionary time. They can be left to drift or they can be involved in community-based programs and activities that contribute to their development. The two Germanys took radically different paths in providing engaging and meaningful experiences of youth during their free time.

Free-Time in West Germany

West Germany of the late 1940s, the 50s, and the early 60s was an adult mediated society. Unlike the East, values and orientations of the previous generation were transmitted to youth through family, school, and governmental organs (Watts, 1989, p. 4). Transferred were those values of a success-oriented system which looked toward a more comfortable, prosperous future. Adults cared more about acquiring goods and recovering economically than looking to the mistakes of the immediate past or to a revolutionary form of government for the future. This was the time of the "Economic Miracle" when Germans, taking advantage of the financial backing of the Marshall Plan, rebuilt their war-torn cities and industry and began to thrive. Life's meaning was tied to work and personal and national economic recovery. The emphasis was on reconstruction, not revolution. Instead of upholding a high socialistic consciousness, West Germans worked themselves into the competitive world market again. Thus, free time was primarily for recuperation so that more work could be done. They were committed to Western democracy because it helped them reach their goals; they focused on concrete accomplishments in gaining economic strength, rebuilding cities, and benefiting from a strong world market. Work was primary, and getting things accomplished dominated until the later 1960s (Opaschowski, 1983, p. 80).

In spite of this focus on work, however, the struggle for more free time begun by workers at the end of the last century continued. The immediate post war period 1945-53 showed a restoration in the long championed 40 hour work week, several weeks vacation period, and retirement with benefits that had been interrupted during the war. From the mid-1950s to the end of the 60s even as economic recovery progressed, the free-time industry and free-time facilities showed a huge growth. Tourism increased; TV sets and automobiles proliferated; more parks, playgrounds, pools, hiking paths, and camping places sprang up (Nahrstedt, 1990, p. 12).

The role of children was seen differently in East and West Germany. In the East, children were seen as the true, unspoiled perpetuators of a new socialist society and untainted by the fascism and capitalism of the older generation; therefore, a large proportion of the country's resources went toward their education. Those in power and others convinced of socialism's superiority devoted much of their attention to the upbringing of youth as socialistic personalities. In contrast, West German adults saw themselves as being responsible for the enormous task at hand--that of rebuilding the country and the economy. While youth were schooled, protected and cared for, they were not central to the rebuilding process and did not, on the whole, take a part in this great work. They grew up apart from the adult world, often having their own play areas, as risk-free as possible. The infant care centers, pre-schools, and kindergartens they attended have been termed a "play course" (*Spiellaufbahn*) (Karst, 1978. p. 85). As they got older, they did not use their free time to take part in rallies or earn money to donate to political solidarity or collect scrap metal to build navy ships. Their schools taught them reading, writing, and arithmetic but did not take responsibility to provide leisure time programs and activities.

As time went on and West Germany prospered, a new social, cultural and political attitude toward free time developed. For younger people who knew nothing of the economic hardships following World War II, free time, not work, became central to their lives. This attitude developed gradually, however. Even as late as 1960, industriousness and accomplishment were values rated most highly in a survey among younger people; but in 1980, private thinking and feeling, enjoyment of life, fun, social contact, and self-realization were the most important values (Opaschowski, 1983, p. 30). As another example, those claiming that they were fully satisfied with work in 1967 was 64%; only 39% agreed in 1982 (Opaschowski, 1983, p. 31). One would want to conclude that young West Germans became more pleasure rather than goal or achievement oriented because they had been left more to themselves, had more free choice, and had the time to do what they wished. But in a survey taken in the 1960s, at a time when youth still claimed work as a top value, 80% said they had "quite a lot" to "very much" free time, especially pupils, and they reported that their free time was used mainly for amusement, entertainment, relaxation, and doing nothing (Blücher, 1966, pp. 13 & 15). Perhaps the attitude of their parents, the rebuilders of post World War II, still influenced them. Conversely, twenty years later only 31% said they "kill time," just let time "run through their hands," or never plan their free time (Psydata/Shell, 1981, p. 22).

The younger generation, then, were the leaders of a new life-style that centered around free time, living for the pleasures of the present, yet keeping before them an interest in nature and the environment. They turned from organization and planning to spontaneity and self-development, from isolation and being a member of organizations to social contact with small or informal groups, from overwork and stress to relaxation, from pressure to succeed to enjoyment of life. (Opaschowski, 1983, pp. 75-85).

As prosperity took over West Germany, much of society accepted the goals of this new lifestyle as well as its idiosyncrasies even though it clearly deviated from what had been an adult-mediated, work-valuing nation. For example, youth magazines institutionalized teen slang or even invented it; industry produced all varieties of youth-specific fashion; churches sponsored jazz worship; and youth centers and free time houses sponsored by communities accepted and encouraged youth behaviors that were on the edge of the adult world.

In spite of a trend among present day youth to reject membership in organizations; nevertheless, some attract young people. In 1986, 32% said they were members of a sport club, 7% claimed to be in political or environmental clubs, 8% said they were members of church groups, and 3% belonged to work unions (Bertram, 1987, p. 33). All in all, more heavily structured groups such as Youth Parliament, Youth Forum, and youth free time facilities (*Jugendfreizeitstätte*) are not as popular as the more unstructured youth clubs such as the House of the Open Door.

Whereas East German schools participated directly in free time offerings for pupils, West German schools mainly stayed out of that area, beyond traditional week-long or day-long class excursions. They did little to guide youth in making free-time choices even though the work week was shortening and vacation time increasing. Some reforms were suggested or attempted. It was suggested that each school class plan out at least one hour a week together during free time where the teacher would hold back and only act as advisor or motivator. Pupils could use this time to talk over school problems, personal concerns, or ways to manage time.

Many recognized that conditions had to be created for improving the free-time situation for a wider level of the population. This was recognized as an important social-political task which should not remain in the private sphere. One proposed solution to this was that the *Hauptschule* would help motivate youth in better utilizing their present and future free time. This aid to life-long learning has never been realized (Opaschowski, 1983, pp. 138, 140).

Other institutions were dedicated to the free-time education of youth and adults. One was the venerable *Volkshochschule*, but it was too work-structured and too similar to regular school to further free time educational needs. Another was the Club of Rome concept, non-school facilities that motivated youngsters to better communication, greater creativity, and expansion of their personalities. Content learning was mixed with fun, and no outward pressure to succeed existed. Free time pedagogues also advocated free-time cultural education, located in neighborhoods and dedicated to development in creativity and communication. Any free-time education, it was argued, must be motivational, be activating and creative to overcome the passive-consumer style of behavior.

The West German government has always backed up the idea that free time and democracy are bound together and that "free time must remain free," is a private matter, and an autonomous area of life. Almost every free-time political program was based on that outlook. But free-time pedagogues and others claim that free time may not be so private after all. The media and leisure-time industry have already invaded the home. Free time is commercialized (Opaschowski, 1983, p. 144).

The same lament heard in the East was also heard in the West: the new generation was influenced too much by TV. In fact, research confirms TV (the hidden teacher) influences young people as much as school does. By 18 years of age the average West German youth has watched 13,000 hours of TV and has attended 12,000 hours of school (Opaschowski, 1983, p. 149). Of the hours spent watching TV, movies and criminal films are most popular. The difficulty with this is that youth is not taught to be critical about what they see on TV, so that they helplessly take in this new teacher's suggestions about opinions and behaviors and this lessens a person's free time competence (Goldschmidt, 1961, p. 89).

Free Time in East Germany

Free time education (*Freizeiterziehung*) was tightly controlled by the GDR and the SED and was closely linked with schools as another means of strengthening socialist ideology. Later in the 1980s, in spite of the regime's effort to keep control of all aspects of the educative process, free-time education changed to expand the possibilities of individual development beyond the defined "socialistic personality."

Marxists did not believe that free time should be regarded as a hedonistic search for pleasure or an area independent from the responsibilities to society. No polarities must exist between work as a productive sphere of life determined from outside the self and free time as a consumptive sphere which was self-determined. According to Marx, the separation between the world of work and the world of leisure time, which was blamed on the capitalistic way of production, would disappear along with class struggle (Laabs & Others, 1987).

The idea was that workers have more time for intellectual development, social interaction, and social and political activities. From a slightly different view, Lilo Steitz (1979, p. 23) emphasized the regenerative nature of free time: the restoration of strength needed for work through relaxation from work stress, the building up of the physical and mental capabilities for work, and the satisfying of needs not directly tied to work.

The Pioneer Organization

A strong maxim of the GDR governing powers was that the successful upbringing process of young people meant close cooperation and correlation between home, school, and youth organizations. Educational institutions were an area easily monitored by the SED, and it was believed that young people's free time could be largely institutionalized into the schools. The task, of course, would be the fostering of the highly educated, socially and politically active, cultured, all-round developed socialistic personality.

Already with the take-over of Eastern Germany by the Soviet army in summer, 1945, anti-fascist youth committees were being formed by the German Communist Party (KPD). A pamphlet published in honor of the thirty year anniversary of the Pioneer organization states that

> from the first day of liberation, children became friends with the soldiers of the red star. Soviet soldiers are our best friends. Not everyone then recognized this truth since the

Fascists spread shameful lies about the country of Lenin. The young anti-Fascists helped children to see through the ruse. And daily they could experience the truth for themselves. Soviet soldiers loved the children. They gave them their bread even though they were hungry themselves. Comsomols (Soviet youth organization members) in uniform visited the future Communist members of children's organizations, played and sang with them, helped them to understand the world and fight for a peaceful life (30 Jahre Pionierorganization, 1978 p. 56).

What began as primarily anti-fascist fledgling groups helped along by young teachers, visitors from the Soviet Union, and sympathetic Germans became an official organization on 7 March 1946, with the founding of the Free German Youth (FDJ). From that time on, the FDJ and later the Pioneer organization operated directly under the party. Motivated by the slogan, "No one is too young to help," FDJ members helped clear rubble, collect nails, and load wood for the rebuilding of destroyed towns and cities. Vacation camps and publications were established and children were put to work converting other children to the cause.

In December 1948, the Pioneer organization was established in the name of slain German Communist hero Ernst Thälmann Primary school members were to wear a blue neckerchief and greet each other with the slogan, "Be prepared." Under the leadership the FDJ--now for older youth--and the SED, the Pioneers joined "a unified political mass organization of children" (30 Jahre Pionierorganization, 1978 p. 60).

At the Fourth Pedagogical Congress of August, 1949, shortly before the founding of the GDR, suggestions were made that schools and the FDJ-Pioneer youth organizations form a close connection as one way of assuring higher academic performance in school. As a result of this recommendation, in January 1950, the SED established Children's Houses in Berlin, Dresden, Halle, Erfurt, and Schwerin. The legal basis for this joining in purpose of schools and youth organization came in February 1950, with the passage of the Law Concerning Participation of Youth in the Building Up of the GDR and the Support of Youth in School, Occupation, Sport, and Recreation. It was known as the first law for youth and included educational standards, political-educational premises, the basic ideas behind the Ernst Thälmann Pioneer Organization, and, in addition, gave authority to the founders of this organization for children 5-14 into fruition. After 1950, many initiatives for the establishment of centers came from the district, city, and community levels. Noteworthy is that the building of Children's Houses was given high priority in the post-war era of scarce building materials and pressure to put industry back in full swing.

The 1950-51 Pioneer mission or charge (these changed yearly) was reflected in the slogan "Young Pioneers--for peace and friendship among peoples--be prepared." That year a Pioneer delegation traveled to the Soviet Union and spent some time with Comsomols and Lenin Pioneers in a summer camp. Then Berlin took its turn as host by sponsoring the II World Festival of Youth and Students with 60,000 youth from 105 countries and two million young people from the GDR (30 Jahre Pionierorganization, 1978, p.65). Children were asked to continue doing their share in building up the GDR by helping to fulfill the country's first five-year plan.

At the 1955 Pioneer Rally in Dresden, the Central Committee of the SED gave Pioneers the charge of helping to build a 3,000 ton freighter to be named "Thälmann Pioneers." During the next five years, Pioneers donated 1.4 million marks and collected 29,000 tons of scrap iron, 295 tons of nonferrous metal, and 290 tons of scrap paper toward this cause (30 Jahre Pionierorganization, 1978, p. 69). Children were constantly involved in projects of one kind or another, local or national--all with the idea of bringing them actively into the building up of the GDR, which was the end goal of schooling, upbringing, and the development of the socialistic personality.

By 1956, 90 Pioneer Houses, 204 Young Technologist Stations, 36 Young Scientist Stations, 40 Young Tourist Stations, and 94

Young Artist clubs had been established by the FDJ/Pioneer Organization throughout the country (Gräßler & Raabe, 1992, p. 12).

The Pioneer Organization offered children rewards for patriotic service and for various accomplishments; for example, the badge for "Good Work at School" or the listing of individuals or groups in the 30,000 page "Red Book of Good Deeds."

By the mid-1970s an increasingly stronger patriotic tone was introduced into the FDJ/Pioneer Organization and schools. Although children participated in the main political commemorations it was recommended to the Ministry of Education that youth organizations and schools increase their efforts. This forced political ideology even more into children's time. In 1974, defense education was introduced into the free time curriculum.

Children were often asked to collect money and even signatures. In 1974, for example, the Pioneers collected signatures against "imperialist aggression" in South Vietnam and Chile and held fund-raising bazaars for the building of schools in North Vietnam; in 1980 Pioneer delegates attended the First International Children's Festival in Moscow and donated over a million marks for solidarity.

FDJ/Pioneer Organization and other extracurricular work with children was supported liberally in materials, technical assistance, and with personnel by the regime; but the regime also insisted its agenda be taught at all such free time organizations.

The Pioneer leader at the school was a well-trained person, a member of the faculty council, who worked closely with the director and class advisors. One such leader, Frau P. graduated from the three-year compressed course at a teachers college in Leipzig. In the 1960s a severe teacher shortage still existed, so the training period was concentrated. She began as a teacher in the lower primary level at Gera, taught 36 pupils for 28 instructional hours weekly, plus she spent one afternoon weekly with the children in pioneer work. After teaching four years she completed a three year course at the *Fachschule* for Pioneer leaders. In 1973 she worked in Berlin to organize the 1973 *Weltfestspiele*, a large international cultural event for pioneers. For two years thereafter she was a colleague at the

Central FDJ Council in Berlin. After more study at Humboldt University, she worked at the Pioneer House in Berlin/Lichtenberg, a free-time facility that provided theater, Russian, English, a hobby corner, a pen-pal exchange center, gymnastics, dance, sports, model building and sponsored vacation camps. Later she returned to teaching because of family responsibilities, where she served as a class advisor, pioneer leader, and did voluntary work with gifted children.

Although the Pioneers had groups in all primary school age level classes and in before and after school care institutions for younger children, the greatest attention was directed toward youth 10-16 years old. All concerned adults were expected to focus their energies toward the upbringing and support of these young people. As one example, on the 25th anniversary of the Pioneer organization, "firm sponsors [of Pioneer work teams and groups], teachers, and parents, the friends of the Free German Youth, came to give congratulations and to ensure the Pioneers that their hearts continued to beat for them" (30 Jahre Pionierorganization, 1978, p. 87).

Work Teams and Firm Sponsorships

Sponsorship relationships (*Patenschaftbeziehungen*) played an important role in the free time education of East German youth. Most generally a "brigade" of 15-30 workers acted as sponsors for a work team--a school class, a group of Pioneers and FDJ, and another group of young people. This was the most widespread extracurricular activity for youth in the GDR (Laabs & Others, 1987, p. 28). Groups of sponsors could be found working with youth in many settings: school, extracurricular facilities, facilities for culture and science, or in the culture houses of firms.

Young people of different ages were often placed in special-interest groups under the guidance of sponsors, who led them in projects, systematic learning, or in activities. Activities were related not only to work but were also of a social, cultural, or athletic nature.

The sponsorship program was under direction of the FDJ/Pioneer organization, but was assisted by teachers and volunteer members of the community. In 1978, 50,000 sponsorships were connected with Pioneer groups alone (30 Jahre Pionierorganization, 1978, p. 83).

The purpose behind the program was a two-way "all-round" development of both youth and sponsors (Laabs & Others, 1987, pp. 290-91), the development of children's ability to work in a collective and to use their free time productively. Sponsors also helped with vocation orientation and participated with their charges in *Appelen* (short formal school assemblies for announcements, awards, etc.) and the *Jugendweihe*.

In later years, sponsorships dwindled because of the discrepancy between school ideals of the workplace and the reality of socialistic production. In addition, a rich supply of "expert" volunteers had dried up. The support of firms and state institutions had disappeared. Volunteers were not so easily given time off work to be with the youth, but more importantly, because youth organizations had been so strongly tied to ideology, there was a loss of relevance with the collapse of that ideology.

The Struggle Toward a More Open System

At the end of the 1970s and beginning of the 80s, an attempt was made at Humboldt University in Berlin to develop a pedagogy that took in leisure time as well as school time. The idea was to develop a free time pedagogy based on research of the real lives and actual needs of youth. Humboldt researchers turned to pedagogical models that were clearly set apart from school instruction; for example, counseling, youth club work, the organization and effects of informal leisure time groups, free time in day care, and work teams.

As the media, particularly Western TV, had a greater influence on East German children, concern was raised by educators and others that interest must be diverted from that to something more worthwhile. It was clear that what once worked in youth organizations was not working anymore. Pupils were not as attracted to set, closed, and ideology-laced activities; the capitalistic idea of free time used for one's own pleasures and purposes seemed to be taking hold of young people. In the 35-40 hours per week that youth, ages 12-16, had at their disposal, much of it was spent on TV, films, and radio--all enticing media that could have lasting, strong effects on their consciousness and behavior (Kompaß, 1989). Indeed, the outlook on the influence, effects, and purposes of free time broadened in the 80s--getting away from the narrower purpose of helping develop firm supporters of the state. Researchers and others believed well-spent free time should awaken and satisfy interests and needs of the individual. It should broaden the mental horizon, aid in acquiring social experience, and in developing gifts and talents. In addition, it should develop social consciousness in areas such as environmental protection, solidarity, and the organizing of intellectual and cultural life in schools and community. Furthermore, it should give the less capable, the weak, and the handicapped a chance to be integrated into the community and, therefore, have more opportunity for development. Each individual should have the opportunity to enfold and express himself in self-chosen activities, and, finally, to rejuvenate his physical and mental strength.

Even as this new thinking opened up new horizons for the adults and children of East Germany, it marked the beginning of the end for unchallenged dictates of the government. The striving of people for freedom, self-determination and affluence, pulled at the tight interweaving of party-state-school, which, in turn, began to have an effect on the curriculum, teaching methods, and organization forms of schools and youth organizations. Although an important reason for the collapse of the GDR was economic, the desire of East Germans to get out from under the social, educational, political, and cultural stagnation was a strong impetus.

A major difficulty preventing free time educators from successfully changing over to a more open system was that the youth organizations of the GDR (as well as schools) remained closed to innovation. Lessons or themes were given in detail to the instructors. Anyone found deviating from this were disciplined. Instructors became technicians within this system.

The Lessening of Political Influence on Youth

In the 1980s as a generation of youngsters became less satisfied with the closed offerings of the FDJ/Pioneers, they took to the streets in search of some imagined new excitements. Leaders did not relinquish the old ways but, in some ways, pushed more strongly on youth. A 1981 published article, "What does a Person Expect from a Youth Club," states in traditional language that "growing interest continues in circles, work teams, and interest groups of the FDJ. It was argued that most young people agreed that free time activities in clubs should be suitably led and well organized and that capable FDJ youth club councils and regulating groups (*Ordnungsgruppen*) exist for this purpose. The wish for constant, concrete, and active participation is related to the self-governing organs, to the exercise of social democracy in their own clubs (Voß, 1981, p. 165). The stern character of the language belies the talk of democracy and self-governance. In reference to FDJ youth clubs based in firms, it goes on to state that such a club "offers members of the working youth many possibilities to pass their free time together in their...collectives with conversation, sociability, relaxation and the development of firm social relationships" (p. 167). Later, however, readers are reminded of the underlying purpose of these clubs which is "to further the personality development of these youth, to make a conscious connection between the socialistic/ideological position and communal activities and cultural interests and behavior" (p 169).

In the early 1980s, though, attempts were made to free youth groups somewhat from the firm hand of the FDJ and the SED. The Department of Free Time Education at Humboldt University in Berlin attempted to establish free time clubs for pupils in their experimental school in Marzahn. In published manuscripts this try was described and analyzed in some detail. The basic Marxist ideas of free time were still honored but the emphasis was on the integration of free time with school, work, and family life. The school was seen as a stimulus for free time interest--not parents, media, or peers; that free time was not a purely private refuge. The goal was to have school clubs organized by pupil initiative, voluntarily joined, free of regimentation or pressure to succeed, and conscious of individual differences. Teachers were only to play an advisory role.

Humboldt researchers conducted an attitude and preference survey of upper form pupils with the following results:

- the most interesting discussion items: partnership, love, and sexuality (37%), school (17%), and politics (11.6%)
- reasons for not doing anything with free time interests: family reasons (31%), school and community reasons (30.6%), too little free time or no possibilities (18%)
- stimulus for free time activities: parents and grandparents (34.3%), friends (33%)
- conditions for getting involved with free time activities: more possibilities and more time (42%), "if they could accept me as I am" (16.7%)
- attitude toward school in general: positive (10.5%), positive critical (21.1%), undecided (23%), moderately negative (24%), clearly negative (21.1%)
- work in Pioneers and FDJ: the main criticism was too few activities, too boring, too little organization, or too few volunteers.

Research was also carried through on how pupils in forms 5 to 9 spent their free time. In order of frequency: TV, listening to the radio and to music, playing and conversation, sports, reading, touring, going to events or performances, and social-political activities. Free time interests in order of preference: touring, going to events and performances, TV, sports, playing and conversation. Not mentioned were reading and social-political activities. Thematic interests on TV: crime, westerns, adventure, and horror (98%), animals and nature (19%), science fiction (15%), entertainment (12%), love (10%), comedy (10%), fairy tales (10%), youth films (2%), documentaries and news (1%). (Reischock, 1982, unpublished).

The work of researchers in East Germany contributed to a foundation upon which free time education in both Germanys could be defined. Even before the collapse, Elke and Harald Gräßler wrote about developing schools into social, cultural, and sport centers of the communities they drew from. They referred to the Program Model of the SED (*Programmenentwurf der SED*, 1947, p. 148) as a basis for their idea that schools in cities or in the country be hubs of community life.

GDR	FRG
Strengthening of the sense of responsibility, of cooperation, and engagement of pupils in school life and learning	Development of pupil personality through individual activities, development of equanimity and self-control
Integration into the political system	Furthering of creativity and individual interests
Strengthening of the class collective	Developing social and political commitment
Expression of free time on a higher cultural plane	Sensible use of free time
Close working together of school and extracurricular institutions	Open schools was only recommended, not required

Sources: School Law, 1965; Ministry of Education of North-Rhine Westphalia, 1988.

But their idea differed from the old, in that activities be less closed, less ideology-based, and more oriented to individual development. In an article published after the collapse, they wrote optimistically about the concept of "open schools" being sufficiently a part of both Eastern and Western tradition to provide a common conceptual ground. However, even though the GDR and FRG both had the concept of the open school, the purposes had been different (Gräßler & Gräßler, 1989).

After the Collapse

By 1990, during the time between the collapse and the reuniting of the two Germanys, several changes were underway in the East which had a dramatic impact on free time education:

- General recognition of East Germany's change from an industrial to a post industrial society.
- Leisure time seen as more than being simply another opportunity to mold the socialistic personality.
- Recognition of the opportunity added free time gives for personal development, and, indirectly from this, the positive affect it can have on society.
- Openness in uniting training procedures for East German and West German free time educators (Dross, 1990, p. 22ff.).

Schools, too, reflected the striving toward more openness. In nearly every school during this time of hope and euphoria, there was a reaching out for new ideas. Old directors who had been strong in the controlling party were replaced by teachers who had not held membership in the SED. Without party pressure teachers got acquainted with alternative pedagogical concepts. Many schools tried to create their own profile or style. Almost immediately the FD-J/Pioneer Organization had lost its grip, so that filling the vacuum left behind became challenging, exiting, and even daunting.

Until the *Wende*, little change occurred within the Pioneers in the way of teaching and organizing. Since teachers were in charge of free time offerings and almost all were only acquainted with traditional teaching methodology and not trained for extracurricular activities, free time activities often seemed little different from extended school. At the time of the collapse, many leaders attempted to change to a more open, less structured approach in their struggle for survival, but it was too late. At this time, sponsorship changed. The GDR regime had given liberally of money, available materials, and staff to officially recognized youth organizations. Now the remaining facilities (many had been closed down) were sponsored much more loosely and with reduced funding by the West Berlin oriented *Schulamt,* German Youth Authority (*Jugendamt*), or private sponsorship. Suddenly, free time educators who had been supplied with money as well as the details of most activities were put in the position of having to scramble for funds and successfully conduct a free-wheeling program that they had no training for Pioneer houses had become leisure time centers.

At this time of collapse, it was clear that there could be no going back to the old ways in free time education nor in the other education processes. Even if the GDR did continue as a separate state, a totalitarian regime and all-powerful SED would have no part in it. The time had come to educate youth about the process of democratic decision making--and that process was a task that continued through a lifetime. In the words of Christa Wolf, an East German writer who had been critical of the regime: Education is an essential prerequisite "to sharpen their critical consciousness in the struggle with other views, to prove their intelligence not only with facts (*Bildungs-stoffen*) but by exerting oneself in meaningful social activities together with others, to experiment even when it fails, their desires to the contrary, their high spirits, their ludicrousness, inappropriateness, and that, whatever gives the vitality to live out this bit of life in a productive way--in other words to become acquainted with themselves (Wolf, 1989).

There is a challenge of creativity and an open-endedness in that tolerance of not having such a sharp division between learners and teachers. It foreshadowed the coming times in such a way that free time educators trained in the old way could not handle. It is important to recognize also that new free time instruction must deal with people who were suddenly thrown into a new world. The peaceful revolution brought with it an extreme change in values. The sense of the life of a GDR citizen lay, according to official ideology, primarily in working for society and through society for oneself. One didn't have to give much thought to free time choices or to unemployment. Now everything is different; the sense of life comes through accomplishing more in one's free time. Free time educators must understand this special situation East Germans find themselves in and help them become part of a *Leistungsfreizeitgesellschaft*, a society that demands accomplishment from leisure hours (Dross, 1990, p. 45).

Several free time educators in both East and West took leadership during this time when idealistic expectations of the reuniting of East and West often turned into cynicism. East German free time educators such as Elke and Harald Gräßler at the teachers' college at Zwickau and Barbara Schöneich at Humboldt University in Berlin took steps to publicize problems and needs of youth with too many unaccustomed free hours to fill. Zwickau became partners with the West German University at Bielefeld and conceptualized a training program for free time educators from both East and West, which was partially put it into practice by 1991.

Two years after the collapse, Elke Gräßler (1992, pp. 1-7) emphasized how necessary it was for the new and the old states of Germany to compare positions concerning free time education and, above all, to come up with concepts that go further than the existing ones. These new ideas must (1) be based on the newest scientific research, yet must also carry over traditions of a particular region or community, (2) be a consequence of united effort both within Germany and internationally, (3) go forward in spite of the reduction in personnel and funding with the recognition that this is a consequence of acute budget deficit and not a lack of need, and, finally, (4) provide a financing model for free time facilities, especially for former socialist countries that had no need of such concerns before.

In spite of the upheaval and uncertainty for the future of free time pedagogy, much discussion has come forth about new roles, expanded areas, and improved training for specialists in leisure time education, particularly from the teachers college at Zwickau in the former GDR. Different emphases in practice are, for example, in the areas of youth centers/recreation areas, cultural activities, sports, and travel. The free time educator is also seen to play many roles including counselor (also for drug dependent clients), motivator, teacher, confidante, organizer, administrator, lobbyist, and researcher. A focal point of this new training would be a joining of pedagogical and psychological training for the specialty area of the free time pedagogue, also courses in administration, communication, play, and media education, knowledge of particular age groups of potential clients from the young to the old, and, finally, an internship or practicum before being fully certified (Dross, 1990, p. 23 ff).

Chapter XIV

Education, Extremism, and the Foreigner

Introduction

One of the vulnerable points in the fledgling German democracy is its tendency toward political extremism. This is best seen in its relationships with those non-Germans living within the borders of Germany. West Germany insists that its model of democracy be imposed on East Germany, yet the West Germans may have much to learn before they serve as a model. The current social crisis of political extremism and unsympathetic relationships with those foreigners living within its boundaries requires some consideration.

Foreigners in the Old States of Germany

As West Germany has become a favored goal of emigrants and foreigners, it has became an increasingly multicultural nation. Since the end of World War II more than 15 million people have settled in West Germany, and by 1989 its population totaled 5 million foreign-born people, making up 6.3 percent of the total population. More than half of these have been residents of West Germany for more than 10 years. People have come to West Germany for different reasons. We shall look briefly at the children of guest-workers, refugees, and foreign students.

Children of Guestworkers and Refugees

The influx of foreigners into Germany in the last half of this century has come mainly through the migration of workers seeking to satisfy the West German need for "guestworkers." These laborers were expected to remain for a short period of time but return to their homelands mainly in Italy, Greece, Spain, Portugal, Yugoslavia, and Turkey. However, by the early 1970s there were clear signs that these foreign people were remaining in West Germany. The average length of stay was increasing and the number of females was nearing the number of males, suggesting that spouses were accompanying their husbands. The most striking signal had to do with births. While the birth rate of Germans was falling by almost 50% in the 1960s and 70s, the share of births of foreigners rose from 4.3% in 1966 to 17.3% in 1974 and neared one third of all births a decade later (Brubaker, 1992, p. 172).

The above signals led to the decision on the part of Germans to begin discouraging immigration, but that decision only contributed to the tendency of those already there to remain. At the time of unification, two thirds of all Turks had been in West Germany for more than ten years. This situation was more extreme for the other nationalities: nearly 90% of Spanish, 80% of Greeks, Yugoslavs, and Portuguese, and about 70% of Italians had resided in the country for more than ten years. Even while fewer foreigners came into Germany, still the numbers of non-Germans continued to rise mainly because of their disproportionately high birthrate. Of the 1.5 million Turks in West Germany just prior to unification, 400,000 had been born there. Moreover, more than one million of the total foreigners had been born in West Germany.

In recent years still another immigration problem has arisen for West Germany. German refugee policies have been relatively liberal, which has led to an unusually large number of refugees. In fact, the various states of West Germany maintained a quota system, which required them to accept a certain percentage of asylum seekers. North-Rhine-Westphalia, for example, maintained an acceptance rate of 28% and Bavaria a rate of 17.4% (Helsinki Watch, 1992, p. 4). Between 1972 and 1987 Germany took in 44% of all refugees in Europe. In more recent years the number Germans have been taking in has accelerated. In 1983 there were only 19,737 asylum seekers, but this increased to 35,278 the next year, to 73,832 in 1985, to 103,076 in 1988, 121,318 in 1989, and 193,063 in 1990

(Statistisches Bundesamt, 1991, p. 73). For comparative purposes, West Germany has historically admitted as many refugees as the USA and Canada combined.

This influx of foreigners into Germany has led to the development of a truly multicultural society, where increasing numbers of people claim to have a social and cultural identity with a country outside Germany, yet claim Germany to be the only land they know and identify with. Many people in Germany carry a dual identity, and institutions must respond to this situation.

The impact of foreigners on West German education has been significant. The number of foreign children in German schools has risen much faster than the number of German children. The percentage of the pupils has been most significant in the primary schools and the *Hauptschulen*. In Figure 2, we see that in 1987, almost 72% of all foreign children were in these institutions, which contained only 54.9% of German pupils. This suggests that foreign children were relegated to this school because only the least was expected from them. One of the significant trends among foreign children is their increasing success rate in the German schools. In the sixties and early seventies few foreign children were expected to complete any school. In 1977/78 only 46% of these children attending the *Hauptschule* were able to receive its school leaving certificate. A decade later (1985/86) the percentage had increased to 83%. In the decades after World War II, foreign children were greatly underrepresented in the *Realschule* and the *Gymnasium*. Generally the only foreign children attending such institutions were the children of diplomats and business leaders who happened to be living in West Germany. A remarkable shift has occurred in the percentage of foreign children attending the *Realschule* and the *Gymnasium*, but we see in Figure 2 that their numbers continue to lag far behind the numbers of German children in these institutions.

The federated system of West Germany has shown divergent policies regarding education for the foreign child. Ray Rist (1978) did a significant study of the situation in two states of West Germany in the 1970s, and he reported that the more conservative Bavarian model was based on the assumption that foreign workers would come and go on a rotation basis; therefore, it was thought that the child would be best served in school by being educated as a Turk, Greek, or Italian. In contrast, the Berlin model was one that aimed at assimilation and eventual absorption of the foreign child into German society. Rist points out that both models are flawed, because neither recognizes the unique nature of the foreign child. That child has typically been born in West Germany but has been reared in a foreign family and often in a neighborhood dominated by foreign residents. The child's identity has been neither completely German nor completely foreign but a mixture of the two--Turkish-German, Greek-German, or Portuguese-German. Children of mixed culture require a unique educational experience and a special pedagogical approach. The German educational policies concerning foreign children rarely addressed these needs.

Figure 1

Percentage of foreign children in various West German school types in 1970, 1975, 1980, 1985, and 1987 .

| | Percentages | | | | |
School Type	1970	1975	1980	1985	1987
Primary school &					
Hauptschule	1.2	3.2	7.8	14.6	13.5
Realschule	0.6	1.2	2.1	4.9	6.5
Gymnasium	0.9	1.4	1.9	3.3	4.0
Gesamtschule	x.x	2.8	4.8	10.5	12.7
Sonderschule	1.2	3.2	7.8	14.6	16.1

In more recent years, the problem of the foreign child has been treated more sensitively. Germans have begun to understand and respond productively to the special situation of foreign children, including their language difficulties. In the past educators assumed that they were specialists in dealing with language problems because the academically oriented schools include so much foreign language training. However, the foreign languages usually studied are French and English, both familiar to Germans. A challenge to the academically oriented schools is to extend options beyond these two languages, including the languages spoken by foreign children living in Germany. A more fundamental problem facing Germans has to do with language programs for those students who are less gifted, a problem not having to do exclusively with foreign children, but involving them in critical ways. This raises important pedagogical issues. Because almost all language instruction has been targeted to a population that might be considered in the gifted range in America, almost no pedagogical understanding exists regarding the teaching of a foreign language to the average and slower pupil. Efforts are now underway, though, to develop new pedagogical approaches for this population and to train and upgrade large numbers of language teachers in appropriate instructional techniques, including an understanding of some of the recurring mistakes, both conceptually and linguistically, that foreign children make. There is also a growing tendency to adopt more current instructional modes, such as the communicative approach to language learning.

The growing sensitivity to foreign children that is reflected in school programs includes awareness of the learning styles of various foreign groups and appropriate ways to interact in classroom settings. German teachers no longer assume that the behavior they expect from pupils is implicitly understood by the foreign child. A troubling note remains, however, in that a disproportionate number of foreign children are in special education programs, but little evidence exists that this is a consequence of discrimination or even poor diagnosis. Educators are becoming more and more aware, too, of attitudes various nationalities have toward male/female relationships. One of the difficult issues German educators now face is how to deal with attitudes Muslim children may bring with them to the classroom. Traditionally, females in that culture have not enjoyed an equal opportunity to exercise independence and to compete directly with males in school. Another problem, not as common among Germans, is the mobility of foreign families, who may move much more and even disappear for months at a time in order to visit their homeland or take an available job in a different location. Conflicting educational programs also raise difficulties. While young German children are at home doing their schoolwork, many foreign children may be attending a school that provides them with a cultural foundation to their homeland.

One of the great shifts that has recently occurred is that many more Germans are taking added responsibility for the way other Germans have interacted with foreigners in the past. That sensitivity has included a willingness on their part to face the negative aspects of their own history more directly and honestly, including the racist and imperialist nature of National Socialism that discriminated against, suppressed, and exploited foreigners both inside and outside Germany. While National Socialism appears to have been an aberration, it may be seen as an extreme example of German hostility toward foreigners (*Ausländerfeindlichkeit*). Since the beginning of the 1980s, such attitudes have been a part of the public discourse, and Germans have been able to examine their shaded past more openly. This has even included an exploration of negative attitudes toward those identified as Germany's best friends, including Americans (e.g., Schwan, 1986). While West Germans are learning how to deal with the multicultural nature of their own society, the situation in the former GDR is more problematic.

Multiculturalism in East Germany

East Germany maintained a more restrictive policy in admitting foreigners than was the case in West Germany. Just prior to the collapse in 1989, there were 191,190 foreigners living in the GDR, or 1.2% of the population. Almost all of these came from five countries: Vietnam, Poland, Mozambique, the Soviet Union, and Hungary

(Helsinki Watch, 1992, p. 3). We shall consider here the issue of foreigners and minority groups.

Foreigners and Minority Groups

East Germany maintained some openness and receptivity toward foreigners, but that was usually restricted to people from the Soviet block and socialist countries from the developing world. The numbers were only a fraction of one percent. They came as contract workers and were usually placed in specified locations so that their presence was not obvious to the typical East German. Consequently, almost no interaction between foreigners and school children occurred. Because East Germany did not maintain a policy of accepting asylum seekers, very few were among the foreigners coming there.

The political system did not provide a mechanism that encouraged sensitivity to those who were different. The situation was further exacerbated in that the curriculum paid almost no attention to minority groups. The focus of the curriculum was almost entirely on the historical conflict between the so-called working class and the leaders of industry and made no mention of minority groups and foreign populations in East Germany.

However, East Germany established a strong policy with regard to its only minority group, the Sorbs, in that instruction in all subjects was to be given Sorbian pupils in their mother tongue. The principle was that language and conceptual orientation are so closely bound together that instruction must be in the language in which the child thinks. The policy was so stressed, that Section X of the Law on the Integrated Socialist Educational System (1966) was devoted to it. Articles 1 and 2 of that section stipulate the following:

> (1) All children and young people of the bilingual territory are guaranteed education and training in accordance with the principles, aims, content and structure of the integrated socialist educational system with the maintenance of the rights of Sorb population.

(2) Secondary schools and extended secondary schools with Sorb language instruction and Sorb secondary schools and extended secondary schools as well as corresponding institutions of pre-school education are to be maintained in the bilingual territory.

While the policy concerning the Sorbs has great merit in recognizing a specific minority group within the borders of East Germany, it could be said that such a policy is all too similar to that in the former states of the Soviet Union, Czechoslovakia, and Yugoslavia. All of these states have fragmented into conflicting and even warring groups in recent years, and we would have to conclude that their language policy may have contributed to the disintegration.

As those in the new states of Germany come to grips with unification, they must recognize that their towns and cities will surely become increasingly multinational. In fact, the Unification Treaty between the two Germanys provides a quota system for the assignment of asylum seekers to the new states. This quota is based on the population distribution (Appendix I, Chapter II, (A)(II)(1)(b)). The numbers were not large. Brandenburg would accept 3.56% of applicants, Mecklenburg-West Pomerania 2.76%, Saxony 6.44%, Saxony-Anhalt 3.94%, and Thuringia 3.3% (Helsinki Watch, 1992, p. 4). In retrospect, even these small percentages were an ill-advised agreement because the East Germans were not prepared to host significant numbers of refugees. The refugees often fled their assigned shelters and migrated to centers in the old states of Germany, where they requested asylum. Apparently international socialism had not prepared the East Germans for this type of global encounter.

Unfortunately, recent survey data appears to confirm that East Germans are not well prepared to deal with foreigners. Some join radical youth groups, such as the so-called skinheads,[1] who express violence and hatred toward foreigners and who have reinforced nega-

---

[1] According to Sturzbecher, approximately 3% of the youth population are skinheads, and another 16% sympathize with the skinheads.

tive stereotypes of German chauvinism. Members of these groups even express a high degree of sympathy for National Socialism and claim their school history has been little more than one-sided propaganda. Sturzbecher's survey data suggests that they think the picture they received of National Socialism was distorted by the GDR regime, and that they identify with the dramatic unemployment situation in Germany prior to the Nazi period because of their own unemployed condition. The parts of both periods that do not fit with their own picture are erased. They are creating a partial historical memory.

The primary reason young people cite for their aggressive behavior toward foreigners is their fear of competition in the job market (Oesterreich, 1992). Consequently, apprentices, who feel the threat most keenly, are much more likely to express animosity toward foreigners than are *Gymnasium* students. There are, of course, other reasons for animosity. Skinheads claim they desire to engage in ethnic cleansing to create and maintain cultural, ethnic, and political homogeneity. For them, Germany is for Germans and the "others" should not be integrated into the German culture. One of the pervasive graffiti slogans in the new states of Germany is "foreigner get out."[2]   The feelings are so intense among some youth that Sturzbecher has found signs of what he calls the apartheid principle to be working, where people who are different are objects of distrust and hostility (Sturzbecher, 1994). Such attitudes appear also to be increasing. A 1991 survey asked young people the question: "Do you feel Germany is for Germans and that foreigners must leave?" More than 27% of the respondents answered yes (Starke, 1991). The same question was posed in 1993 and more than 42% of the youth answered in the affirmative (Sturzbecher, 1994).

While violence and suicide appear to be increasing, youth assistance programs have largely disappeared in the new states. In addition, many parents of troubled youth have recently lost their professional identity and often have been unable to function as guides and

---

[2]Ausländer heraus.

supporters of their children. This is usually compounded by an increasingly repressive family climate (Sturzbecher 1993). Schools are also being criticized for contributing to disorientation. The current educational system encourages individualism, which requires adjustments on the part of pupils, who often fail to see how they must change and what is expected of them (Kühnel, 1991).

One of the remarkable findings of Sturzbecher (1994) in his surveys of youth is that the Polish are seen in a poorer light than the Vietnamese in terms of dichotomous labels such as intelligent/dumb; conscientious/lazy; disciplined/undisciplined; self assured/unsure. From the Western vantage point, it may well be that Western multicultural education is and has been ultimately integrative and incorporative (Olneck, 1990). Such a claim may sound heretical, but the purpose of multicultural education is to harmonize relationships among culturally diverse groups by cultivating attitudes of empathy, appreciation, and understanding on the part of individuals for various cultures. Further, it attempts to break down barriers so that all people, regardless of cultural background, have access to the rewards of society (Banks, 1988; Bullivant, 1981).

German Citizenship and the Foreigner

Closely related to the changing attitudes of Germans to multiculturalism are German policies concerning citizenship. Current German policy regarding citizenship was set prior to World War I and has held constant since that time. A law was established in 1913 which allowed Germans, who emigrated out of Germany, to retain their right to return to Germany as fully recognized citizens, but it also refused to allow all but a miniscule number of non-Germans moving into Germany to obtain German citizenship.[3] That policy has held until this period, and it has implications for the current situation in Germany. The influx of guestworkers and refugees into Germany

---

[3]Naturalization requires that the individual provide a "valuable addition to the population" (*wertvollen Bevölkerungszuwachs*).

has resulted in millions of people who have been in the country for generations, yet who are unable to make any claim to German citizenship. At the same time, the collapse of the barriers between East and West has resulted in the influx of large numbers of people who claim German heritage. By law they must be accepted as German citizens. Large numbers of these people have no idea what it means to be German. German language proficiency and cultural identity were lost with previous generations. Discussions with teachers in the *Hauptschulen* of the old states of Germany indicate the greatest assimilation difficulties are no longer the children of guestworkers but with the children of Eastern Europeans claiming German ancestry.

The dual problem of a settled non-German immigrant population and the surge of an ethnic German population underscores what Brubaker (1992, p. 172) calls the "ethnocultural inflection of citizenship law." In 1990 there was a small liberalization of the naturalization law, but its restrictions remain prohibitive and biased. In order to obtain citizenship, a person must renounce any other state citizenship. And the notion *jus sanguinis* pertaining to automatic citizenship for those of German heritage remains in force. Even though Germany has experienced large influxes of foreign people, the norm of its people and public policy makers remains that "Germany is not a country of immigration."[4] Even those Germans favoring inclusion tend to argue against full recognition of citizenship. They recommend such accommodations as "voting rights of non-citizens" and "partial civic inclusion" rather than full citizenship (Keskin, 1984). This perpetuates attitudes and encourages relationships that leave the country ill-prepared to function as a multicultural society, in spite of its many ethnic groups.

Action Must Be for All Germans

Both the old and new states, then, have serious problems to overcome if a united Germany is to become multicultural in spirit and

---

[4]*Deutschland ist kein Einwanderungsland.*

fact. However, some positive signs are appearing. Recent survey data indicate that although there is a good deal in common between East and West German youth, great differences still exist in their values, sense of optimism, and interest in each other. More than 70% of young people (13 to 29) in both the old and new states reject violence as a means of settling differences. They reject terrorist activities by an overwhelming rate of almost nine to one. Large numbers of young people sympathize with peace movements. They also have great distrust for the politicians, feeling that they do not have the people's interest at heart and simply use them for their own personal gain. They are optimistic about the future. Whereas 96% of the youth of the new states have visited the West, only 66% have taken the time to visit the new states (Kanders & Rolff, 1994).

At the school level, some good developments can be found. The Janusz-Korczak School in Altenstadt, which has 21 different nationalities represented among its 370 pupils, has a declared objective to include multiculturalism in every subject and area of their school program. Art, geography, history, their free-time program, and even eating times reflect a conscious effort to include, as far as possible, the heritages of the children in the school (Student, 1993, p. 9).

Section V

Beyond the New States of Germany

Chapter XV

A United Germany Faces the Future in a United Europe

Germany in the European Community

So far the authors have concentrated on the story of the unification of East and West Germany. While this must necessarily be the focus of attention, that drama is taking place in the context of a larger unification process, a quest for a united Europe. In 1987 the twelve member nations of the European Community passed the Single European Act, which aimed to formalize the creation of a "Europe without internal frontiers" by 31 December 1992.[1] The Act symbolized another major step toward European unity. Prior to the time the Act went into effect, The GDR had become a part of the Federal Republic of Germany, making it automatically a part of the Community. Brigid Laffan (1992) explains the consequences in the following way: "Put simply, there is a *de facto* enlargement of the Community, complicated by the fact that the economy of the GDR is not compatible with the economy of the other parts of the community." Much of its social and political structure was also incompatible.

The notions of "European unity" vary greatly. The British, for example, want as little as possible, while the Germans support a relatively high degree of integration. Commitments toward unification cluster around two major orientations. On the one hand, there are those who see unity from what Rust (1991) calls a "technocratic" perspective. That is, their commitments are reserved almost entirely for the establishment of reciprocal agreements related to employment,

---

[1]Belgium, Denmark, France, Germany, Greece, Ireland, Italy, Luxembourg, the Netherlands, Portugal, Spain, and the United Kingdom.

a common currency, reduced trade barriers, shared technology, etc. In fact, the four basic freedoms to be realized through the Single European Act are directly related to this technocratic perspective: free movement of capital, service commodity exchange, the freedom for any inhabitants to live where they wish, and the freedom to work where they desire (Schmidt, 1992). Such a point of view is not insignificant because there are impressive indications that these agreements will result in increased jobs, accelerated economic development, more stable prices, and greater trading power outside the European Community. On the other hand, there are those who argue that unity must extend beyond technocratic matters and include a more general development toward European social integration, which suggests a genuine "United States of Europe." From this vantage point, those living in a United States of Europe would be expected to have a common sense of purpose, a certain patriotic feeling, and an emotional and mental identification with being European.

Germany's role in the movement toward a united Europe has been crucial. Prior to the collapse of the Soviet Union, Germany had led the way toward a type of normalization of relations with Eastern European countries while at the same time remaining absolutely committed to Western European integration. Germany has come to exemplify the goal of trying to live in peace and cooperation both with its neighbors in the East and in the West. With regard to the European Community, Germany has pulled for a stronger integration, but it has held to a new type of federalism with the countries of the European Community. The West German vision was of a Europe that would not require individual countries to abandon their unique traditions and histories but to maintain that more can be accomplished by joining together for mutual benefit and interest.

When the Soviet block began to unravel, West Germany's role was also critical. It insisted that "Eastern Europe's nations can develop toward democracy and well-being without violent discontinuities" (Hacke, 1992, p. 79). West Germany's political tone was accepted by other Western European countries. However, the revolutionary changes taking place in Eastern Europe have disrupted the much talked-about new European order. Whereas in the past the idea had been that Europe would grow together gradually, now the joining of East and West Germany has quickened the process and Germany has become the catalyst for this new fast-paced European order (Fritsch-Bournazel, 1992).

Education has never been a direct target of the Single European Act. At the time it was passed in 1988, most Europeans felt education was not a "European issue." In fact, in a "Eurobarometer" survey in 1991 asking whether people felt various issues were best handled on a national level or a European level, only 32% of respondents indicated that education was best handled on a European level, while the majority of people felt that science and research, foreign politics, environmental protection, and currency were best handled at a European level (Eurobarometer, 1991, p. 30). However, certain aspects of education in the Single European Act, particularly regarding testing, certification, and technical standards, have been recognized as being important. They require harmonization of education at least to the point that reciprocity agreements can be reached regarding the recognition and honoring of educational and professional accomplishments and the certificates of adults and their children who move from country to country.

Most of the tangible educational programs that have been established focus directly on the technocratic side of the debate, although some deference is usually given to emotional elements of being European (Rust, 1991). Without question, the most active cooperative educational programs have occurred at the higher education level. A number of acronyms have become widely known in recent years, the two most popular are COMETT (Community in Education and Training for Technology) and ERASMUS (European Action Scheme for the Mobility of University Students). All of these programs concentrate on the exchange of students between countries; their major difference having to do with fields of study. The recent Maastricht Treaty had significant implications for further integration of higher education, mainly through the cultivation of exchanges and the recognition that university diplomas and study time required for these diplomas must be further integrated.

Some attention is being given in Germany to a European orientation at the secondary level. A major barrier to change is the feeling on the part of many in academic schools that their secondary schools are already European oriented, mainly because they place great weight on first, second, and third foreign language learning. That is, the pupils in the *Gymnasium* learn one or two languages spoken in Europe. In addition, secondary programs systematically expose their pupils to some other culture through direct experience. Almost 80% of all *Realschulen* and *Gymnasien* in the old states of Germany have formal partnerships with comparable schools somewhere outside Germany. These partnerships involve regular exchange of pupils, letters between pupils, and information. France is the most popular country for such partnerships, although strong relations also exist with the United States and Great Britain. In the 1980s great strides were made in making contact with schools in Italy and Spain (Baumert and Others, 1990, p. 103).

In vocational education, considerable progress has been made toward more universal training and competence standards. However, progress is generally seen at the large and multinational enterprises, while the small and medium-sized firms remain fixed in local ways. The most important aspect of the newer developments is a recognition that general and vocational requirements in some areas of Europe must be upgraded to become more equivalent to requirements in countries such as Germany (Schaumann, 1993).

To this point almost no attention has been given to the curricular implications of unification for primary school pupils. This is the clearest indication that schooling remains largely focused on national interests.

As further steps are taken toward a united Europe, education has begun to take a more central role. Article 126 of the Maastricht Treaty on a European Union, signed on 7 February 1992, specifically states that the European Community shall be aimed at:

- developing a European dimension in education...;
- encouraging mobility of students and teachers...;
- promoting cooperation between educational establishments;
- developing exchanges of information and experience on issues common to the education system of the Member States;
- encouraging the development of youth exchanges and of exchanges of socio-educational instructors;
- encouraging the development of distance education.

However, those signing the treaty hedged on a psychological commitment for a united Europe. In Article 128, they stress that the intention of the treaty is to "contribute to the flowering of the cultures of the Member States, while respecting their national and regional diversity and at the same time bringing the common cultural heritage to the fore." That is precisely the position taken by educational policy makers in West Germany, who maintain that cultural life belongs to regions and nations, while economic and political structures should be supranational. Because schooling is largely within the cultural sphere, Germans agree that it ought to remain largely specific to nations.

Certain common European values and cultural aspects ought to be re-emphasized throughout Europe. In Germany, Wolfgang Mickel (1992, p. 252) suggests that a set of "minimum common foundation values" might include peace, justice, international cooperation, common heritage, personal and political freedom, and the rule of law and democracy. In Great Britain, Martin McLean (1992) has attempted to translate some of this into curricular possibilities, but he concludes that the multiplicity of traditions and orientations dictate an allegiance to local and even traditional school-based instructional processes and curriculum. The types of governments and institutions that convey values and the aims of these governments and institutions are diverse. They include the highly centralized state, the federated state, and the confederated state, and reflect the presidential model, the dual parliamentary model, the monarchy, and so forth. At the higher education level, Germans appear to be committed to an internationalization of scientific research activities (Schaumann, 1993).

Klaus Schleicher (1992, pp. 304-8), suggests that the content of school curricula will inevitably be decided at the national level, although some attention will be given to specific European dimensions. However, he maintains that as the European Community grows in institutional unity, some harmonization of national and regional interests will evolve naturally and voluntarily. The consequent outcome of a United Europe will not be a Europeanization of the various educational systems. Rather, the goal will likely be toward greater openness to contacts and exchange, to flexibility, and to receptivity. In this way, the various state systems will not remain alien to those whom the schools are intended to help, but they will at the same time serve as a bridge to mutual understanding, to greater appreciation, and ultimately to an unforced sense of being European.

While West Germans have taken a cautious and open position with regard to their role in the European Community, they remain the most important voice in the European Community. Historical events during the twentieth century related to German militarism and hegemonic ambitions have raised concerns about abuses they could exercise as a dominant partner in the European Community. The unification of East and West Germany tend to exacerbate these concerns because a unified Germany promises to become even more dominant than West Germany alone would have been.

Most experts of the German scene, however, feel that the Germany of today has little resemblance to the country that produced National Socialism, two world wars, and attempts to exterminate an entire race of people. We agree with Wolf D. Gruner (1992, p. 61), who observes:

> They know of the fears still prevailing among their neighbors that they might attempt a German Europe once again, maybe this time by other means. Thus, they will do their best to become good and reliable European Germans, working for the European ensemble.

Such a tragic legacy appears to have been a good teacher. Germans appear to have learned from their own history, and they have shown extraordinary constraint in the way they have worked with their neighbors. However, the question remains whether Germans will be able to resolve differences among themselves.

Dual Unification

In recent years the old Federal Republic of Germany has been engaged in unification at two levels. They have joined together with the former German Democratic Republic and at the same time they have participated as willing and active leaders in a movement toward a unified Europe. One might expect a consistent point of view with regard to the two unification processes. Curiously, the West German political leaders appear to behave in a contradictory manner. On the one hand, they have espoused unification of Europe through a process of mutual respect and cooperation, emphasizing technical arrangements while insisting that the cultural integrity of each nation state be respected. On the other hand, they have let unification of the two Germanys take place by the complete capitulation of the former German Democratic Republic. While they have supported economic and political unification coupled with cultural diversity and local choice in Europe, they have demanded that East Germans conform to West German cultural norms. Schooling is a primary case in point. Even though West Germany is a federated system and proclaims that it tolerates educational diversity, the West German political leaders insisted as a condition of unification, that nearly all agreements concerning education made by the old states be accepted by the five new states. Unfortunately, the post-*Wende* period was such a time of confusion, that East Germans reflected too little on the implications of these conditions before agreeing.

Another study could be devoted to analyzing the approach of West German political leaders, but a few simplistic observations may be in order. An explanation for West German politicians' different behavior toward East Germany and Western Europe lies in two tightly intertwined beliefs. The first being that West Germans believe East Germany is not a separate culture, that Germany is a unified whole that was temporarily divided and is now put back to its natural configuration. The second being the belief that old East German political and economic structures were so corrupt that it was necessary to clean house and start over.

On closer examination, though, East Germans had not only moved sharply away from West Germany in their political and economic systems, but they had also developed their own culture. Lynne Chisholm and her colleagues (1990) have made the following observation regarding youth in East Germany, but it holds for the entire population:

> ...East and West Germany have been moving in different directions *culturally* [their italics] as well as economically over the past decades. Young people in the GDR cannot be regarded primarily as 'deprived' versions of their western neighbors, as simplistic analyses might suggest, even though they would wish greater and freer access to elements of western consumer and youth lifestyles.

While Chisholm rejects the deprivation theory, Peter Schneider (1990) rejects the refrigeration theory, which suggests that the real German in the East Germans has been in kind of deep freeze for the past forty years, waiting to be thawed. This view also suggests that all the elements of Marxism and communism were just patched onto the East Germans, but when they were warmed, all of that would fall away like old snow.

Immediately following the *Wende,* the euphoria of the time demanded that East and West come together like separated lovers. Studies even appeared to confirm such a phenomenon. Psychology professor, Peter Becker, from the University of Trier, for example, selected a representative sample of East Germans just one month after the *Wende*, and he gave them a battery of psychological tests dealing with self identify, behavioral tendencies, and the ability to overcome emotional and physical stress. He concluded that there is a "relationship of the souls in East and West" because the outcomes indicated greater commonality with West German findings than differences. Becker downplayed the differences: East Germans tended toward the need for greater order and a normative orientation, they placed greater worth on having a set of principles that guides their life, they were more dependable in interactions with others, they were more future oriented, they based their decisions on rational choices, and they saved more and were less wasteful (Degen, 1991).

Serious cultural differences between the two Germanys showed up immediately. The Germans in the East and the Germans in the West had each been molded by their political cultures, their living conditions, their economic systems, and their own media. These experiences created quite different identities and ideals that would be hard to reconcile. In July, 1992, for example, Berlin residents were asked in a survey about the degree of political, economic and cultural integration in the two Berlins. The consensus in both parts of the city was that economic and political integration was more advanced than cultural integration. Only 13% of West Berliners felt cultural integration was completely or primarily accomplished, while 35% said there had been no integration. In East Berlin only 11% of the East Berliners believed cultural integration was completely or primarily accomplished, while 43% said there had been no integration. A shocking 64% claimed Berlin was not yet a unified city, while only 7% believed it had been unified (Bauschke, 1992, p. 5). Within a year after formal unity, it was clear to almost everyone that Germany was not only divided in spirit but did not even want the unity offered by the Unification Treaty. In fact, German intellectuals said that they identified less with being German than with being Europeans, as if such identity would resolve the differences between the two Germanys (e.g., Schmidt, 1991). Friedrich Schorlemmer (1991), co-founder of Democratic Awakening describes unification in picturesque terms:

The West Germans had to take us. And we gladly allowed ourselves majority-wise to be swallowed whole. Now we lie rather heavily in the stomach of the well-nourished and groomed Federal Republic -- with heavy metals, asbestos-palaces, rooted landscapes, *kaputt* cities, *Stasi*-snares that reach all the way to Bonn, and with broken down unsalable factories. Now it's a question of digestion. Cramps are unavoidable. For many it is a gall-bladder attack.

Today, the differences between East and West Germans do not appear to be diminishing. Thomas Gensicke (1992) surveyed East Germans in May 1990, October 1990, and again in October 1991, and he found a remarkable stability in values related to family, children, the environment, tolerance, and money. However, he also found a drop in collegiality and politics, which is understandable in view of the conditions under which East Germans were expected to survive.

Attitude differences between the two states regarding schooling appear to be accentuating. The Institute for Research of School Development conducted a survey of attitudes toward education in 1991 and again in 1993 and found a growing reluctance among East Germans to accept the West German school model and a growing sentiment to restore a form of the old unified school, without the ideological press of the old German Democratic Republic POS. Only 19% of East German respondents in November 1993 favored the school system that has been imposed on the East Germans (Kanders & Rolff, 1994, p. 6).

Emphasis has been placed here on the mistakes West Germany made in the unification process. The curious thing we find is that most demands made by the West Germans would have been unnecessary. The East Germans, of their own volition, had chosen much of the West German educational model shortly after the collapse of the East German regime. The error made by the West Germans was that they failed to recognize this choice. In essence they insisted that the East Germans hadn't the capacity to change themselves and that

change must be imposed upon them. Because of that patriarchal attitude, East Germans take little responsibility for the situation in which
they find themselves, claiming they are not responsible for what now
exists.

It would be futile to dwell on blame for the present situation; the
main issue making positive what is now negative. The authors of this
volume maintain that a major responsibility lies with the East Germans themselves if something productive is to come from the experiences of the past four years. Only through their own efforts will they
satisfy their own ideals. To mourn for what might have been, to cling
to the old system and ideology, to resist change and hold rigidly to
the old forms would all be unproductive. Equally fruitless would be
to accept without question the West German life-style and values.
East Germans cannot adopt a new life-style that alienates them from
their own past. Trying to conform to an external standard that they
do not fully comprehend would hamper their ability to create and
mold.

The above message is especially critical for teachers to understand. They do a disservice to their pupils by romanticizing the past
or the unquestioned value of an alien system. If the East Germans are
going to transform their education, they must reject the tendency to
move backward or to accept uncritically what has been thrust upon
them. They must adapt and adjust, certainly, but that includes utilizing the good from the old system, from West Germany, and from
other cultures as well. In addition, they must learn to appreciate that
which was good in their past and be willing to share this with their
fellow Germans in the old states. The transformation will require
constant effort and the journey will never be finished.

NEW FORMULATION OF THE SCHOOL LAW OF THE STATE OF SAXONY-ANHALT

June 30, 1993

PART ONE: General Provisions
Section I: Scope and Mission of Education
1: The mission of education

(1) The mission of the school will be determined through the Basic Education Law of the Federal Republic of Germany and the constitution of the state of Saxony-Anhalt. In particular, all young people have the right, without regard to their origin or economic situation, to education and training appropriate to their talents, capabilities, and interests. This includes preparing them to take on the responsibilities and duties and to observe the rights related to state and society.

(2) In fulfilling this mission, the school is especially obliged to:

1. educate students to respect the worth of people; to think for themselves but, at the same time, remain responsive to the rights of others to think differently; to recognize and hold ethical values; to respect religious differences; to use their freedom in a responsible manner; and maintain an attitude of peace,

2. prepare students to take political and social responsibility defined by the fundamental principles of a free democracy,

3. impart knowledge, competencies, and proficiencies with the aim of allowing the free unfolding of the personality and talents and to encourage pupils in self-responsible behavior and a willingness to achieve,

4. qualify the pupils with the capacity to be aware, to judge, and to make decisions in an information society of new media and new communication techniques,

5. prepare students to meet the challenges of vocation and work, public life, family, and leisure time,

6. impart knowledge, capabilities, and values which advance equality of the sexes and mutual respect,

7. make pupils capable of behaving responsibly in regard to health, nature, and the environment,

8. help pupils become more tolerant of cultural diversity and more

understanding of others, as well as to be more cognizant of the meaning of the homeland (*Heimat*) in a unified Germany and a united Europe.

(3) Within the scope of feasibility, the school will consider the individual learning requirements and needs of pupils and in this way improve their chance for success.

(4) In fulfilling this educational mission the schools must observe the constitutional right of parents to determine the education of their children.

(5) The state and the communities (*Kommunen*) will take responsibility for providing an adequate and multi-faceted public school system. Under the terms of this school law, the state encourages schools under private sponsorship.

2: Scope

(1) This law is valid for public schools, and to the degree that other laws are not in force, for schools under private sponsorship in the state of Saxony-Anhalt.

(2) Public schools, according to this law, are those named in # 3, whose sponsors are the counties (*Landkreise*), the communities (*Gemeinden*) or the state. They are public institutions without legal autonomy.

(3) Schools under private sponsorship, according to this law, are the schools whose sponsors are natural persons or legally constituted bodies or religious or ideological organizations that have the rights of a public law corporation and whose legal relationships are determined in accordance with the provisions of Part One, Section III.

Section II: Division of the School System
3: Division of the school system

(1) The school system is divided into school types and divisions.

(2) The school types are:

1. General education schools
   a. primary school,
   b. secondary school with the differentiated promotion stage (*Förderstufe*), main school track (*Hauptschulbildungsgang*) and secondary general school track (*Realschulbildungsgang*),
   c. *Gymnasium* (college preparatory track),
   d. special education school (*Sonderschule*),
   e. schools of the second educational path (*Schulen des zweiten*

Bildungsweges): evening secondary school, evening *Gymna-sium.*

2. Vocational preparatory schools (*Berufsbildende Schulen*),
    a. vocational school (*Berufsschule*),
    b. special vocational school (*Berufsfachschule*),
    c. promotion type vocational school (*Berufsaufbauschule*),
    d. technical school (*Fachschule*),
    e. advanced technical school (*Fachoberschule*),
    f. specialized *Gymnasium* (*Fachgymnasium*).

(3) The school divisions are:

1. The primary division, which comprises forms 1 through 4,
2. The secondary division I, which comprises forms 5 through 9 in the *Gymnasium*; otherwise through form 10; and the evening secondary school,
3. The secondary division II, which includes forms 10 through 12 in the *Gymnasium*; otherwise forms 11 and 12; the vocational preparatory schools, the evening *Gymnasium*, and the *Kolleg*.

4: The primary school

(1) Pupils in forms 1 through 4 are instructed in the primary school.

(2) Through a common course of education, the primary school imparts basic knowledge and skills to its pupils and helps them develop their various capabilities. Methods of instruction include, but are not limited to, elements of play.

(3) Parents of children completing form 4 will receive a recommendation from the school for the choice of their children's continued type of schooling.

(4) A preparatory class (*Vorklasse*) may be established in a primary school for children who have reached the compulsory age of attendance but who are not yet ready for form 1. This class shall develop their readiness for school.

(5) A primary school has at least one complete sequence of forms.

5: The secondary school

(1) Pupils in forms 5 through 9 or 10 are instructed in the secondary school.

(2) In forms 5 and 6 of the secondary school (differentiated orientation stage), pupils are assisted in their individual capabilities and introduced to the focal points of learning and to the learning challenges of extended schooling. Instruction within the individual subjects should take

place in differentiated groupings. Parents of children completing form 6 will receive a recommendation from the school for choosing the main school track (*Hauptschulbildungsgang*), secondary general school track (*Realschulbildungsgang*), or university preparatory track (*Gymnasium*).

(3) After form 7 in the secondary school, pupils will either follow a secondary general school track or a main school track.

1. The main school track comprises forms 7 through 9. It imparts a fundamental general education, offers vocational guidance, and leads to vocational qualifications. Its curriculum is tailored specifically to pupils in whom the focal point of their abilities and accomplishments is characterized by concrete thinking and a practical· approach to things. In connection with vocational qualifications, training and supplemental vocational or educational qualifications, the main school track can lead to entry into preparation for advanced vocational qualifications and to higher education qualifications. The qualifying main school leaving certificate is earned through examination and authorizes attendance of form 10 of the secondary general track.

2. The secondary general school track comprises forms 7 through 10. It imparts a general and vocationally oriented education which is the basis for practicing a vocation that requires a complete vocational training and is suited to coping with practical and advanced theoretical challenges. With supplemental vocational or academic qualifications, the secondary general school track can lead to a specialized higher education qualifying certificate (*Fachhochschulreife*) or a higher education qualifying certificate (*Hochschulreife*). The secondary general school track leaving certificate (*Realschulabschluß*) is earned by examination.

(4) Graduation from the main school track as well as from the secondary general school track enables pupils to continue their education in the vocational area. By submitting certain completed work (advanced secondary general school leaving certificate (*erweiterter Realschulabschluß*), pupils in the secondary general school track have the right to enter the specialized *Gymnasium* or form 10 of the *Gymnasium*.

(5) The secondary school will have at least two complete sequences of forms; school authorities can allow exceptions if the number of pupils in a particular secondary general school track falls short of the determined minimum for setting up a class. Then, with permission of school authori-

ties, these pupils can be instructed in an overlapping type of schooling that provides differentiated school leaving examinations.

6: *Gymnasium*

(1) Pupils of forms 5 through 12 are instructed in the *Gymnasium*.

(2) The *Gymnasium* offers an in-depth general education that qualifies pupils to continue their education at an institution of higher learning. With permission of the Ministry of Education, a school can place instructional emphasis on certain subjects.

(3) Forms 10 through 12 comprise the advanced levels. Form 10 is the introductory phase. In forms 11 and 12 (*Kursstufe*) instruction will be divided into that taught to the class as a whole and that taught in specialized groups.

(4) The *Gymnasium* is concluded with a leaving exam (*Abitur*). In certain subjects, written examinations will have particular topics, which are defined by authorities at the state level.

(5) The *Gymnasium* will have at least three form sequences; however, school authorities may grant exceptions for two form sequences.

(6) The Ministry of Education is authorized through ordinance to regulate the specifics of carrying out Items 2 and 3.

7: Schools of the second educational path

(1) The evening school (evening secondary school, evening *Gymnasium*) is for employed individuals who need evening instruction that leads towards a main school or secondary general school leaving certificate or the *Abitur*.

(2) The *Kolleg* is a type of school which leads to the *Abitur* for adults who have already proved themselves in an occupation.

(3) The Ministry of Education is authorized to withdraw any ordinance relating to schools of the second educational path.

8: Special education schools

(1) Pupils of all forms can be taught in special education schools. The goal of these schools, which are based on rehabilitation-oriented influences, is individual, developmentally effective, future-oriented, and kindly assistance to children who are given to their care. Specific therapy-oriented instructional strategies can be applied according to handicap. With the agreement of the Ministry of Education, special education schools can be offered with certain emphases in curriculum.

(2) Pupils who attend special education schools are those impaired in one or several functions. In addition, they are not able to be assisted ade-

quately through special help in other types of schools, and for this reason require special instructional support for an extended period. Depending on individual preconditions, all general education leaving certificates can be earned through special education schools.

(3) In particular, special schools are schools for:

a. the blind and visually handicapped,
b. the deaf,
c. the hearing handicapped,
d. the physically handicapped,
e. the learning handicapped,
f. those needing speech therapy,
g. those requiring support classes, and
h. the mentally retarded.

(4) At special education schools, preparatory classes and residential homes for pupils can be established. According to need, before and after school care can also be offered. Special schools can also be set up as day schools. Approval is given by the Ministry of Education.

(5) At special education schools, pupils with different kinds of handicaps can be instructed together if a better pedagogical advancement of the handicapped pupils can be expected.

(6) Special education schools can work together with other general education and vocational training schools. This applies especially for programs where handicapped pupils are integrated into regular courses.

(7) Special education guidance centers (*Beratungsstellen*) can be established at special education schools. These provide support in early assistance, in intraregional social pedagogical services, and aid in the combined instructing of normal and handicapped pupils.

(8) With permission of the Ministry of Education, a preschool for children not of compulsory age can be set up at special education schools.

(9) The Ministry of Education is authorized through ordinances of the enrollment laws (*Aufnahmevoraussetzungen*) to regulate the design of this type of schooling as well as regulate the leaving requirements.

9: Vocational preparatory schools

(1) Vocational preparatory schools offer vocational training and expand already acquired general knowledge. They confer vocational or general leaving certificates and entitlements. These vocational preparatory schools contribute continuing and further vocational training.

(2) Within the dual system framework of vocational training, the vo-

cational school (*Berufsschule*) has the responsibility to train and educate pupils for a specific vocation. In so doing, requirements of practical training in firms and of vocational practice will be taken into consideration. The vocational school program is divided into general education and specialized training. The lower level lasts one year and normally is given in related blocks of instruction, either part- or full-time. In addition to this, the possibility exists of completing a voluntary vocational basic training year (*Berufsgrundbildungsjahr*) with full-time instruction in related areas. A year-long, full-time vocational preparation course of instruction can also precede the apprenticeship year. Depending on budget considerations, the state may cover the cost of board and room in the implementation of block instruction.

(3) In the course of one or more years of specialized vocational training in full-time schools, and in accordance with their type of school leaving certificates, pupils will be introduced to one or more occupations or will be trained in one occupation. In the specialized vocational school, pupils will also acquire school leaving certificates that allow them, depending on the leaving certificate of their particular educational path, to continue in other schools of the secondary division II.

(4) During or following vocational training, the promotion-type vocational school (*Berufsaufbauschule*) offers pupils general and theoretical education that go beyond that of the vocational school. After successfully attending the promotion-type vocational school together with the acquiring of the vocational leaving certificate (*Berufsabschluß*), pupils are granted a school leaving certificate that allows them, depending on the leaving certificate of their particular educational path, to continue in other secondary division II schools.

(5) Depending on their school leaving certificates and after vocational training or adequate and relevant practical occupational experience, the technical school (*Fachschule*) offers pupils with more in-depth continuing vocational education. In the technical school, pupils may also earn school leaving certificates that qualify them, depending on the leaving certificate of their educational path, to continue in other schools of the secondary division II or at an advanced technical school (*Fachoberschule*).

(6) In the advanced technical school, pupils with the secondary general school leaving certificate (*Realschulabschluß*) or the equivalent will be instructed:

1. without vocational training in forms 11 and 12,
2. after vocational training in form 12.

The advanced technical school enables pupils to have a technical emphasis in their education that makes it possible for them to continue their education at a specialized institution of higher learning (*Fachhochschule*).

(7) In the specialized *gymnasium* (*Fachgymnasium*), pupils who have gained entrance to form 10 will have instruction for three years. The specialized gymnasium offers pupils an in-depth general education with vocational emphases that qualifies them to continue their educational path at an institution of higher education (*Hochschule*). The specialized *gymnasium* terminates with the *Abitur*. In certain subjects, written examinations will be given which will be defined by authorities at the state level.

(8) Handicapped pupils with special needs may be instructed in their own classes or in their own schools.

(9) The Ministry of Education is empowered through ordinances of the enrollment laws to regulate the design of this educational path as well as the possible leaving certificates and their entitlements.

10: Framework and time-table

(1) The Ministry of Education determines the framework guidelines for goals, content, procedure, and organization of instruction which

1. ensures the fulfillment of the educational mission of the schools,
2. is in accord with the findings of pedagogical research,
3. takes into account parents' rights and the various possibilities of upbringing in family and school,
4. contributes to healthy physical, intellectual, and emotional development in children and youth.

(2) The Ministry of Education will publish the formal curriculum plan, in which, above all, the instructional subjects, their scope, and the designation of required or elective will be determined.

(3) Before publication of the framework guidelines, the Ministry of Education will inform the regional legislature (*Landtag*) in a timely manner regarding the plan and decision of the state department of education (*Landesschulbeirat*).

10a: Approval and adoption of instructional material

(1) Textbooks may be used in schools only if they have been approved by the Ministry of Education. They will be approved if they are compatible with the framework and are not contrary to legal provisions. Approval can also be denied if acquisition is not economically justifiable.

(2) The school will decide on the adoption of an approved text and other instructional materials used by that school.

11: School experiments

(1) Experiments may be undertaken for further development of school types and for trial of new pedagogical and organizational concepts.

(2) Experiments must have the permission of the regional school authorities.

12: Establishment of full-day schools, extra-curricular activities

Extra-curricular educational offerings exist at schools. The setting-up of these must have the approval of the school authorities. A prerequisite for approval is that material and personnel requirements exist.

13: The merging of schools

(1) With the approval of the Ministry of Education, in exceptional cases, school sponsors can merge schools organizationally. The merged schools must be organized to correspond with the school types. Schools of different divisions as well as different types can be merged.

(2) With permission of the Ministry of Education, in special cases, school sponsors can establish and maintain secondary schools with only a main school track or a secondary general school track (in accordance with # 3, Item 2, Point 1b).

(3) In the case where minimum numbers of pupils in certain subjects are not met, instruction in those subjects can be given in groups that extend through several forms.

(4) Enrollment in a school can be cut off when it can be determined that the number of enrolles is lower than the minimum number required for the establishing of a class.

Section III: Schools under Private Sponsorship

14: Relationship to the public school system

(1) Schools under private sponsorship work in conjunction with public schools in fulfilling the mission of education as outlined in Article 28 of the State Constitution (*Landesverfassung*) and Article 7, Sections 4 and 5 of the Basic Law of the Federal Republic. They are subject to state control. Cooperation between recognized schools under private sponsorship and public schools is to be aided and encouraged.

(2) School organization, especially the determination of a particular pedagogical, religious, or ideological character, is the duty of the private sponsors. The determination of instructional methods and curriculum as

well as the organization of instruction may also deviate from public school regulations, as far as they do not state otherwise.

15: Designation of schools under private sponsorship

Schools under private sponsorship must be designated in such a way that they cannot be confused with public schools. Schools under private sponsorship are to be termed alternative schools (*Ersatzschulen*) (# 16) or schools of further education (*Ergänzungschulen*) (# 18b). An additional type of school is permissible if it is allowed or recognized by the state.

16: Alternative schools

(1) Schools under private sponsorship are termed alternative schools if their educational goals correspond to public schools as described in Section II. Their internal and external organization can deviate from requirements placed upon similar public institutions if, all told, the organization is regarded as equivalent.

(2) They may be established and operated only with the prior permission of school authorities.

(3) Permission must be granted when

1. the school is not inferior to state schools in instructional goals and organization, as well in the academic training of its teachers.
2. segregation of pupils according to the material circumstances of their parents is not encouraged, and
3. the economic and legal position of the teaching staff is sufficiently guaranteed.

(4) Whoever would like to establish, operate or lead a school in private sponsorship under the provisions of the school law must offer a guarantee that he will hold to the constitutional rules.

(5) Permission may be recalled if one of these prerequisites is not met.

17: Recognized alternative schools

(1) An alternative school that, upon application, ensures consistent compliance with the terms of approval is to be given the status of recognized alternative school. This is to be conferred after three years of uninterrupted operation. Recognition must be given in writing. This will state the type of the school and the special course of study (*Fachrichtung*) that has been endorsed.

(2) Recognition can be granted before the end of the three-year time period in # 1, if public interest is served or if a school sponsor has already met the terms of approval in another school in the state of Saxony-Anhalt.

(3) Recognized private alternative schools are obliged to abide by regulations applicable to public schools or state approved decisions, especially concerning enrollment and transfer of pupils as well as the administration of examinations. A deputy from the school authorities will supervise the administration of leaving examinations. As a stipulation of recognition, alternative schools are given the right to give school credits and marks that have the same validity as those given in public schools. Upon application, the right to organize secondary leaving or *Abitur* examinations can be limited.

(4) The Ministry of Education is empowered by ordinance to regulate the specifics of the terms for approval and recognition, in particular and including the factual findings which lead to the recall of the approval or recognition.

18: Financial aid

(1) Upon application, the state will grant to a recognized alternative school under private sponsorship financial aid to help cover day-to-day personnel and operating costs.

(2) Also receiving financial aid are alternate schools of special pedagogical significance which assure consistent compliance with the terms of approval. Aid will begin after three years of continuous operation. Financial aid can be granted before the end of the three year period if it serves the public interest.

(3) The granting of financial aid requires that the sponsor be a non-profit institution in terms of # 52 of the presently valid version of the tax regulations (*Abgabeordnung*). The claim for financial aid can no longer be in force or can expire if the school is run for profit or the attempt is made to run it for profit.

(4) State financial aid according to Item 1 will be honored only in so far as no claim is made by the institution to other public financial aid.

18a: Extent of financial aid

(1) Grants of financial aid are appropriated according to the number of pupils who attend a school, in so far as the average of the respective class numbers do not exceed those of comparable public schools by 20%.

(2) Financial aid may total 90% of the day-to-day personnel and operating costs of comparable public schools.

(3) The Ministry of Education is empowered by ordinance to regulate the requirements and arrangements for the granting of financial aid.

18b: Schools of further education

(1) Schools under private sponsorship that are not alternative schools according to # 16 are schools of further education.

(2) School authorities must be notified of the establishment of a school of further education before instruction is begun. Notification must be given of curriculum, proof of sponsorship, school organization, the educational background of the administrators and teachers, as well as the projected number of students.

(3) School authorities must be notified of each change of sponsorship and administration, each hiring of a teacher, as well as each fundamental change in school facilities. Upon hiring of administrators and teachers, proof of their educational backgrounds must be presented.

18c: Prohibition of organization or continuation

The organization or continuation of a school of further education may be prohibited by school authorities if the sponsor, administrator, a teacher, or the facility of the school does not meet requirements for the protection of pupils or the general public affected by it. This prohibition will take place if, in spite of the request of school authorities, faults are not corrected within a certain period of time.

18d: Recognized schools of further education

(1) A school of further education can become recognized if instruction is given according to the curriculum plan approved by school authorities. If the leaving examination follows officially approved test regulations, then a recognized school of further education can present leaving certificates whose occupational designation (*Berufsbezeichnung*) is annotated with the term "state recognized."

(2) School officials can authorize a recognized school of further education to free pupils from their obligation to attend public schools. Claim to financial support as described in Item 4 does not exist.

(3) The Ministry of Education is empowered by ordinance to determine the maximum numbers of pupils per class or per corresponding organizational units. No higher requirements may be set than for corresponding public schools.

(4) Recognized schools of further education can, upon application, be granted financial support depending on budget considerations. An ordinance of the Ministry of Education outlines the specifics.

18e: Granting of leave for teachers

(1) Public school teachers may, with agreement of their schools, be granted leave to teach at an alternative school for a period of up to ten

years. The leave can be termed salaried or unsalaried leave. The leave time counts as state-recognized teaching activity for these teachers.

(2) No allowance for personnel costs is granted to the alternative school for those teachers there on salaried leave.

Section IV: Religious and Ethics Instruction
19: Religious and ethics instruction

(1) Religious instruction and ethics instruction are regular subjects in public schools.

(2) Pupils must take part in either religious instruction or ethics instruction.

(3) Religious instruction is given in accordance with the principles of the religious communities. School authorities publish guidelines and adopt texts which are in agreement with the religious communities.

(4) In ethics instruction, pupils will engage in the understanding of ethical values and norms and will concern themselves with philosophical and religious questions.

(5) Instruction in these subjects is to be established as soon as the required courses are developed and trained teachers are available.

20: Review of religious instruction

The state Industrial Law (*Arbeitsrecht*) notwithstanding, religious communities have the right to determine for themselves whether religious instruction given is in agreement with their basic tenants. The specific conditions for review must be coordinated in advance with school officials.

21: Participation in religious and ethics instruction

According to # 19, Item 1, parents or guardians will determine which kind of instruction their children will take part in. After their fifteenth birthday, pupils are entitled to make this decision.

Section V: School Development Planning, School Calendar, Holidays
22: School development planning

(1) School development planning should provide the foundation for the development of a regionally balanced educational offering in the state and should also be the skeletal plan of long-range school construction. Schools under private sponsorship are also to be included in this plan.

(2) The county (*Landkreis*) and county-independent cities (*kreisfreie Städte*) will draw up school development plans for their areas, in agree-

ment with school authorities and with the communities that belong to the county. Mid-range and long-range school needs, as well as school locations, will be presented in the plans. To be specified for each school location are the available educational offerings and the physical space (districts and catchment areas) for which they are valid. Educational needs are also to be taken into consideration, which cannot be reasonably satisfied by the schools established for only one county or county-independent city.

(3) School development plans must have subject approval of the regional school authorities. They can approve parts of the physical space and content areas of the school development plans in advance. At least every two years, school development plans need to be examined and modified further. They can be modified independently if there are sufficient grounds to demand an alteration of the existing, approved school development plans. In case an educational offering is relevant for a catchment area that extends beyond the boundaries of a county or a county-independent city, and in case the school development plan doesn't provide the necessary specifications, then regional school officials, rather than failing to approve it, may act on it after a hearing with the county or the county independent city with appropriate additions or modifications.

(4) The Ministry of Education is empowered through ordinance to regulate:

1. which zoning regulations are to be applied to school locations and school catchment areas, that is, school districts,
2. what size schools or school subdivisions must be to qualify for differentiated instruction,
3. how the school catchment areas and locations of schools of a single type should be determined in relationship to each other,
4. how the formation and coordination of school development plans are to be handled,
5. which kind of descriptive and graphic representation are to be used in the school development plan.

23: School calendar and holidays

(1) The school year begins on August 1 each year and ends on July 31 of the following year.

(2) The Ministry of Education regulates school holidays. Regulation of holidays for pupils of privately sponsored schools can deviate from public schools.

PART TWO: The School Constitution
24: General information

Schools are independent in the planning and carrying through of instruction, and in educating and in administrating within the framework of state responsibility and legal and administrative regulations.

25: School decisions

School decisions will be made according to standards of the following provisions concerning administrators and conferences.

26: Position of the administrator

(1) The administrator is the external representative of the school, carries the overall responsibility for the school, manages day-to-day administrative duties, and looks after the remaining responsibilities which are not reserved for conferences. He sees to compliance with legal and administrative regulations, as well as order in the school.

(2) The administrator is chairman of the general conference (*Gesamtkonferenz*). He prepares for sessions of this conference and carries out its decisions.

(3) In pressing cases where a previous decision of the appropriate conference cannot be met, the administrator takes the necessary action. He is to inform the appropriate conference forthwith.

(4) If, according to the judgment of the administrator, a conference decision violates legal and administrative regulations, an official ordinance, or generally-recognized pedagogical principals or norms, the administrator must file an objection within three days. The objection has a delaying effect. If the conference upholds its original decision, the school administrator must turn to school authorities to settle the matter.

(5) The administrator is the superior, in the sense of # 3 of the Civil Servant Law (*Beamtengesetz*) of Saxony-Anhalt, of the teachers employed in that school.

(6) The administrator manages funds transferred to him by the sponsor, exercises domestic authority and supervision over the school site for the sponsor, and is the superior of the sponsor-employed school staff.

27: Responsibilities of the conferences

(1) The conferences organize and coordinate education and instruction within the framework of the entire school. They advise on and decide all essential concerns of the school that require collaboration of teachers, parents and pupils. Especially included are:

1. basic questions of education and instruction in the school,
2. principles of evaluation and judgment,
3. special assistance for pupils,
4. regulations for school events,
5. general rules of behavior in school,
6. standards for discipline (*Erziehung*) and order,
7. internal organization of the school (establishing the order of business and sub-committees of conferences),
8. rules for assigning instruction and for schedules,
9. important questions about working relationships with sponsors,
10. important questions about working relationships with parents,
11. decisions regarding the adoption of texts,
12. the procurement and distribution of instructional materials
13. suggestions for the arrangement and equipping of the school,
14. the distribution of budgetary funds at the disposal of the school,
15. important issues in working with external organizations (public authorities, business organizations, and associations.)

(2) The conferences must take into consideration the pedagogical freedom and responsibility of teachers (# 30, Item 1, Sentence 1).

28: Division of responsibilities of conferences

(1) The general conference (*Gesamtkonferenz*) decides all matters as described in # 27, in so far as the responsibility of a conference is not expressly stated in Items 2 and 3 following.

(2) The general conference will organize department conferences (*Fachkonferenzen*) for subjects or groups of subjects. These will make rulings, within the framework of general conference decisions, about matters that have to do exclusively with the specialized area in question.

(3) A class conference (*Klassenkonferenz*) is to be organized for each class. This will make rulings, within the framework of the decisions made by the general conference, about matters that have to do exclusively with the class or individual students belonging to that class. Especially included are:

1. collaboration of subject teachers,
2. coordination of homework,
3. evaluation of student behavior as a whole,
4. certificates, transfers, graduation, and promotion.

29: Makeup and procedure of conferences

(1) Members of the general conference with voting rights:

1. the administrator
2. the faculty
3. parent representatives and pupil representatives numbering half the conference representatives in Point 2. In schools where no pupil representation is set up, the number of parent representatives may double,

with advisory rights:

4. two representatives of the instructional support staff and supervisory staff (*Betreuungspersonal*),
5. a representative from the remaining staff,
6. a representative of the sponsor,
7. at vocational schools, two representatives, respectively, of employers and employees,
8. teacher candidates and junior teachers working at the school.

(2) Members of class conferences and specialized conferences are:

with voting rights:

1. teachers active in the respective areas,

with advisory rights:

2. in the class and specialized conferences, at least three parent representatives and three pupil representatives; their number will be decided through the general conference,
3. at vocational schools, two employer representatives and two employee representatives,
4. teacher candidates or junior teachers working in their respective areas.

(3) The Ministry of Education regulates the specific duties and procedures of conferences according to directives drawn from conference rules of procedure (*Konferenzordung*). A regulation pertains to these rules of procedure which defines the circumstances under which pupil representatives can be barred from class or specialized conferences, as well as the procedures for reducing the size of the general conference.

PART THREE: Teachers and Other Staff Members
30: General information

(1) The teacher has the right to instruct under his own responsibility and with pedagogical freedom. He is bound by legal and administrative regulations, as well as the decisions of the conferences.

(2) The teacher in public schools is in direct service to the state.

Teachers are required to impart the basic values of the constitution to the children and youth entrusted to them and stand up for the state and for a free, democratic, just, and public-minded national order.

(3) The teacher ordinarily gives instruction in the subjects and in the types of schools for which he is credentialed. In addition he is to give instruction in other subjects and types of schools if, from preparatory training or previous experience, it can be expected of him and if it is required for the orderly operation of the school. Sentence 2 is not valid regarding religious instruction.

(4) The teacher will constantly improve his teaching competency and should, outside his instruction time, also engage in necessary further education that is commensurate with his teaching credential. Offerings by the state in continuing and further education are available to teachers in recognized alternative schools as well as teachers in public schools. The Ministry of Education is empowered through regional ordinance to regulate the standards of continuing and further education.

(5) Teacher training is given in courses appropriate to different school types for

1. teacher candidates at primary schools,
2. teacher candidates at secondary schools with main school or secondary general school as a focus,
3. teacher candidates at special education schools,
4. teacher candidates at *Gymnasien*,
5. teacher candidates at vocation training schools

and consists of theoretical study in the first phase and teacher preparation in the second phase. The first and second phases of teacher training end with examinations conducted by the state testing office (*Prüfungsamt*). The Ministry of Education is empowered to regulate through ordinance the test regulations for teacher candidates as well as the leaving certificates, and to establish regulations regarding admission to teacher preparation where there is limited capacity.

31: Appointment of school administrators and their representatives

(1) The state appoints school administrators and their representatives.

(2) A teacher who is part of the school staff may be appointed as the school administrator only if special reasons warrant it.

(3) Before the appointment of the positions, school officials will try to have approval from the sponsor and the general conference. If this has

not been done within six weeks, officials make the decision. The filling of the position must be made known to the sponsor in a timely manner.

32: Other staff members

Staff members and supervisory staff employed in public schools are employed directly by the state. Other staff members are employed directly by the sponsor.

PART FOUR: Pupils

33: The right to an education

(1) The state of Saxony-Anhalt organizes and assists the educational system so that the pupils can benefit from their right to an education as completely as possible. Varying educational opportunities and talents should be addressed through special assistance to the pupils in question .

(2) In carrying out their constitutional rights, the parents and guardians support pupils by placing them in educational tracks that are appropriate to their capabilities and interests.

34: Choice of school system, transfer, and graduation

(1) Parents and guardians choose the educational track, taking into consideration the interests and capabilities of their children and the recommendation of the school.

(2) Acceptance to the secondary school II can be made dependent on the pupil's having earned a certain leaving certificate or having demonstrated occupational experience. This is not valid for acceptance into vocational school.

(3) In the secondary school division I, a pupil can change from one track to another if successful work can be expected from him.

(4) A pupil can transfer to the next highest school form only if the class conference has decided that successful work in this form can be expected (promotion). Between individual school years, exceptions to the requirements for promotions can be made. A pupil of the secondary general school track or the *Gymnasium* who hasn't been promoted twice or for two years in a row, should be transferred to another track that is more fitting. Pupils of the fifth form at the *Gymnasium* should already have been transferred if a successful participation in this track, even after one repetition, cannot be expected.

(5) A pupil of the secondary division I of the *Gymnasium*, who has been held back twice, can be transferred to a more appropriate educational path if the class conference decides that successful attendance at the *Gym-*

nasium cannot be expected. Pupils of the secondary school, who after two repetitions, again cannot be promoted, should, in as far as the full-time compulsory requirement is satisfied, be transferred to an appropriate vocational training track.

(6) Pupils can earn only the leaving certificates that are provided by the schools they have attended.

(7) Through examination, non-enrolled pupils can earn leaving certificates from general education schools and vocational training schools.

35: Rules of the educational paths (tracks)

(1) The Ministry of Education is empowered through ordinances to govern/direct:

1. admission into the schools of the secondary division I and II as well as the special education school,
2. transfers between types of schools or tracks including transfers in cases described in # 34, Items 4 and 5,
3. promotion, skipping of a form, voluntary repetition and voluntary withdrawal,
4. termination of schooling (leaving or being let go), including the longest allowable time of attending a school type or division,
5. leaving certificates and their authorization, including the leaving examination for pupils and non-pupils; in regard to this, it can be determined that a failed examination may be repeated,
6. determination of a need for special educational assistance, transference to a special education school, as well as the obligation to take part in specialized instruction (# 39, Item 1),
7. admission requirements for schools with a content emphasis approved by the Ministry of Education in accordance with # 6, Item 2, Point 2 and # 8, Item 1, Point 4.

(2) The empowerment of the content and extent of the ordinances emerge in general from the educational mission of the school (# 1) and from the duty to encourage the development of the individual pupil as well as the pupils as a whole.

PART FIVE: Compulsory Education
36: General information

(1) Attendance at a school is compulsory for all children and youth in the state of Saxony-Anhalt.

(2) This duty can be fulfilled through attendance at a public school

or an authorized school in private sponsorship. School officials may allow exceptions.

37: Beginning of compulsory education

(1) All children who will turn six by June 30, must begin school the following school year. Children who will turn five by June 30, can, by parent application, be admitted to school if they possess the required physical and intellectual prerequisites and are sufficiently developed in social relationships. When these children are accepted, then education becomes compulsory for them.

(2) As part of the decision-making process in admitting under-age children to school, examinations will be carried out by a public health doctor. To ascertain school readiness, recognized tests may be used and certificates from experts in the field may be brought in.

(3) Children within the age of compulsory education who are too physically, intellectually, and socially immature to take part successfully in instruction at the primary school, may be excused by school officials for one year from compulsory education with agreement of the parents. They may be compelled to attend preschool classes.

38: School health care

Pupils must take part in programs of school health care under the department of public health, including addiction and drug counseling.

39: Attendance at special education schools
and special education instruction

(1) Pupils who require special pedagogical considerations are for the time of their impairment to attend special education schools or special education instruction at their own schools if the special pedagogical requirement can not be met in another school.

(2) School officials decide whether the obligation according to Item 1 exists and determine, by examination procedures and a hearing with the parents, which special education school the pupils will attend or what special education instruction he should take part in. For the decision, a medical examination may be conducted, recognized testing procedures used, and certificates from experts in the field brought in.

(3) Children and youth of compulsory age who are not able to attend school because of a long-term illness, are to be given instruction at home or in the hospital to the appropriate extent.

40: Duration and end of compulsory attendance

(1) Compulsory attendance remains in effect for twelve years after it

begins.

(2) To begin with, all compulsory age pupils attend at least nine years of school in the primary division and in the secondary division I (full-time compulsory attendance).

(3) In as far as they do not attend general education schools following that, they fulfill their compulsory attendance by attendance at a vocational training school.

(4) If a pupil attends a vocational training school with full-time instruction for at least one year, his compulsory attendance is fulfilled. After conclusion of compulsory attendance, whoever begins vocational training according to the vocational education law (*Berufbildungsgesetz*) or crafts ordinance (*Handwerksordnung*), is obligated to attend the vocational school for the duration of the training.

(5) After the conclusion of compulsory school attendance, a pupil may begin a practice-based retraining in a specific vocation as defined by the work assistance law (*Arbeitsförderungsgesetz*), which is concluded by an examination according to # 34 of the vocational education law or # 31 of the crafts ordinance. The pupil is entitled to attend vocational school for the duration of the retraining requirement if material and personal costs are repaid.

(6) The time spent in civil service preparation training will be counted toward obligatory attendance at a vocational training school.

41: School districts, school catchment areas

(1) The school sponsor, with the agreement of school officials, sets the school boundaries for primary and secondary schools. A pupil must attend the school in the school district where he lives to fulfill his compulsory attendance. School officials decide exceptions.

(2) For other general education schools the sponsor can, with agreement of the school officials in regard to the goals of the school development plans, establish catchment areas. The admission of a pupil who does not live in the catchment area can be denied if no special reasons exist for admission.

42: Further rulings on compulsory attendance

The Ministry of Culture is empowered to make specific determinations regarding fulfilling compulsory school attendance, including deferments outlined in # 37, Item 3, as well as content, scope and prerequisites having to do with imparting instruction, outlined in # 39, Item 3.

43: Duties of parents and pupils

(1) Parents and guardians must see to it that pupils take part in instruction as well as other events of the school and fulfill their duty as pupils; they need to supply the pupils with the means to carry this out.

(2) Educators and their representatives must guarantee pupils the required time to fulfill their school duties, to take part in conferences, and to take part in pupil councils.

44: Disciplinary measures and provisions for keeping order

(1) If a pupil disrupts instruction, a teacher can use appropriate disciplinary measures against him.

(2) Provisions for keeping order are especially permissible if a pupil persistently disrupts instruction, refuses to conform to the required performance standards, has unexcused absences, or if it is necessary to protect people or things in the school. They are to be warned of the penalties.

(3) The provisions for keeping order are:
1. transfer into a parallel class,
2. transfer to another school of the same type,
3. suspension from instruction up to three months,
4. expulsion from all schools.

(4) The Ministry of Education is empowered to regulate the requirements and the procedures through ordinances.

PART SIX: Pupil Representation
Section VI: Pupil Representation in the School
45: General information

Pupils take part in the fulfillment of their education in schools of the secondary divisions I and II through involvement in class associations as class spokesmen, in the school council as its spokesmen, and as school representatives at conferences.

46: Class associations

Pupils of each class (class association) from the fifth form on will choose their class spokesman and his delegate, as well as the pupil representatives for the class conference.

47: School council

Class representatives make up the school council. This group elects its spokesman and one or several deputies from among themselves, as well as a pupil representative for the general conference.

48: Voting and removal

(1) The spokesman, his deputies and the pupil representatives in the conferences are elected for one year.

(2) The spokesman, his deputies and the pupil representatives in the conferences can be removed from office

1.   if they are recalled by a majority of 2/3 of the eligible voters, or
2.   if they leave their position, or
3.   if they don't attend the school anymore.

(3) Pupil representatives, who have not left the school continue in their offices for up to three months until voting is over and until new representatives are chosen.

(4) The Ministry of Education is empowered through ordinance to regulate voting and removal.

49: Participation of pupils in the school

(1) All school questions can be discussed in the class associations and student councils, as well as in pupil meetings.

(2) School council and class associations are to be attended by the school administrator or by the responsible conference when basic decisions are being made; above all when matters dealing with the organization of the school and with evaluation are being discussed. Content, planning, and organization of instruction are to be discussed with the class associations.

(3) The school council has the right to make decisions and to put proposals before the general conference. These proposals must be handled by the general conference.

(4) Administrators and teachers must give necessary information to the school council and class associations.

(5) The spokesmen represent the pupils to teachers, conferences, administrators and school officials. Pupils can entrust spokesmen and pupil representatives with the safeguarding of their interests.

(6) Pupil representatives to the conferences report to school council or to the respective class associations regularly about their activities.

(7) The school council can choose one or several advisors from among the teachers in the school.

Section II: School representations in the community and county

50: Community and county school councils

(1) A community school council will be established in communities,

and a county school council will be established within counties. In cities, the community school council will be named the city school council.

(2) The school councils within a community area will each elect one member and a representative for the community school council. If only one school exists within a community, the school council becomes the community school council. If a general education school consists of several school tracks (*Schulezweige*) (# 13, Item 2), then the school council elects one member and one representative from each school track for the community school council. Comprehensive schools (*Gesamtschulen*) elect two representatives.

(3) The school councils in schools within the district each elect one member and one representative for the county school council, commensurate with Item 2, Sentence 3.

(4) The community or the county school council chooses from among themselves one or several spokesmen.

51: Voting and removal

Members of the community or county school councils will be elected for two school years, commensurate with # 48, Items 2 to 4.

52: Responsibilities of the community and county school councils

(1) The community and county school councils can advise on questions that have special relevance to pupils in their area. Sponsors and school officials must give them necessary information and give them the opportunity to share their opinions and suggestions.

(2) The community and county school councils must be aware that the concern of everyone in the community or county needs be taken into consideration.

53: Financing of pupil representation

(1) The sponsor provides the necessary operating funds and facilities to pupil representations of individual schools (# 47) that are engaged in their duties. The sponsor offsets necessary travel costs for the members of the school council and the pupil representatives.

(2) The community and the county provide the community school councils and the county provides the county school councils with the necessary facilities and operating funds. The community or county offsets necessary travel costs for members of the school council.

(3) The Ministry of Education is empowered by ordinance to regulate the specific details of operating costs and facilities for pupil representations, as well as the allowance of travel costs.

54: Publication of pupil newspapers

(1) Pupil newspapers are newspapers that are written by pupils and published for pupils in one or several schools.

(2) Pupil newspapers may be offered on school property.

(3) Pupil newspapers exist outside the responsibility of the school and are subject to press guidelines and other general legal conditions. Pupils who publish the newspapers must adhere to these conditions.

PART SEVEN: Parent Representation
Section I: Parent Representation in the School
55: General information

(1) Parent representations are independent, self-elected or formed groups that keep parents informed about their work and interest them in working with the group to improve relationships both within and outside the school. They accept suggestions and ideas from parents, advise, and take these suggestions to the school or the school sponsor, and help the public to better understand the school instructional and educational work.

(2) Parents and guardians participate in the school through class parent groups (*Klassenelternschaften*) and as class parent representatives, through parent school council, and as parent conference representatives.

(3) In elections and voting, parents or guardians have only one vote between the two of them for each child.

56: Class parent groups and class parent representation

(1) Parents and guardians of the pupils of a class (*Klassenelternschaft*) elect the chairman and his deputy. In addition, these parents and guardians elect parent representatives for the class conference, as well as a corresponding number of deputies. Sentences 1 and 2 are not valid for classes where more than half the children are not of compulsory age.

(2) At least twice yearly, the chairman invites the parents and guardians of the class to meet and takes charge of the proceedings. A parent meeting is called if a third of the parents or guardians, the school administrator, or the class teacher ask for it. If the chairman agrees, the school administrator, teachers who are active with the class, and pupil representatives can take part in the class parent meeting.

57: School parent council

(1) The school parent council consists of the chairmen of the class parent groups.

(2) The school parent council elects the school parent council chair-

man and one or more deputies from their members, as well as the parent representative who stands in for parents at the general conference.

58: Election and removal

(1) Those who are authorized to vote and be elected are parents and guardians. Staff or administrators of the school are not eligible.

(2) Chairmen of the class parent groups and school parent council, their deputies, and parent representatives to conferences generally are elected for two school years.

(3) Parent representatives must leave office,

1. if they are recalled by a two-thirds majority of the voters, or
2. at the end of the school year in which their child is no longer of compulsory age, or
3. if they resign from their office, or
4. if their child doesn't attend the school anymore.

(4) The Ministry of Education is empowered through ordinances to regulate the voting procedure.

59: Participation of parents in the school

(1) All questions pertaining to the school can be discussed in the class parent groups and the school parent council, as well as in general parent meetings.

(2) Parent conference representatives report to the school parent council or the class parent groups regularly about their activities. The school parent council can report about its activities in general parent meetings of the school.

(3) The school parent council has the right to make decisions and to put proposals to the general conference. These proposals must then be handled by the general conference.

(4) The school parent conference and the class parent groups are to be attended by the school administrator or the responsible conference when making basic decisions; above all, concerning the organization of the school and evaluations. School administrators and teachers must share required information with them.

(5) Teachers must make the content, plans and organization of instruction known to the class parent groups. This is valid, in particular, for subjects that concern parental rights. On this point, parental rights and personal rights of pupils have to be taken into consideration. Discretion, openness, and tolerance toward different values must be shown.

(6) After arrangements are made with the school administrator and

the class advisor, it is possible for parents to sit in on instruction.

Section II: Parent Representation in Communities and Counties
60: Community and county parent councils

(1) A community parent council will be established in communities and a county parent council will be established in counties. In cities, the community parent council will be named the city parent council.

(2) The parent councils lying within a community area will each elect one member and a representative for the community school council. If only one school exists with a community, the parent council becomes the community parent council. If a general education school consists of several school tracks (*Schulzweige*) (# 13, Item 2), then the parent council elects one member and one representative from each school track for the community parent council. Comprehensive schools elect two representatives.

(3) The school parent councils in schools within the county each elect one member and one representative for the county parent council, commensurate with Item 2, Sentence 3.

(4) The community or the county parent council chooses from among themselves one or several spokesmen.

61: Voting and removal

Members of the community or county parent councils will be elected for two school years, commensurate with # 58, Items 2 to 4.

62: Responsibilities of the community and county parent councils

(1) The community and county parent councils can advise on questions that have special relevance for schools in their areas. Sponsors and school officials must give them necessary information and give them the opportunity to share their opinions and make suggestions.

(2) The community and county parent councils must be aware that the concern of everyone in the community or district must be taken into consideration.

Section III: Financing of Parent Representation
63: Costs

(1) The school sponsor provides the necessary operating costs and facilities to parent representations that are engaged in their duties. The sponsor offsets necessary travel costs for members of the parent council and for parent representatives.

(2) The community provides the community parent council and the county provides the county parent council with the necessary facilities and operating funds.

(3) The Ministry of Education is empowered by ordinance to regulate the specific details of operating costs and facilities for parent representations, as well as the allowance for travel costs.

PART EIGHT: School Sponsorship
64: School sponsorship

(1) The school sponsors must proffer school offerings and school plants to the required extent and equip them with the necessary facilities and maintain them according to specifications, as well as expand them or reduce them, in consideration of the goals of the school development plan. Required school plants that belong to an interregional catchment area may also have school residence halls, if such a need is determined by school officials and is in agreement with the sponsor.

(2) The school sponsorship entails a special sphere of activity of school sponsors. They need to provide their schools the necessary operating resources. The sponsor can name a school, with agreement of the school officials.

(3) The Ministry of Education can make recommendations concerning the extent to which school property and school structures are equipped, as well as recommendations concerning the construction of school buildings and the equipping of the schools, above all in regard to teaching and learning materials for instruction.

65: Sponsors

(1) Primary school sponsors are the communities. Before and after school child care centers can also be under private sponsorship.

(2) Sponsors of the other types of schools are the counties or county-independent cities. The sponsor of the state agricultural technical schools is the Ministry for Food, Farming, and Forests, that also exercises jurisdiction over these schools.

(3) On request of the county communities and after a county hearing, school officials can take over the sponsorship of the school, in so far as this action corresponds to the goals of the school development plan. Similarly, sponsorship can also be taken over by the communities of the county. In a case where one community in conjunction with other communities is not able to provide the necessary financial and administrative

resources to build or maintain the necessary schools, then the county is obligated to take over the sponsorship.

(4) The state can have special significance to sponsors of schools.

(5) Counties must transfer the location of a school which is in the sponsorship of the county to the communities belonging to the county, on request of the present administration of this school. The communities administer the schools in the name and at the cost of the county. The county can give directions for the performance of this task. The participants regulate the details through agreement, especially in the case of liability.

#66: Consolidation of sponsors

(1) Sponsors can come to agreement among themselves as to what constitutes the fulfilling of their individual duties.

(2) With the assent of school officials, neighboring sponsors can agree to take in students from catchment areas of another sponsor.

(3) Such agreements commensurate with Items 1 and 2 must be in harmony with the school development plan. School officials need to give their assent to these agreements.

(4) School officials can direct that outside pupils be taken in if a genuine need exists and an agreement between the sponsors cannot be reached. Outside pupils are pupils who do not have their place of residence or their living quarters in the area of the sponsor.

(5) The Ministry of Education regulates the compensation of necessary expenditures for sponsors of vocational training schools from Sachsen Anhalt for the admission of pupils who do not come from Sachsen Anhalt. The admission of such pupils necessitates permission from the Ministry of Education.

#s 67 and 68: (Deleted)

PART NINE: Meeting of Costs

#69: Personnel costs

The state carries the costs for personnel, for teachers, for instructional aides, and supervisory staff at public schools. The sponsor carries the remaining costs for personnel.

#70: Operating costs

(1) The sponsor carries the operating costs of public schools.

(2) If a school of the secondary divisions I and II is attended by outside pupils, according to #66 Items 2 and 4, or provides an residential

hall, then this sponsor is entitled to demand compensation for ensued costs from the sponsor responsible for the outside students. The Ministry of Education is empowered through ordinances to establish lump sums appropriate for the types of schools, the tracks, the school forms, and, if required, also for occupational fields and specialized subjects of the vocational training schools. Property and development costs are not to be considered in setting the costs.

(3) If the location of a primary school, whose catchment area covers several communities, is established in a certain community, then the school sponsorship is transferred to this community. The communities involved must agree how costs will be met. If they cannot come to an agreement, school officials decide.

71: Pupil transportation

(1) The county and county-independent cities are responsible for transportation costs of pupils.

(2) They are required to provide for pupils living in their area
1. general education schools through the tenth form,
2. school part of the foundation year of vocational training and the preparation year for vocational practice,
3. the first school years of the vocational technical school that do not require the general secondary school leaving certificate,

given anticipated conditions, for the nearest school of their track or educational path, or to refund the necessary expenses for school transportation to their parents.

(3) Pupils not indicated in # 2 can receive allowed costs for school transportation from the sponsor. The Ministry of Education regulates the specifics through ordinance.

(4) The counties and county-independent cities determine the minimal distance between home and school upon which the transportation or reimbursement is determined. The strength and safety of the student have to be taken into consideration. If pupils, because of a chronic or temporary handicap, must receive transportation, then the transportation or reimbursement obligation exists.

(5) The state shares the costs of pupil transportation according to the provision of the community financial law.

72: Cost of learning materials

(1) Parents should be relieved of the cost of learning materials.

(2) The Ministry of Education is empowered through ordinances to

set conditions on the kind, the extent, and the time period.

73: Advancement of school construction through the state

The state can assist sponsors, according to conditions of the state budget appropriations, with new buildings, reconstruction of buildings, and expansion of buildings, with the purchase of buildings for school purposes as well as the initial equipping of schools, in order to guarantee equal provisions of school locations.

74: Sharing of school construction costs and
setting up of a district school building fund

(1) The counties set up a county school building fund to finance school construction. It is an appropriated special purpose fund of the county. Out of it, the county and county-independent cities obtain the means to carry out the plans in # 3.

(2) The county school building fund must be raised to two-thirds of that of the county communities, if the backflow from the guaranteed loans is not sufficient. The county regulates the maximum amount.

(3) The counties guarantee from the funds of county communities:

1.   in the primary division appropriations of at least one third of the necessary costs for new buildings, reconstruction of buildings, and expansion of buildings, with the purchase of buildings for school purposes and the initial equipping of schools,

2.   in the secondary division appropriations in the amount of at least one half the necessary costs as subsidy or as an interest free loan.

74a: Other costs

For costs of pupils in the secondary division not covered under # 74, the counties guarantee the county communities allocations in the amount of 50 from one hundred as subsidy.

**PART TEN: Representation to the Ministry of Education
and the county school council
Section I: Make up and duties**
75: General information

(1) Under the Ministry of Education will be founded a state parents' council as a representation of the parents and a state pupils' council as a representation of the pupils, as well as a state school advisory board, in which those groups directly associated with the schools and those organizations and associations indirectly concerned may work together.

(2) The Ministry of Education provides the necessary personnel and

the material resources for the state parents' council. On recommendation of the state parents' council, it appoints personnel to work in their office.

(3) The Ministry of Education provides the necessary personnel and provisions for the activities of the state pupils' council.

76: State parents' council

(1) In the state parents' council will be represented parents and guardians of

1. primary schools through six members, secondary schools through six members, the *Gymnasium* through six members, and special education schools through three members,
2. vocational training schools through six members,
3. schools under private sponsorship through three members.

(2) Voting will be conducted in this manner: in each government district, two members as well as two deputy members will be elected from among the primary schools, the secondary schools, the *Gymnasien*, and also from among the vocational training schools; one member and one deputy member from among the special education schools and from among the schools under private sponsorship; one member and one deputy member from among the county parent councils and from among the parent councils of county-independent cities.

(3) The state parents' council cooperates in all important questions that touch upon matters concerning parents and pupils. The following especially pertains:

1. general decisions about training and educational goals and paths of the schools and the structure of the school system,
2. guidelines for the establishment of school locations.
3. measures to eliminate or reduce crises in the education system,
4. the decree of general guidelines for rules of behavior (# 27, Item 1, Number 5)
5. General decisions about learning materials.

The Ministry of Education puts forward related general rules to the state parents' council and discusses them in confidence and with the intent of achieving mutual understanding. This cooperation is related also to appropriate legal and ordinance proposals of the Ministry of Education.

77: State pupils' council

(1) In the state pupils' council will be represented students from

1. secondary schools through six members, *Gymnasien* through six members, and special education schools through three members,

2. vocational training schools through six members,
3. schools under private sponsorship through three members.

(2) The members of the state pupils' council will be elected according to # 76, Item Two.

(3) The state pupils' council cooperates in all important general questions of the school system, in so far as they relate to pupil interests. For other matters, # 76, Items 3 and 4 are in force.

78: State school advisory board

(1) The state school advisory board consists of

1. six teachers who are called by the Ministry of Education on the recommendation of the associations, whereby all school types are represented,
2. six parents or guardians elected by the state parents' council,
3. six pupils elected by the state pupils' council,
4. a) one representative each from schools under private sponsorship and from institutions of higher education (*Hochschulen*),
    b) two representatives of churches,
    c) two representatives from sponsors, as well as from the organization of employees and the organization of employers, who are called by the Ministry of Education on the suggestion of the appropriate organizations.

(2) The state school advisory board cooperates in all general questions that are of fundamental meaning for the school system. The Ministry of Education instructs the state school advisory board on appropriate issues and gives them the necessary information. The state school advisory board can give the Ministry of Education suggestions and stimulation. It has the opportunity to give an opinion about the laws and ordinances decreed by the Ministry of Education that have to do with the school system.

Section II: Ordinances of Procedure
79: Tenure of office, election and recall

(1) The tenure of office for pupils is two years, otherwise three years. Membership in the representations or on the state school advisory board ends as soon as an elected or called member is no longer a teacher, a parent, or a pupil or steps down from office.

(2) The Ministry of Education is empowered to regulate through ordinance the procedure of election and recall.

80: Procedures

(1) Representations and the state school advisory board will hold meetings according to need.

(2) Meetings are not public.

(3) The state parents' council and the state pupils' council elect an executive board that consists of a chairman, a deputy chairman, and up to four members.

(4) In the state school advisory board the Minister of Education or his deputy is the chairman.

81: Costs

(1) Activity in the state parents' council, state pupils' council and in the state school advisory board is honorary.

(2) Necessary costs of activities of the representation and the state school advisory board will be borne by the state.

(3) The Ministry of Education is empowered to regulate through ordinance the specific details of the allocation of operating supplies, the required facilities, as well as reimbursement of travel costs to representations and the state school advisory board.

PART ELEVEN: State school authorities
82

(1) The state has control over the school system. Planning, order and development of the school system belong to the state school authorities.

(2) Boundaries of state school authority over the schools under private sponsorship is a function of Article 7 of the Basic Law of the Federal Republic of Germany.

(3) School authorities are

1. The Ministry of Education as the top-most authority,
2. The district government as the higher authority,
3. The school supervisory offices (*Schulaufsichtsämter*) as the lower authority.

83: Duties and responsibilities

(1) School authorities must plan the development of the school system and establish and advise schools and sponsors. They must consider the advice of the school psychologists within their realm of jurisdiction.

(2) School authorities must act so that the school system is in compliance with current regulations.

(3) School authorities exercise supervision over staff and over certifi-

cated personnel. This authority should be exercised in such a way that the independence of the individual school is not impaired.

(4) The department of the state supervisory office is the employment office of the teachers.

(5) School authorities exercise authority over the administration and maintenance of the schools through the school sponsor.

(6) The state supervisory officers work together in a cooperative manner. The coordination of the internal and external offices should rotate every four years. The officers should in framework of their assigned duties make the final decisions.

PART TWELVE: Temporary and permanent regulations
84: Irregularities of order

(1) One acts contrary to order if one deliberately or carelessly
1. does not comply with compulsory school attendance,
2. in disregard of # 43, Item 1, does not encourage those of compulsory school age to attend instruction or other events of school regularly or fulfill their duty as pupils,
3. as educator in disregard of # 43, Item 2 does not encourage a pupil to fulfill his school duties or does not give him the recommended time to do this,

(2) Irregularities of order can be punished by a monetary fine.

(3) Within the meaning of the law concerning irregularities of order, responsible school administrative authorities are the counties and county-independent cities.

84a: Statistical surveys and the processing of personal data

(1) For purposes of the school administration and school authorities, school derived statistical surveys can be carried out. Sponsors, administrators, faculty, and other school employees, pupils, as well as parents and guardians, are obligated to provide information.

(2) The confidentiality in processing data drawn from individuals is maintained according to the law of 12 March, 1992 (GVB1 LSA page 152), in so far as information from Items 3 and 4 is not revealed.

(3) Schools, school authorities, school sponsors, pupil representations and parent representations may process the personal data of pupils and their parents in so far as it is useful to satisfy the educational mission and welfare responsibilities; the departments of health also have the same authorization, insofar as they observe #s 37 and 38 in their work, and the

sponsors of the pupil transportation office, insofar as they observe # 71 in their duties. Medical and psychological information may not automatically be processed.

(4) The right to information, examination of records, adjustments, sealing, or destruction of data will be carried out by the parents and guardians of minor children. Examination of records can be limited or denied insofar as it is necessary to protect a third party.

(5) The Ministry of Education is empowered by ordinance to regulate specifics concerning the kind of statistical surveys, the characteristics of the surveys, the obligation to give information, the time limitations, the deadlines, and the recurrence of the report.

85: (Deleted)

86: Linguistic equalization

Person or role designations in this law are valid in either the masculine or feminine form.

86: Transitional regulations

(1) Until a separate legal regulation for school day care centers is adopted, the following will be in effect for primary schools: In the school day care center, parents who wish their children to have day care, may receive it before and after school. A day care center is a part of every primary school.

(2) On application the school sponsor receives a state grant to be used for pedagogical personnel in residential homes of special education schools (# 8, Item 4), to the degree that these personnel costs had been previously carried by the state. The grant will be guaranteed for up to two years. It consists of 60% of the gross salaries in the first year after the taking effect of this law, and 40% in the second year.

(3) Deviating from # 65, Item 1, the county community sponsorships are only for primary schools until 30 June, 1995.

87: (The taking effect)

Bibliography

1. POS. 1990. Schwischenbericht zum Projekt: Äußere Differenz-
   ierung. DIPF. 1989b. BBF/Archiv. APWA. Sign.: 1234, Reg.
   11.438.
2. POS. 1990. Zur Neuprofilierung der Schule - Überlegungen der
   Fachgruppe Schulmodell für das Leistungsangebot ab Schuljahr
   1990/91. DIPF. 1989b. BBF/Archiv. APWA. Sign.: 1234, Reg.
   11.438.
5. POS. 1990. Konzeption zur Entwicklung der 5. Oberschule
   'Mathias Thesen,' dated 6 June 1990.
12. POS. 1990. A file of documents including memos, proposals,
    and letters of the 12. POS in Blenheimstr. 53 in Berlin-Marzahn.
25. POS. 1989. Diskussionsangebot zur weiteren Arbeit im Berich
    Volksbildung. Draft dated Dec. 19, 1989 under the signatures of
    Koll. Beyer, Koll. Rudolph & Koll. Westphal (Director).
28. POS. 1990. A file of documents including memos, proposals,
    and letters of the 28. Karl-Grünberg Oberschule in Berlin-
    Köpenich.
30 Jahre Pionierorganisation 'Ernst Thälmann.' 1978. Berlin: Ver-
    lag Junge Welt.
32. POS. 1990. Konzeption zur Profilierung der 32. Oberschule
    'Arthur Pieck.' Beginn Schuljahr 1990/91, dated June in Berlin.
37. POS. 1990. Schulprojekt der 37. Oberschule Berlin-Hohen-
    schönhausen, dated May. DIPF. 1989b. BBF/Archiv. APWA.
    Sign.: 1234, Reg. 11.438.
Abusch. 1966. Our Educational System Corresponds to the National
    Mission of the German Democratic Republic. In *Education and
    Training in the German Democratic Republic*, a publication of
    the Government of the German Democratic Republic. Berlin:
    Staatsverlag der Deutschen Demokratischen Republik, pp. 7-31.
Adl-Amini. B. 1976. *Schultheorie: Geschichte, Gegenstand, und
    Grenzen.* Weinheim: Beltz.

APW. 1983. *Pädagogik.* Berlin: Volk und Wissen.

Alt, Robert. 1946. Zur gesellschaftlichen Begründung der neuen Schule. *Pädagogik* 1, pp. 12-28.

Ansorg, L. 1968. *Kinder im Ehekonflikt,* nr. 69 of pamphlet series *Elternhaus und Schule.*

Anweiler, Oskar. 1990. Die 'Wende' in der Bildungspolitik der DDR. *Bildung und Erziehung* 43, nr. 1, pp. 97-107.

APW. 1989. Proposal for Discussion regarding a Changed Content Conception for History Discussion in the Classes 8 to 10 in the Schoolyear 1990/91. Memo, dated December 1989, under the name of H. Iffert from the Research Group in History of the APW.

APW. 1989. Unpublished document, dated 6 December 1989, entitled Auswertung der Aushänge an den Wandzeitungen der AP-W/BPO von Mitte Oktober bis 30.11.1989.

APW. 1990. Memo from Rolf Hanisch & Gisela Weiß to the Leadership of the APW dated 25.6.1990.

APW. 1990. Memo from Rolf Hanisch & Gisela Weiß to the Leadership of the APW dated 27.6.1990

APW. 1990. Unpublished document, dated March, 1990, entitled Erste Überlegungen in Richtun der Entwicklung dines komplexen Projektvorschlages 'integrierte Gesamtschule,' from the Institut für Didaktik, authored by Hilbrich/Walter/Westphal at the APW.

Babing, Heide. 1990. Von der Differenzierungsforschung zur Entwicklung eines Schulmodells der Humboldt-Universität in Berlin-Marzahn. *Gesamtschul-Information* 3/4.90, pp. 49-63.

Babing, Heide. 1990. Europäische Friedensschule--Eine Vision? *Deutsche Lehrerzeitung* nr. 33 (August/September), p. 7.

Bachmeier, Christine & Fischer, Thomas. 1992. *Wer sind die Deutschen?* Frankfurt a/M: Alexander Horn Verlag neues Forum.

Banathy, Bela H. 1988. Matching Design Methods to System Type. *Systems Research* 50, nr. 1, pp. 27-34.

Banks, James A. 1988. *Multiethnic Education: Theory and Practice* Boston: Allyn & Bacon.

Basic Law for the Federal Republic of Germany, officially proclaimed on May 23, 1949.

Baske, Siegfried. 1990. Die erweiterte Oberschule in der DDR. In Anweiler, Oskar & Others. *Vergleich von Bildung und Erziehung in der Bundesrepublik Deutschland und in der Deutschen Demokratischen Republik.* Köln: Verlag Wissenschaft und Politik, pp. 210-217.

Bathke, G.-W. 1990. Sozialstruktur - Soziale Herkunft - Persönlichkeitsentwicklung. In Timmermann, H. (ed.). *Sozialstruktur und sozialer Wandel in der DDR.* Saarbrücken.

Baumert, Gerhard, & Hunniger, Edith. 1954. *Deutsche Familien nach dem Kriege.* Darmstadt: E. Röther.

Baumert, Jürgen. & Others. 1990. *Das Bildungswesen in der Bundesrepublik Deutschland: Ein Überblick für Eltern, Lehrer und Schüler.* Arbeitsgruppe Bildungsbericht am Max-Planck-Institut für Bildungsforschung. Hamburg: Rowohlt Taschenbuch Verlag.

Bausch. 1966. Our Educational System Corresponds to the National Mission of the German Democratic Republic. In *Education and Training in the German Democratic Republic*, a publication of the Government of the German Democratic Republic. Berlin: Staatsverlag der Deutschen Demokratischen Republik, pp. 7-31.

Bauschke, Christian. 1992. Einig in der Beurteilung der Uneinigkeit. *Berliner Zeitung* nr. 173 (27 July), p. 5.

Beck. U. 1987. Beyond Status and Class. In Mega, W, & Others. *Modern German Sociology.* New York: Columbia University Press.

Bell, Michael. 1978. *Teachers' Pay.* Geneva: International Labour Office.

Bender, Klaus-Peter. 1990. Europäische Friedenschule, Antrag auf einen universitären Schulversuch an der 12. und 14. Oberschule, Berlin-Marzahn.

Bereday, George, Z. F., Brickman, William W., Read, Gerald H. 1960. *The Changing Soviet School.* Boston: Houghton Mifflin.

Bergner, Wolfgang. 1990. Zur Krise der Volksbildung in der DDR. *Päd Extra & demokratische Erziehung* (May), p.42-5.

Berlin Ministry of Education. 1991. *Fort- und Weiterbildung für die Berliner Schule* I/91: Februar 1991 bis Juli 1991. Berlin: Senatsverwaltung für Schule, Berufsbildung und Sport.

Berlin Ministry of Education. 1991. *Fort- und Weiterbildung für die Berliner Schule* II/91: September 1991 bis Januar 1992. Berlin: Senatsverwaltung für Schule, Berufsbildung und Sport.

Berthold, Michael & Schepp, Heinz-Hermann (ed.). 1973. *Politik und Schule von der Französischen Revolution bis zur Gegenwart: Eine Quellensammlung zum Verhältnis von Gesellschaft, Schule und Staat im 19. und 20. Jahrhundert.* Frankfurt a/M.

Bertolt-Brecht POS. 1990. Letter to Karin Pinel of the APW, dated 20 June 1990.

Bertram, Hans. 1987. *Jugend Heute.* München: C. H. Beck.

Blücher, Vigyo Graf. 1956. *Jugend: Bildung und Freizeit.* Stuttgart: EMNID Institut für Sozialforschung.

Boettcher, H. 1965. *Das Familienklima.* Berlin: Volk und Wissen.

Bourdieu, Pierre, & Passeron, Jean-Claude. 1977. *Reproduction in Education, Society and Culture.* London: Sage Publications.

Brandenburg Ministry of Education. 1991. *Fortbildungsprogamm für Lehrerinnen und Lehrer im Land Brandenburg: November 1991 bis Februar 1992.* Ludwigsfelde: Pädagogisches Landesinstitut Brandenburg.

Breer, Dietmar. 1982. *Die Mitwirkung von Ausländern an der politischen Willensbildung in der Bundesrepublik Deutschland durch Gewährung des Wahlrechts, insbesondere des Kommunalwahlrechts.* Berlin: Duncker & Humblot.

Brodbeck, M. 1992. *Zur Reflexion psychosozialer Konflikted durch Schuljugendliche.* Frankfurt a/M.

Bronfenbrenner, Urie. 1970. *Two Worlds of Childhood: U.S. and U.S.S.R..* New York: Touchstone Books.

Brubaker, Rogers. 1992. *Citizenship and Nationhood in France and Germany.* Cambridge, MA: Harvard University Press.

Bruce, Michael G. 1986. The Place of Europe's Women. *Phi Delta Kappan* 67 (June), pp. 761-2.

Bullivant, Brian M. 1981. *The Pluralist Dilemmas in Education: Six Case Studies* Sydney: George Allen & Unwin.

Carneiro, Robert L. 1982. Successive Reequilibrations as the Mechanism of Cultural Evolution. In *Self-Organization and Dissipative Structure,* Schieve William C., & Allen, Peter M. Austin, TX: University of Texas Press, pp. 110-31.

Carnoy, Martin & Levin, Henry (ed.). 1976. *The Limits of Educational Reform.* New York: McKay.

Cerny, Karl H. 1978. *Germany at the Polls: The Bundestag Election of 1976.* Washington, D.C.: American Enterprise Institute for Public Policy Research.

Chisholm, Lynne & Others. 1990. *Childhood, Youth and Social Change: A Comparative Perspective.* London: Falmer Press.

Cramer, Alfons. 1982. *Familie und Familienpolitik in der Bundesrepublik Deutschland.* Opladen: Leske Verlag + Budrich GmbH.

Dahrendorf, Ralf. 1965. *Bildung ist Bürgerrecht.* Bramsche/Osnabrück: Die Zeit Bücher.

Dalin, Per. 1978. *Limits of Educational Change.* London: Macmillan Press.

Dalin, Per & Rust, Val D. 1983. *Can Schools Learn?* London: Nelson-NFER.

Darnton, Robert. 1991. *Berlin Journal: 1989-1990.* New York: W. W. Norton.

Degen, Rolf. 1991. Verwandtschaft der Seelen in Ost und West. *Berliner Zeitung* #277.

Deuerlein, Ernst. 1957. *Die Einheit Deutschlands.* Frankfurt a/M: Alfred Metzner Verlag.

Deutsch, Karl. 1961. Social Mobilization and Political Development, *The American Political Science Review,* LV (Sept., 1961), pp. 493-514.

Deutscher Bildungsrat. 1969. *Einrichtungen von Schulversuchen mit Gesamtschulen.* Bonn.

Deutscher Bildungsrat. 1970. *Strukturplan für das Bildungswesen: Empfehlungen der Bildungskommission.* Stuttgart: Klett.

Deutscher Industrie- und Handelstag. 1988. *Dual Vocational Training in the Federal Republic of Germany.* Bonn: Deutscher Industrie- und Handelstag.

Die Zeit. 1992. (7 February).

Dieter Vaupel. 1990. Es gibt etwas herüberzuretten. *Päd Extra & demokratische Erziehung* (May), p. 46.

DIPF (Deutsches Institut für Internationale Pädagogische Forschung). 1989a. Bibliothek für Bildungsgeschichtliche Forschung; Archiv. Bestand der früheren Akademie der Pädagogischen Wissenschaften; BBF; Archiv. APWA. Sign.: 1234, Offener Brief, Reg. No. 3.

DIPF. 1989b. BBF/Archiv. APWA. Sign.: 1234, Reg. 11.351.

DIPF. 1989c. BBF/Archiv. APWA. Sign.: Reg. nr. 13II.

DIPF. 1990a. BBF/Archiv. APWA. Sign.: 1234, Feb.

DLZ. 1988. Erfahrungsaustausch vor IX. Pädagogischen Kongreß. *Deutsche Lehrerzeitung* 47 (Nov. 3), p. 1.

DLZ. 1990. Gesamtschule in Berlin-Köpenick, *Deutsche Lehrerzeitung* (March).

Döbert, Hans & Manning, Sabina. 1994. The Transformation of the East German School and Its International Educational Developments. In Rust, Val D., Knost, Peter & Wichmann, Jürgen (ed.). *Education and the Values Crisis in Central and Eastern Europe.* Frankfurt a/M: Peter Lang.

Dross, Joachim. 1990. *Freizeit und Schule.* Zwickau: Gesellschaft für Freizeitforschung e.V.

Dürr, Karlheinz. 1992. East German Education: A System in Transition. *Phi Delta Kappan* 73, nr. 5 (January), pp. 390-93.

Eggers, Gerd. 1992. Unterricht zu Lebensfragen: Ostdeutsche Konzepte und Entwicklungen nach der Wende. In Lott, Jürgen (ed.). *Religion--Warum und wozu in der Schule?* Weinheim: Deutsche Studien.

Ehrenberg, R. 1916. *Die Familie in ihrer Bedeutung für das Volksleben.* Jena: Archiv für exakte Wirtschaftsforschung Thunen-Archiv.

Einicke, Dörte, & Boose, Anett. 1990. Allgemeine Verunsicherung. *LehrerInnen in Ost und West* 44, nr. 4/5 (March 1), p. 12.

Eisbrenner, 1991. Was hat sich an meiner Schule seit Sommer 1989 verändert. *Pädagogik*, nr. 11, pp. 18-21.

Erlebach, E. 1969. *Damit sie sich selbst erziehen können*, nr. 63 of pamphlet series *Elternhaus und Schule*. 1969.

Ernst Schneller Grimma EOS. 1990. Pläne zur Neuprofilierung unserer Bildungseinrichtung, dated 23 May. DIPF. 1989b. BB-F/Archiv. APWA. Sign.: 1234, Reg. 11.438.

Etzold, Sabine. 1991. Wieder eine Chance verpaßt, *Die Zeit* , 1 Jan., p. 1.

Falk, Waltraud. 1990a. Stellungnahme zur Arbeit der Gesellschaftswissenschaftler. *Das Hochschulwesen* 38. Jahrgang (Januar 1990), p. 1-2.

Falk, Waltraud. 1990b. Erneuerung des Wissenschafts- und Hochschulsystems der DDR. *Das Hochschulwesen* 38. Jahrgang (Februar), p. 45-8.

Fallon, Daniel. 1980. *The German University: A Heroic Ideal in Conflict with the Modern World.* Boulder: Colorado Associated University Press.

Faust, Helmut. 1992. Von der Abwicklung betroffen. In Himmelstein, Klaus & Keim, Wolfgang (ed.). *Jahrbuch für Pädagogik: 1992.* Frankfurt a/M: Peter Lang, pp. 167-78.

Fend, H. Gesellschaftliche Bedingungen schulischer Sozialisation, *Soziologie der Schule.* Weinheim: Beltz.

Fink, Heinrich. 1990. Die Universität und ihre Rolle in dieser Zeit. *Das Hochschulwesen* 38. Jahrgang, Heft 7 (Juli), p. 217-9.

Fischer, Andreas. 1992. *Das Bildungssystem der DDR: Entwicklung, Umbruch, und Neugestaltung seit 1989.* Darmstadt: Wissenschaftliche Buchgesellschaft.

Fischer, Bernd-Reiner & Schmidt, Norbert. 1992. Das zweifache Scheitern der DDR-Schule. *Aus Politik und Zeitgeschichte: Beilage zur Wochenzeitung Das Parlament* B 37-38 (6 September), 27-36.

Foucault, Michel. 1978. *The History of Sexuality*. New York: Pantheon Books.

Foucault, Michel. 1980. *Power/Knowledge*. New York: Pantheon Books.

Friedrich, W. & Schubarth, W. 1991. Ausländerfeindliche und rechtsextreme Orientierungen bei ostdeutschen Jugendlichen: Eine empirische Studie, *Deutschland-Archiv*, 10, pp. 1052-1065.

Fritsch-Bournazel, Renata. 1991. German Unification: Views from Germany's Neighbors. In Heisenberg, Wolfgang (ed.). *German Unification in European Perspective*. London: Brassey's (UK), 70-87.

Fuchs, G. 1987. Die weiteren Aufgaben bei der Entwicklung des theoretischen Niveaus und der Praxiswirksamkeit der pädagogischen Ausbildung der Diplomlehrerstudenten. *Pädagogik* 42, pp. 658-83.

Geißler, Rainer. 1990. Entwicklung der Sozialstruktur und Bildungswesen. In Anweiler, Oskar & Others. *Vergleich von Bildung und Erziehung in der Bundesrepublik Deutschland und in der Deutschen Demokratischen Republik*. Köln: Verlag Wissenschaft und Politik, pp. 83-111.

Gensicke, Thomas. 1992. Lebenskonzepte im osten Deutschlands. *BISS Public* 9, nr. 2, pp. 101-122.

German Research Service. 1992. East Germans Becoming Increasingly Pessimistic. *Deutscher Forschungsdienst*. vol. VIII, nr. 9/92, pp. 9-10.

Giesen, Heinz, & Others. 1992. Die Bedeutung der Koedukation für die Genese der Studienfachwahl. *Zeitschrift für Pädagogik* 38, pp. 65-81.

Glaser, Hermann. 1993. The Future Requires an Origin: East-West German Identity, the Opportunities and Difficulties of Cultural Politics. In Eigler, Friederike & Pfeiffer, Peter C. *Cultural Transformations in the New Germany: American and German Perspectives*. Columbia, SC: Camden House, Inc., pp. 64-80.

Gleick, James. 1987. *Chaos, Making a New Science*. New York: Viking.

Gräfin von Bethusy-Huc, Viola. 1987. *Familienpolitik.* Tübingen: J.C.B. Mohr.

Gräßler, Elke, & Raabe, Marion. 1992. Vom Pionierhaus zum Schülerfreizeitzentrum. *Freizeitpädagogik* 14 nr. 1, pp. 19-26.

Gräßler, Elke, 1992. *Freizeitpädagogik: Eine neue Ausbildungs-disziplin an der Pädagogischen Hochschule Zwickau.* Zwickau: Gesellschaft für Freizeitforschung e.V., Band 1, pp. 21-30.

Gräßler, Elke & Gräßler, Harald. 1989. Pädagogische Aspekte der Freizeit in der Systemauseinandersetzung. *Pädagogische Rundschau* Sonderdruck, pp. 651-658.

Günther, Karl-Heinz & Others. 1973. *Geschichte der Erziehung* (eleventh edition). Berlin: Volk und Wissen.

Hacke, Christian. 1992. German: Locomotive for European Integration or Pacemaker for Detante with Eastern Europe? In Nelson, Brian, Roberts, David & Veit, Walter (ed.). *The European Community in the 1990s.* New York: Berg.

Hancock, M. Donald. 1989. West Germany: The Politics of Democratic Corporatism. Chatham, NJ: Chatham House Publishers.

Heitmeyer, W. 1991. Wenn der Alltag fremd wird: Modernisierungsschock und Fremdenfeidlichkeit, *Blätter für deutsche und internationale Politik,* 36, Nr. 7, pp. 851-858.

Helwig, Gisela. 1982. *Frau und Familie in beiden deutschen Staaten.* Bielefeld: Verlag Wissenschaft und Politik.

Hermann, Ulrich & Others. 1989. *Familienpolitik.* Berlin: Verlag W. Kohlhammer.

Hitpass, Josef. 1980. *Gesamtschule oder Gymnasium.* Bonn: Bonn Aktuell.

Honecker, Margot. 1986. *Zur Bildungspolitik und Pädagogik in der DDR.* Berlin: Volk und Wissen.

Honecker, Margot. 1989. Unser sozialistisches Bildungssystem - Wandlungen, Erfolge, neue Horizonte. *Deutsche Lehrerzeitung* 25, pp. 7-16.

Hurrelmann, Klaus. 1991. Zwei Schulen für das eine Deutschland. *Die Zeit* nr. 45 (1 November), p. 64.

ILO. 1980. *Employment and Conditions of Work of Teachers*. Geneva: International Labor Organization.

Ines, Horst. 1992. Abgewickelt--Aufgewickelt--Abgewickelt. In Himmelstein, Klaus & Keim, Wolfgang (ed.). *Jahrbuch für Pädagogik 1992*. Frankfurt a/M: Peter Lang, pp. 151-164.

IPOS. 1990. *Einstellungen zu Fragen der aktuellen Innenpolitik*. Mannheim: Institut für praxisorientierte Sozialforschung.

Jantsch, Erich. 1980. *The Self-Organizing Universe*. Oxford: Pergamon.

Kaack, Haike. 1992. Keine Antwort - M.f.S: Briefe an den pädagogischen Kongreß '89. Unpublished paper, written in 1992.

Kaltenborn, Carl-Jürgen. 1990. Der Denkansatz stimmt nicht. *Deutsche Lehrerzeitung* 30.

Kanders, Michael & Rolff, Hans-Günter. 1994. All Schulimporte haben an 'Image' verloren. *Frankfurter Rundschau* 28 (3 February), p. 6.

Karst, Uwe Volker. 1978. Spielen, Toben, Lernen. Freizeit für Kinder. *Hessische Blätter für Volks- und Kulturforschung* Band 7/8. Gießen: Wilhelm Schmitz Verlag, pp. 81-100.

Kauermann-Walter, Jacqueline & Others. 1990. Formal Equality and Discrete Discrimination. *Western European Education* 22, nr. 1 (Spring), pp. 67-79.

Keiser, S. & Lindner, B. 1991. Jugend im Prozeß der Vereinigung: Erfahrungen, Empfindungen und Erwartungen der Neubundesbürger aus der Sicht der Jugendforschung. In Muszynski, B. (ed.). *Deutsche Vereinigung: Probleme der Integration und der Identifikation*. Opladen: Leske und Budrich, pp. 27-43.

Kempowski, Walter. 1979. O Gott, was macht der den da? *Der Spiegel* 14, pp. 60-5.

Keskin, Hakki. 1984. *Menschen ohne Rechte? Einwanderungspolitik und Kommunalwahlrecht in Europa*. Berlin.

Kienel, Hartmut. 1991. Aspekte der Schulpolitik in Brandenburg im Jahre 1991: Ein Erfahrungsbericht. Unpublished report.

Klapper, John. 1992. German Unification and the Teaching of Modern Languages: The Methodological Legacy of the German

Democratic Republic. *Comparative Education* 28, nr. 3, pp. 235-47.

Koch, Thomas. 1992. Chancen und Risiken von Modellen einer 'getrennten' Entwicklung der beiden Gesellschaften in Deutschland. *BISS Public* 9, nr. 2, pp. 5-22.

Köhler, Helmut & Schreier, Gerhard. 1990. Statistische Grunddaten zum Bildungswesen. In Anweiler, Oskar & Others. *Vergleich von Bildung und Erziehung in der Bundesrepublik Deutschland und in der Deutschen Demokratischen Republik.* Köln: Verlag Wissenschaft und Politik, pp. 112-55.

Kompaß, J. & Others. 1989. *Freizeitpädagogik und Freizeitforschung.* Berlin: Akademie der Pädagogischen Wissenschaften.

Kossakowski, Adolf. 1992. Abwicklung der Akademie der Pädagogischen Wissenschaften. In Himmelstein, Klaus & Keim, Wolfgang (ed.). *Jahrbuch für Pädagogik: 1992.* Frankfurt a/M: Peter Lang, 1992, pp. 87-102.

Krohn, Wolfgang, Küppers, Günter & Nowotny, Helga (ed.). *Self-organization: Portrait of a Scientific Revolution.* Dordrecht: Kluwer Academic Publishers.

Krzyweck, Hans-Jürgen, 1991, Berlin. *Recht der Jugend und des Bildungswesens* 39, nr. 3, pp. 290-4.

Kuhn, Hans-Jürgen. 1992. Der Gesamtschule Freud und Leid. *Deutsche Lehrerzeitung* 46/92 (2. November), p. 13.

Kühnel, W. 1991. Doppelte Identität: Jugendliche im Vereinigungsprozeß, *Blätter für deutsche und internationale Politik* 36, Nr. 11, pp. 1333-1344.

LA Times. 1994. Endangered Motherhood in Unified Germany, *Los Angeles Times.* March 13, p. A10.

Laabs, Hans Joachim & Others. 1987. *Pädagogisches Wörterbuch.* Berlin: Volk und Wissen.

Laffan, Brigid. 1992. *Integration and Co-operation in Europe* London: Routledge.

Land, Rainer. 1989. Überlegungen zu Problemen und Perspektiven des gesellschaftlichen und wirtschaftlichen Wandels des Sozialismus und der Weiterentwicklung gesellschafstragischer Konzeptionen in der DDR und anderen sozialistischen Staaten des RGW. Humboldt-Universität zu Berlin, Juli/November.

Lask, Berta. 1926. Vom Geist der Schule des gegenwärtigen Deutschland und Sowjetrußlands. *Die neue Erziehung* 8, p. 11f.

Le Gloannec, Anne-Marie. 1991. Like Fire and Water? Two Germanies in One. In Heisenberg, Wolfgang (ed.). *German Unification in European Perspective*. London: Brassey's (UK), 57-69.

Lemke, Christiane. 1993. Old Troubles and New Uncertainties: Women and Politics in United Germany. In Huelshoff, Michael G, Markovits, Andrei S & Reich, Simon (ed.). *From Bundesrepublik to Deutschland*. Ann Arbor: University of Michigan Press, pp. 147-65.

Lemmens, Markus. 1990. Vorgriff auf die Länderkompetenz vermeiden. *Deutsche Universitätszeitung* 12, pp. 24-5.

Lengkeek, George. 1992. Heute stirbt jeder für sich alleine. Unpublished manuscript of interviews with history teachers in Saxony.

Leonhardt, Rudolf Walter. 1962. *X-mal Deutschland*. München: Bertelsmann Lesering.

Leschinsky, Achim, & Mayer, Karl Ulrich (ed.). 1990. *The Comprehensive School Experiment Revisited: Evidence from Western Europe*. Frankfurt a/M: Peter Lang.

Lewin, Rosemarie. 1991. Zur Anerkennung und Äquivalenz der in der DDR verliehenen Abschlüsse und akademischen Grade. *Das Hochschulwesen* 39, Nr. 1 (Februar), pp. 3-6.

Liegle, Ludwig. 1990. Vorschulerziehung. In Anweiler, Oskar & Others. *Vergleich von Bildung und Erziehung in der Bundesrepublik Deutschland und in der Deutschen Demokratischen Republik*. Köln: Verlag Wissenschaft und Politik, pp. 157-70.

Littell, Franklin. 1960. *The German Phoenix*. New York: Doubleday.

Lorentzen, Uwe. 1991. Mecklenburg-West Pomerania. *Recht der Jugend und des Bildungswesens* 39, nr. 3, pp. 285-90.

Lorenz, Bärbel. 1991. Mecklenburg-Vorpommern: Die konservative Reform. *Pädagogik* 43, nr. 10 (November), pp. 30-35.

Luckmann, Waltraud. 1991. Eine Direktorin zieht sich zurück. *Pädagogik* 43, nr. 11, pp. 22-24.

Makarenko, A. S. 1971. Ein Buch für Eltern - Vorträge über Kindererziehung: Reden und Aufsätze über Familienerziehung. In *Werke*, Bd. IV, Berlin: Volk und Wissen.

Mann, Horace. 1844. Seventh Annual Report. *Common School Journal* 6.

Mannschatz, Eberhard. 1970. *Einführung in die sozialistische Familienerziehung.* Berlin: Volk und Wissen.

Markovits, Andrei S. & Gorski, Philip S. The New Women's Movement. In Huelshoff, Michael G, Markovits, Andrei S, & Reich, Simon (ed.). *From Bundesrepublik to Deutschland.* Ann Arbor: University of Michigan Press, pp. 137-45.

Marshall, Tyler. 1993. Mothers on a Social Banana Peel. *Los Angeles Times* (April 27), pp. 1 + A9.

Mattern, Cornelia. 1979. Zur Situation der in Verbänden organisierten privaten Schulen: Einige quantitative Aspekte. In Goldschmidt, Dietrich & Roeder, Peter Martin (ed.). *Alternative Schulen?* Stuttgart: Klett-Cotta, pp. 197-212.

Meier, Barbara. 1990. Ethik oder Lebensgestaltung oder Religion? *Deutsche Lehrerzeitung* nr. 30/90, p. 4.

Meixner, Harald. 1990. *Deutsche Lehrerzeitung* 21/90.

Menlo, Allen, & Poppleton, Pam. 1990. A Five-country Study of the Work Perceptions of Secondary School Teachers in England, the United States, Japan, Singapore and West Germany (1986-88). *Comparative Education* 26, nrs. 2/3, pp. 173-82.

Merkl, Peter H. 1963. *The Origin of the West German Republic.* New York: Oxford University Press.

Ministerium für Bildung und Wissenschaft. 1990. *Arbeitsgrundlage für den Geschichtsunterricht in den Klassen 5 bis 10*, Berlin, 1990.

Ministerium für Volksbildung. 1949. *Der 4. Pädagogische Kongreß vom 25. August 1949.* Berlin: Volk und Wissen.

Ministerium für Volksbildung. 1988. *Lehrplan der zehnklassigen allgemeinbildenden polytechnischen Oberschule: Geschichte: Klassen 5 bis 10.* Berlin: Volk und Wissen.

Ministerium für Volksbildung. 19889a. *Geschichte, Lehrbuch für Klasse 9.* Berlin: Volk und Wissen, pp. 279-80.

Ministerium für Volksbildung. 1989b. *Geschichte,* Lehrbuch für Klasse 10. Berlin: Volk und Wissen.

Ministry for Education, Youth, & Sport. 1991 *Vorläufiger Rahmenplan: Lernbereich 'Gesellslchaftslehre' politische Bildung: Sekundarstufe I.* Manual for the state of Brandenburg, (June).

Ministry of Education of North-Rhine Westfalia. 1989. *Entwurf einer Rahmenkonzeptes zur 'Gestaltung des Schullebens und Öffnung von Schule.'* Düsseldorf: Kultusminister von Nordrhein-Westfalen.

Ministry of Education. 1981. *Development of Public Education in the German Democratic Republic* Berlin: Ministry of Education, p. 16.

Mitter, Wolfgang. 1990. Allgemeinbildendes Schulwesen: Grundfragen und Überblick. *Vergleich von Bildung und Erziehung in der Bundesrepublik Deutschland und in der Deutschen Demokratischen Republik.* Köln: Verlag Wissenschaft und Politik, pp. 171-200.

Mitter, Wolfgang. 1994. Secondary Graduation and Entry into Higher Education in Germany: Trends and Conflicts in the Light of German and European Educational Policies. Paper prepared for the Annual Conference of the Comparative and International Education Society in San Diego, CA, March 21-24.

Mitter, Wolfgang. 1992. Educational Adjustments and Perspective in a United Germany, *Comparative Education* 28, nr. 1, pp. 45-52.

Münch, Joachim. 1990. Probleme der Lehrlingsausbildung in der Bundesrepublik Deutschland. *Vergleich von Bildung und Erziehung in der Bundesrepublik Deutschland und in der Deutschen Demokratischen Republik.* Köln: Verlag Wissenschaft und Politik, pp. 316-25.

Mushaben, Joyce Marie. 1993. Citizenship as Process; German Identity in an Age of Reconstruction. In Eigler, Friederike & Pfeiffer, Peter C. (ed.). *Cultural Transformations in the New Germany: American and German Perspectives.* Columbia, SC: Camden House, Inc., pp. 42-63.

Nahrstedt, Wolfgang. 1972. *Die Entstehung der Freizeit.* Göttingen: Vandenhoeck & Ruprecht.

Nahrstedt, Wolfgang. 1978. Der Kampf um die Freizeit. *Hessische Blätter für Volks- und Kulturforschung* Band 7/8. Gießen: Wilhelm Schmitz Verlag, pp. 7-19.

Nelan, Bruce W. 1993. Europe Slams the Door. *Time* (July 19), pp. 38-40.

Oestreich, D. 1992. Im Osten nicht rechtsextremer als im Westen *Erziehung und Wisssenschaft* Heft 3.

Olneck, Michael R. 1990. The Recurring Dream: Symbolism and Ideology in Intercultural and Multicultural Education. *American Journal of Education* 98, nr. 2, pp. 147-75.

Opaschowski, Horst W. 1983. *Arbeit, Freizeit, Lebenssinn?* Leverkusen: Leske.

Open Letter on the Central Committee of the SED, 31 October 1989, by the members of Parteigruppe I der APO VIII der APW der DDR.

Paterson, William E. & Smith, Gordon. 1992. German Unity. In Smith, Gordon, Paterson, William E., Merkl, Peter H. & Padgett, Stephen (ed.). *Developments in German Politics.* Durham: Duke University Press.

Peisert, Hansgert. 1990. Entwicklung und Struktur des Hochschulwesens in der Bundesrepublik Deutschland. *Vergleich von Bildung und Erziehung in der Bundesrepublik Deutschland und in der Deutschen Demokratischen Republik.* Köln: Verlag Wissenschaft und Politik, pp. 394-413.

Peter, Volkhard. 1990. Famulus Wagner Missioniert Thüringer Volks-ildung. *Ad Hoc* 5/90 (12 march), pp. 1-2.

Schaarschmidt, U. 1991. Wie könnte eine kinderfreundlichere Schule aussehen. In Schmidt, H.D., Schaarschmidt, V. & Peter, V.

(ed.). *Dem Kinde zugewandt.* Hohengehren: Schneider, pp. 24-34.

Philipsen, Dirk. 1993. *We Were the People: Voices from East Germany's Revolutionary Autumn of 1989.* Durham: Duke University Press.

Pinder, John. 1991. *European Community: The Building of a Union* Oxford: Oxford University Press.

Poppleton, Pam. 1992. The Significance of Being Alike: The Implications of Similarities and Differences in the Work-Perceptions of Teachers in an International Five-country Study. *Comparative Education* 28, nr. 2, pp. 215-23.

Präsidium der hochschulrektorenkonferenz. 1991. Förderungsprogramm für die Hochschulen in den fünf neuen Bundesländern. *Das Hochschulwesen* 39, Nr. 1 (Februar), pp. 1-3.

Programmenentwurf der SED für die Schaffung einer neuen deutschen Schule. 1947. In *Allen Kindern das gleiche Recht auf Bildung.* Dokumente und Materialien zur demokratischen Schulreform. Berlin: Dietz.

Psydata/Shell. 1981. *Jugend '81. Lebensentwürfe - Alltaskulturen - Zukunftsbilder.* Hamburg.

Rabinow, Paul (ed.). 1984. *Foucault Reader.* New York: Pantheon Books.

Raddatz, Rolf. 1991. In-Company German Vocational Education from a Teaching, Economic, & Labor-Market Viewpoint. In Rust, Val D., Silberman, Harry F., & Weiner, Marijana B. (ed.). *Vocational Education: Germany and the United States.* Berkeley, CA: National center for Research in Vocational Education at the University of California, Berkeley, pp. 49-54.

Reischock, Wolfgang. 1982. Ablauf einer empirischen Untersuchung, unpublished manuscript.

Resch, Roland. 1993. *Grundschule in Entwicklungsprozeß.* Press release of the Minster of Education, Youth and Sport for the state of Brandenburg, on March 25.

Richter, Christine. 1991. Rektor Fink fällt über die Staatssicherheit. *Berliner Zeitung* Nr. 276 (27 Nov.), p. 1.

Richtlinien der Deutschen Verwaltung für Volksbildung zur pädagogischen Bewegung Freunde der neuen Schule. 1981. In *Allen Kindern das gleiche Recht auf Bildung*. Dokumente und Materialien zur demokratischen Schulreform. Berlin: Dietz.

Riehl, W. H., 1855. *Die Familie*. Reproduction as a part of a series on the *Naturgeschichte des Volkes as Grundlage einer deutschen Sozialpolitik*. Stuttgart: 1904.

Rist, Ray C. 1978. *Guestworkers in Germany*. New York: Praeger.

Rolff, Hans-Günter. 1992. Schulentwicklung als Entwicklung von Einzelschulen? *Zeitschrift der Pädagogik* 37, nr. 6, pp. 865-86.

Rolff, Hans-Günter. 1988. *Ansätze zu einer Theorie der Schulentwicklung*. Dortmund: Institut für Schulentwicklungsforschung.

Rosenberg, Dorothy. 1991. The Colonization of East Germany. *Monthly Review* Volume 43 (Sept.), pp. 14-33.

Rust, Val D. 1991. Educational Response to European Integration. *Educational Horizons* 70 (Fall).

Rust, Val D. 1989. *The Democratic Tradition and the Evolution of Schooling in Norway*. Westport, CN: Greenwood Press.

Rust, Val D. 1967. *German Interest in Foreign Education Since World War I*. Ann Arbor, University of Michigan, Comparative Education Dissertation Series, No. 13.

Rust, Val D. 1968. The Common School Issue--A Case of Cultural Borrowing. In Correll, Werner & Süllwold, Fritz (ed.). *Forschung und Erziehung*. Donauwörth: Ludwig Auer, pp. 86-97..

Rust, Val D. 1992. School Reform in the Russian Republic, *Phi Delta Kappan*, 73, Nr. 5 (January), p. 377.

Rust, Val D. 1992. An Interview with Edward Dneprov, *Phi Delta Kappan* 73, No. 5 (January), pp. 375-77.

Rytlewski, Ralf. 1990. Entwicklung und Struktur des Hochschulwesens in der DDR. *Vergleich von Bildung und Erziehung in der Bundesrepublik Deutschland und in der Deutschen Demokratischen Republik*. Köln: Verlag Wissenschaft und Politik, pp. 414-24.

Sächsisches Staatsministerium für Kultus. 1991. *Lehrplan Geschichte: Klassen 5-12: Allgemeinbildende Schulen Schuljahr 1991/92.* Dresden: Union Druckerei Dresden GmbH.

Sarup, Madan. 1989. *An Introductory Guide to Post-Structuralism and Postmodernism.* Athens, GA: University of Georgia Press.

Schaefer, Hans-Dieter & Others. 1990. Die Hochschullandschaft in den ostdeutschen Bundesländern--Herausforderungen--Empfehlungen--Projekte. *Das Hochschulwesen* 38, Nr. 12 (December), pp. 381-6.

Schäfer, Hans Peter. 1990. Probleme der Lehrlingsausildung in der DDR. *Vergleich von Bildung und Erziehung in der Bundesrepublik Deutschland und in der Deutschen Demokratischen Republik.* Köln: Verlag Wissenschaft und Politik, pp. 326-35.

Schäfer, Hans Peter. 1990. Vollzeitschulischen Ausbildungsgänge (Fachschulen) in der DDR. *Vergleich von Bildung und Erziehung in der Bundesrepublik Deutschland und in der Deutschen Demokratischen Republik.* Köln: Verlag Wissenschaft und Politik, pp. 340-46.

Scharnhorst, Erna. 1970a. *Süppchen kochen...Zeitung lesen,* nr. 67 of pamphlet series *Elternhaus und Schule.*

Scharnhorst, Erna. 1970b. *Erzieherische Grundhaltung der Eltern - wichtigster Faktor der familiären Erziehung.* nr. 3 of pamphlet series *Elternhaus und Schule.*

Scharnhorst, Erna. 1970c. *Die Familie als Kollektiv.* nr. 5 of pamphlet series *Elternhaus und Schule.*

Scharnhorst, Erna. 1970d. *Die Frau in sozialistischen Gesellschaft.* Herausgegeben von der Akademie der Pädagogischen Gesellschaft der DDR, Berlin.

Scharnhorst, Erna & Schille, H. 1989. *Von Autorität bis Zärtlichkeit.* Berlin: Verlag für die Frau.

Schattenfroh, Sylvia. 1993. Streit um ein Professoren-Gutachten: Die Zukunft der Berliner Kliniken. *Frankfurter Allgemeine Zeitung,* Nr. 38 (Monday 15 Feb.), p. 5.

Schaumann, Fritz. 1993. Die Konsequenzen der Beschlüsse von Maastricht für die Hochschul- und Forschungspolitik in Europa. *Das Hochschulwesen* nr. 1, pp. 11-15.

Schissler, Hanna. 1993. Women in West German from 1945 to the Present. In Huelshoff, Michael G, Markovits, Andrei S, & Reich, Simon (ed.). *From Bundesrepublik to Deutschland.* Ann Arbor: University of Michigan Press, pp. 117-36.

Schmidt, Helmut. 1991. Zur Lage der Nation. *Die Zeit* 41 (3 October), p. 4.

Schmidt, Hermann. 1991. German Vocational Education and the Dignity of Work. In Rust, Val D., Silberman, Harry F., & Weiner, Marijana B. (ed.). *Vocational Education: Germany and the United States.* Berkeley, CA: National center for Research in Vocational Education at the University of California, Berkeley, pp. 3-18.

Schmidt, H. D. 1991. Das Bild des Kindes und seine pädagogischen Konsequenzen. In Schmidt, H.D., Schaarschmidt, W. & Peter, V. (ed.). *Dem Kinde zugewandt.* Hohengehren: Schneider, pp. 1-12;

Schmidt, Gerlind. 1990. Lehrerbildung und Lehrerschaft in der DDR. In Anweiler, Oskar & Others. *Vergleich von Bildung und Erziehung in der Bundesrepublik Deutschland und in der Deutschen Demokratischen Republik.* Köln: Verlag Wissenschaft und Politik, pp. 526-38.

Schneider, Peter. 1990. Gibt es zwei deutsche Kulturen? Die Kühlschranktheorie und andere Vermutungen. *Extreme Mittellage: Eine Reise durch das deutsche Nationalgefühl.* Reinbeck bei Hamburg: Rowohlt, pp. 120-150.

School Law. 1966. The 1965 Law on the Integrated Socialist Educational System. In *Education and Training in the German Democratic Republic.* Berlin: Staatsverlag der Deutschen Demokratischen Republik, pp. 74-118.

Schorlemmer, Friedrich. 1991. Graben statt Mauer: Wir brauchen euch -- ihr braucht uns nicht. *Die Zeit,* 5 July.

Schriewer, Jürgen. 1994. World-System and Interrelationship Patterns: The Internationalization of Education and the Role of Comparative Inquiry. Paper prepared for the Annual Conference of the Comparative and International Education Society in San Diego, CA, March 21-24.

Schulz, Dieter. 1990. Lehrerbildung und Lehrerschaft in der Bundesrepublik Deutschland. Anweiler, Oskar & Others. *Vergleich von Bildung und Erziehung in der Bundesrepublik Deutschland und in der Deutschen Demokratischen Republik.* Köln: Verlag Wissenschaft und Politik, pp. 526-38.

Schwan, Gisine. 1986. Das deutsche Amerikabild seit der Weimarer Republik. *Aus Politik und Zeitgeschichte* 26, pp. 3-15.

Schwarz, Gislinde & Zenner, Christine (ed.). 1990. *Wir wollen mehr als ein 'Vaterland.'* Hamburg: Rowohlt Taschenbuch Verlag.

Sckleicher, Klaus. 1992. *Zukunft der Bildung in Europa* Darmstadt: Wissenschaftliche Buchgesellschaft.

Sheridan, Alan. 1980. *Michel Foucault: The Will to Truth.* London: Tavistock Publications.

SPD. 1947. *SPD Parteitag Protokoll 1947.*

Spiegel, Der. 1991. Laßt die Studenten selber denken. *Der Spiegel.* Nr. 4, pp. 72-77.

Spiegel, Der. 1992. Medaille im Ofen. *Der Spiegel.* Nr. 52, pp. 75-6.

Standing Conference of Ministers of Education. 1978. *Empfehlungen zur Arbeit in der gymnasialen Oberstufe gemäß Vereinbarung zur Neugestaltung der gymnasialen Oberstufe in der Sekundarstufe II.* Neuwied: Hermann Luchterthand Verlag.

Standing Conference of Ministers of Education. 1990a. Mitteilung über die Sitzung der Gemeinsamen Bildungskommission am 16. Mai 1990 in Bonn. Unpublished manuscript.

Standing Conference of Ministers of Education. 1990b. Zur 1. Sitzung der Unterkommission Allgemeine schulische Bildung der Gemeinsamen Bildungskommission der Bundesrepublik Deutschland und der Deutschen Demokratischen Republik am 17. Juli 1990 in Bonn. Unpublished manuscript.

Standing Conference of Ministers of Education. 1990c. Gemeinsame Mitteilung über die dritte und abschließende Sitzung deer Gemeinsamen Bildungskommission der Bundesrepublik Deutschland und der Deutschen Demokratischen Republik am 26. September 1990 in Bonn. Unpublished manuscript.

Standing Conference of Ministers of Education. 1990d. Grundsätze und Empfehlungen zur Neugestaltung des allgemeinbildenden Schulwesens in den Ländern Brandenburg, Mecklenburg-Vorpommern, Sachsen, Sachsen-Anhalt und Thüringen sowie in Berlin (Ost). 26.09.90. Unpublished manuscript.

Stares, Paul B. (ed.). 1992. *The New Germany and the New Europe.* Washington, DC: Brookings Institute.

Starke, U. 1991. *Jugend in Leipzig: 1991.* Unpublished manuscript from the Laboratorium für Studentenforschung und Gesellschaft für Jugend- und Sozialforschung, Leipzig University.

Statistisches Bundesamt. 1987. *Berufliche Bildung 1987.* Fachserie 11, Reihe 3 . Bonn: Statistisches Bundesamt.

Steitz, Lilo. 1979. *Freizeit - Freizeit?* Berlin.

Stöhr, Prof. Dr., Vorschlag einer Stundentafel für eine erneuerte allgemeinbildende zehnklassige Schule, circulated through the APW in January, 1990.

Stowe, Calvin E. 1930. Report on Elementary Public Instruction in Europe. In Knight, Edgar (ed.). *Reports on European Education.* New York: McGraw Hill.

Student, Sonja. 1993. Mach mir mal Mut! *Deutsche Lehrerzeitung* nr. 43/93 (4 October), p. 9.

Sturzbecher, D. & Dietrich, P. 1992. *Freizeitverhalten Jugendlicher und Freizeitangebote im Land Brandenburg,* Research Report. Potsdam: Potsdam Universität, Institut für Familien- und Kindheitsforschung.

Sturzbecher, D., Dietrich, P. & Kohlstruck, M. 1992. *Jugendszene und Jugendgewalt im Land Brandenburg,* Research Report. Potsdam: Potsdam Universität, Institut für Familien- und Kindheitsforschung.

Sturzbecher, D. 1993. Der Familien-Interaktions-Test für Vorschul-kinder (FIT-K) und erste Ergebnisse seiner Erprobung, *Psychologie in Erziehung und Unterricht*, 40, in press.

Sturzbecher, D. & Kalb, D. 1993. Vergleichende Analyse elterlicher Erziehungsziele in der ehemaligen DDR und der alten Bundesrepublik, *Psychologie in Erziehung und Unterricht*, 40, in press.

Struzberg, Peter. 1991. Aus dem Westen kommt das Licht. *Berliner Lehrerinnenzeitung* 45. Jahrgang, Nr. 1: 10-11.

Tiedtke, Michael & Zschommler, Christiane. 1990. Die Entwicklung der 'I. Gesamtschule Hellersdorf' - politischer Aufbruch, Konzeption und pädagogische Praxis, *Gesamtschul-Information* 3/4 90, pp. 29-47.

Tomae, H. 1984. Formen der Auseinandersetzung mit Konflikt und Belastung im Jugendalter. In Olbrich, E. & Todt, E. (ed.). *Probleme des Jugendalters*. Berlin/ Heidelberg/ New York/ Tokyo.

Toro, Taryn. 1991. A University in the Former East Germany Struggles to Sweep Away the Influences of Its Communist Past. *Chronicle of Higher Education* 38, Nr. 17 (18 December), pp. A37-38.

Volksmund (anonymous). 1992. Impressionen zur Entwicklung der Humboldt-Universität zwischen Oktober 1989 und Ende 1991. In Himmelstein, Klaus & Keim, Wolfgang (ed.). *Jahrbuch für Pädagogik 1992*. Frankfurt a/M: Peter Lang, pp. 79-86.

Vollstädt, W. 1990. Letter to Karin Pingel, dated 19 June 1990.

Völschow, Uwe. 1992. Ein umstrittenes Thema. *Berliner Zeitung*, nr. 57, 7/8 March, p. 42.

von Dohnanyi, von Klaus. 1992. Der Notplan Ost. *Die Zeit* nr. 28, (3 Juli), p. 11.

Voß, Peter & Autorenkollektiv. 1981. *Die Freizeit der Jugend*. Berlin: Dietz.

Wagner, Christian. 1992. Die Humboldt-Universität zwischen Erneuerung und Dauerkrise. In-house publication from the Institut für Romanistik der Humboldt Universität, (March).

Waldrop, Mitchell. 1992. *Complexity*. New York: Touchstone Books.

Wallach, H. G., & Francisco, Ronald A. 1992. *United Germany: The Past, Politics, Prospects*. Westport, CT: Praeger.

Waterkamp, Dietmar. 1990. When Teaching Fails: Ideological Training in the German Democratic Republic. Paper read at the annual Comparative and International Education Society conference, held in Anaheim, CA in March.

Watts, Meredith & Others. 1989. *Contemporary German Youth and Their Elders*. Westport, CN: Greenwood Press.

Weiler, Hans. 1994. New Conceptions of Knowledge and Old Institutional Realities: Reflections on the Creation of a New University in Eastern Germany. Paper prepared for the Annual Conference of the Comparative and International Education Society in San Diego, CA, March 21-24.

Weschler, Lawrence. 1993. Slight Modifications. *New Yorker* (July 12), pp. 59-65.

Will, Rosemarie. 1992. Die Humboldt-Universität im vereinigten Berlin. *Das Hochschulwesen*. Nr. 1, p. 21.

Wirth, Günter, Letter, dated 19 February 1990, to H. Iffert of the APW regarding the history program under development.

Wissenschaftsrat. 1990. *Empfehlungen und Stellungnahmen*. Köln: Wissenschaftsrat.

Zimmer, Dieter E. 1992. Die Verbitterung. *Die Zeit* 28 (3 July), pp. 49-50.

Zimmer, Dieter E. 1992. Sag mir, wo die Forscher sind. *Die Zeit*. Nr. 32 (7 August), p. 17.

Index

Printed in the United States
by Baker & Taylor Publisher Services